TEACHER'S ANNOTATED EDITION
Vocabulary Workshop

Level F

Jerome Shostak

Senior Series Consultant

Alex Cameron, Ph.D.
Department of English
University of Dayton
Dayton, Ohio

Series Consultants

Sylvia A. Rendón, Ph.D.
Coord., Secondary Language Arts
  and Reading
Cypress-Fairbanks I.S.D.
Houston, Texas

Mel H. Farberman
Supervisor of Instruction
Brooklyn High Schools
New York City Board of Education
Brooklyn, New York

John Heath, Ph.D.
Department of Classics
Santa Clara University
Santa Clara, California

Sadlier-Oxford
A Division of William H. Sadlier, Inc.

Reviewers

The publisher wishes to thank for their comments and suggestions the following teachers and administrators, who read portions of the series prior to publication.

Anne S. Crane
Clinician, English Education
Georgia State University
Atlanta, GA

Susan W. Keogh
Curriculum Coordinator
Lake Highland Preparatory
Orlando, FL

Mary Louise Ellena-Wygonik
English Teacher
Hampton High School
Allison Park, PA

Lisa Anne Pomi
Language Arts Chairperson
Woodside High School
Woodside, CA

Arlene A. Oraby
Dept. Chair (Ret.), English 6–12
Briarcliff Public Schools
Briarcliff Manor, NY

Susan Cotter McDonough
English Department Chair
Wakefield High School
Wakefield, MA

Sr. M. Francis Regis Trojano
Sisters of St. Joseph (CSJ)
Educational Consultant
Boston, MA

Keith Yost
Director of Humanities
Tomball Ind. School District
Tomball, TX

Patricia M. Stack
English Teacher
South Park School District
South Park, PA

Joy Vander Vliet
English Teacher
Council Rock High School
Newtown, PA

Karen Christine Solheim
English Teacher
Jefferson High School
Jefferson, GA

NOTE: ALL RIGHTS RESERVED. NO PART OF THIS BOOK MAY BE REPRODUCED, STORED IN A DATABASE OR RETRIEVAL SYSTEM, OR TRANSMITTED IN ANY FORM BY ANY MEANS, ELECTRONIC, MECHANICAL, PHOTOCOPYING, RECORDING, OR OTHERWISE, WITHOUT THE PRIOR WRITTEN PERMISSION OF WILLIAM H. SADLIER, INC. COPYRIGHT INFRINGERS WILL BE PROSECUTED TO THE FULL EXTENT OF THE LAW AND MAY BE LIABLE FOR DAMAGES OF UP TO $150,000. REPORT ALL VIOLATIONS, IN CONFIDENCE, TO THE PUBLISHER AT THE ADDRESS SHOWN BELOW.

Copyright © 2002 by William H. Sadlier, Inc. All rights reserved.

This publication, or any part thereof, may not be reproduced in any form, or by any means, including electronic, photographic, or mechanical, or by any sound recording system, or by any device for storage or retrieval of information, without the written permission of the publisher. Address inquiries to Permissions Department, William H. Sadlier, Inc., 9 Pine Street, New York, New York 10005-1002.

s is a registered trademark of William H. Sadlier, Inc.

Printed in the United States of America.
ISBN: 0-8215-7621-6
456789/05 04 03

Contents

Introduction T4

Overview T5
Systematic Vocabulary Instruction T5
Grade-Level Placement T7
Word Lists T8

Program Components T10
Student Texts T10
Supplemental Assessment Components T19
Test Generator CD-ROM T19
Test Booklets T20
TEST PREP Blackline Masters T20
Interactive Audio Pronunciation Program T21

Implementing the Program T22
Schedule for the Year T22
Weekly Lesson Plans T26
Alternative Approaches to Using the Program T29
Writing Approach T29
Literature-Based Approach T30
Content-Area Approach T31
Useful Classroom Techniques T33
Alternative Types of Assessment T34

Teacher Resources T36

**Explanations for Answers to Exercises in Reviews and
Cumulative Reviews** T38

Introduction

VOCABULARY WORKSHOP has for more than five decades been the leading program for systematic vocabulary development for grades 6–12. It has been proven a highly successful tool in helping students expand their vocabularies, improve their vocabulary skills, and prepare for the vocabulary strands of standardized tests.

This new edition of VOCABULARY WORKSHOP preserves and improves upon those key elements of the program that have made it so effective *and* introduces important new features that make the series more comprehensive in scope and current in approach to vocabulary instruction.

Key Elements

- At each Level, a **word list** of 300 main entries, plus hundreds of synonyms, antonyms, and other related words
- Proven and effective **five-step approach to instruction**, leading students to mastery of word meanings and usage
- Excellent **preparation for SAT I** and other standardized tests with strong correlations between word lists and words that frequently appear on the SAT, as well as practice in types and formats of exercises found on the SAT I
- Frequent **review and assessment** in both Student Text and in supplementary programs

New Features

- In each Unit and Review, **Vocabulary in Context**, a reading passage formatted to the SAT I reading comprehension sections that provides examples of how Unit words are used in context
- **Building with Classical Roots**, a Review exercise that acquaints students with Latin and Greek roots, and provides a strategy for finding the meaning of words derived from these roots
- In each Review, **Writer's Challenge**, an exercise that helps students improve their writing skills by applying what they have learned about the meaning and proper usage of selected Unit words
- **Enriching Your Vocabulary**, a Cumulative Review feature designed to broaden and enhance the students' knowledge and understanding of the relationships, history, and origins of the words that make up our rich and dynamic language
- Instruction in and examples of key vocabulary **strategies**—using context and using word structure—for decoding word meaning

- In the Units, expanded **Definitions** sections, which now include synonyms, antonyms, and complete, illustrative sentences for each part of speech of every taught word
- **Synonyms and Antonyms** sections that offer more examples of range of contexts and distinctions of usage
- Stress marks in **Pronunciation** sections that now reflect the system used in most leading dictionaries
- **Photographs** and color to engage student interest and illustrate reading and enrichment features

New Components

- For each Level, an **Annotated Teacher's Edition** that includes answers to all exercise items in the Student Text as well as valuable background information to help in lesson planning, instruction in vocabulary strategies, and assessment
- For each of Levels A–F, a **Test Generator CD-ROM** adds a new, secure assessment option to the program, eliminating the risk of "second-hand" tests that may distort assessment results
- For each of Levels A–F, an **Interactive Audio Pronunciation Program** now available in CD format as well as cassette—ideal for English Language Learners of all cultures and backgrounds, and for use in ESL classrooms

In the following pages of this Teacher's Edition, you will learn more about the VOCABULARY WORKSHOP program, including these new features and components, as well as how to get the most out of the program in your classroom.

OVERVIEW

"Pure Vocabulary" Approach: Systematic Vocabulary Instruction

The VOCABULARY WORKSHOP program focuses on words themselves, their meanings (both literal and figurative), their ranges of application (or usage), and their relationships with other words.

The approach is systematic in the sense that it begins with and builds upon a word list compiled to provide students with vocabulary they will encounter in their reading both in and out of the classroom. It is designed to prepare students with the vocabulary skills they will need in order to achieve higher-level reading proficiency and to succeed at standardized tests.

The VOCABULARY WORKSHOP systematic approach differs from a literature-based approach in that each Unit begins with a thorough consideration of the words themselves rather than with a reading selection featuring words to be studied. (This is not to say that VOCABULARY WORKSHOP cannot be profitably used as a complement to a literature-based approach. See pages T30–T31 for suggestions on how this might be done.)

Rather than in the circumstantial context of literature, VOCABULARY WORKSHOP introduces and exemplifies vocabulary usage in varied and controlled contexts. These range from short phrases to full sentences to the Vocabulary in Context reading passages that are new to this edition of the program.

For effective study, the "pure vocabulary" approach also offers these advantages:

- It provides unlimited flexibility in the choice and placement of grade-appropriate material.
- It avoids the problem of trying to deal with a literary passage both as literature and as a vehicle for vocabulary instruction.
- It focuses more directly and completely on the words themselves, their meanings, their usage, and their relationships with other words.
- By economizing space, it allows a greater range of practice, reinforcement, and enhancement.
- It allows maximum coverage to a maximum number of key words.

One of the cornerstones of the VOCABULARY WORKSHOP approach is intensive practice through varied and abundant "hands-on" exercises. This method ensures that students are provided with:

- maximum exposure to different meanings of the key words studied;
- maximum coverage of the range of each key word through its appearance in many different contexts;

- fullest understanding of the key words' relationships to other words.

The aim of the pattern of intensive practice is to include the words in the students' active, daily-use vocabulary. This implies the ability to use a given word not only in its literal, or narrow, sense but also in a figurative way as well. Furthermore, it means that students will be able to use the word with confidence both as speakers and as writers.

Grade-Level Placements

The chart below shows the suggested grade placement for each level of VOCABULARY WORKSHOP, depending on the overall ability of the student population involved.

In determining "proper" placement of a particular level of VOCABULARY WORKSHOP in a given situation, the following considerations should be taken into account:

- Grade placements are based on actual teacher experience and recommendations throughout the long course of VOCABULARY WORKSHOP's history.
- Differences in grade are reflected not only in the "difficulty" of the words presented but also in the "maturity" of the sentences and other contexts in which those words are used.
- Grade levels indicated in the chart should not be taken in too literal or rigorous a sense. A certain amount of experimentation, as well as the use of the diagnostic materials provided in the program, will establish the "correct" placement of a particular level in a given situation.
- The use of Level H with "above-average" students is designed to enhance preparation for the SAT I and other college-entrance examinations.

Grade Placements			
"Average" Students		"Above-Average" Students	
Level	Grade	Level	Grade
A	6	A	5
B	7	B	6
C	8	C	7
D	9	D	8
E	10	E	9
F	11	F	10
G	12	G	11
		H	12

Word Lists

Each Student Text in the VOCABULARY WORKSHOP program for Levels A–H contains 300 words organized in 15 Units.

Criteria for Selection

The selection of words for the VOCABULARY WORKSHOP program is based on four major criteria:

- currency in and usefulness for present-day American oral or written communication;
- frequency on recognized vocabulary lists;
- applicability to standardized tests, especially the SAT I;
- current grade-placement research.

General Sources

The lists of key words were developed from many sources:

- traditional, classic, and contemporary literature including novels, short stories, essays, newspaper and magazine articles, plays, films, videos, TV programs;
- spelling and vocabulary lists recognized as valid bases for teaching language skills at the middle and secondary levels;
- current subject-area textbooks, glossaries, and ancillary materials (especially for general, nontechnical terms).

Dictionary and Reference Sources

The following were the primary dictionary resources used for word (and definition) selection:

- *Webster's Third International Dictionary of the English Language* (unabridged)
- *Merriam-Webster's Collegiate Dictionary* (ninth and tenth editions)

Other supplementary dictionaries consulted included:

- *The American Heritage Dictionary of the English Language* (all four editions)
- *The Random House Dictionary of the English Language* (unabridged; both editions)
- *The Compact Edition of the Oxford English Dictionary*

Standard Word-Frequency Sources

Standard word-frequency studies were employed to evaluate and revise the words on the tentative lists. These included:

- *Primary*
  Dale-O'Rourke: *The Living Word Vocabulary*
  Carroll-Davies-Richman: *Word Frequency Book*

- *Supplementary*
  Harris-Jacobsen: *Basic Reading Vocabularies*
  Thorndike-Lorge: *The Teacher's Word Book of 30,000 Words*
  Zeno-Ivens-Millard-Duvvuri: *The Educator's Word Frequency Guide*

"Sliding-Scale" Placement

Each word list works on a sliding scale based on these principles:

- No word that Dale-O'Rourke indicates as known in a given grade is presented in that grade. Instead, where possible, it is presented 2 or 3 grades earlier.

- Each grade level contains a preponderance of words not known (according to Dale-O'Rourke) 2 or 3 grades later, with an admixture (in decreasing numbers) of words not known 4 or more grades later.

- The higher the grade, the larger the percentage of more difficult words contained on the word list. This was done to accommodate as many "SAT-type" words as possible in the key word lists for Grades 10–12.

Program Components

This new edition of Vocabulary Workshop, Levels A–H, consists of the following components:

> **Components of the Vocabulary Workshop Program***
>
> - **Student Texts,** 8 Levels (A–H)
>
> - **Teacher's Annotated Editions,** 8 Levels (A–H)
>
> - **Test Booklets**
>   - Form A, 8 Levels (A–H)
>   - Form B, 8 Levels (A–H)
>   - Combined Answer Keys, 8 Levels (A–H)
>
> - **Test Generator CD-ROM,** 6 Levels (A–F only)
>
> - SAT-Type **TEST PREP Blackline Masters** (answers included), 8 Levels (A–H)
>
> - **Interactive Audio Pronunciation Program,** 6 Levels (A–F only)

The components have been designed for use in an integrated year-long vocabulary program, as suggested in the chart on pages T23–T25.

*Note that, in its entirety, the Vocabulary Workshop program now includes Student Texts, Teacher's Editions, and Supplementary Testing Programs for Grades 3–5 (Levels Green, Orange, and Blue).

The Student Texts

All eight Student Texts (Levels A–H) present 300 key words and are organized in the same way: 15 Units of 20 words each; 5 Reviews (following Units 3, 6, 9, 12, and 15); and 4 Cumulative Reviews. Preceding the first Unit is a section titled The Vocabulary of Vocabulary and a Diagnostic Test. Concluding each Student Text is a Final Mastery Test.

Vocabulary of Vocabulary (Student Text pages 7–17)

The purpose of this section is to familiarize students with some of the terms, concepts, and strategies that will be introduced and applied in the program. The practice exercises that accompany the discussions are meant to clarify and consolidate the concepts involved.

Some of these terms (for example, *synonyms* and *antonyms*) will already be familiar to most students. However, teachers should not hesitate to review these terms if doing so seems advisable, even at the upper levels of the program. Other, more complex concepts (such as analogies and context), however, may require more instruction and practice, both as preparation for related exercises and as review or re-teaching for any students who have difficulty in successfully completing those exercises.

This is particularly true of analogies, which many students find especially challenging. Four pages of Vocabulary of Vocabulary are devoted to this important critical-thinking exercise so often found on standardized tests.

Diagnostic Test (Student Text pages 18–20)

A Diagnostic Test has been provided at the beginning of each Level as a means of assessing the students' overall vocabulary and test-taking skills. The Test covers a selection of key words introduced in the Level in question, and is presented in the form of 50 synonym and antonym items.

Although the Diagnostic Test may be presented as a timed speed test, with the specific aim of determining how many items students can answer in 10 or 15 minutes, it is better used as an informal assessment and/or motivational device. Speed will come when confidence and vocabulary fluency have developed.

The Units

At the heart of the Student Texts—and of the VOCABULARY WORKSHOP program—are the 15 Units in which the 300 key words are introduced.

The work of each Unit is divided into a unique 5-part structure designed to give maximum coverage to each of the key words given the space available.

Structure of the Unit
(20 words)
1. Definitions
2. Completing the Sentence
3. Synonyms and Antonyms
4. Choosing the Right Word
5. Vocabulary in Context

The following descriptions of the individual exercises in a typical Unit of Levels A–H are designed to aid the teacher in using the text to maximum effect in the classroom.

1. DEFINITIONS

The first section of each Unit provides definitions, parts of speech, pronunciation, synonyms, antonyms, and illustrative sentences.

DEFINITIONS

The definitions provided are not of the dictionary type. They are, for the most part, relatively brief and simple. The intent is to give students a reasonably good "core" idea of what each word means, without extensive detail or secondary connotations.

Generally, only a single meaning of maximum usefulness is given the student. However, several meanings may be indicated if they are distinct, if they appear to be more or less equally useful, or if they will enable students to prepare for the vocabulary-in-context strand of the Critical Reading section of the new SAT I.

PART OF SPEECH

The part of speech of each word is indicated at the beginning of the definition, using a simple set of abbreviations. When a word functions as several parts of speech, the appropriate abbreviation appears before the corresponding definition. (An explanation of the abbreviations used can be found on page 6 of each Student Text).

PRONUNCIATION

With each word listing, the pronunciation is indicated by means of a simple set of diacritical marks presented at the beginning of every Student Text (page 6).

The practice has been to indicate only 1 pronunciation, even where alternate pronunciations are sanctioned by the dictionary. There are only a few exceptions to this—for example, when a word changes its pronunciation in accordance with its use as different parts of speech (ob′ ject and ob ject′).

Note that once they have completed the first section of each Unit, students may utilize the **Interactive Audio Pronunciation Program** (Levels A–F only) for that Unit. This program provides about four hours of spoken material per Student Text, including pronunciations, part(s) of speech, definition(s), and illustrative usages. For further details about the use of the Audio Program in this and other ways, see page T21.

SYNONYMS AND ANTONYMS

A list of synonyms and/or antonyms is given for each key word for which there is one or more of either. Some of these synonyms and antonyms will reappear in the Synonyms and Antonyms section (see page T13). By studying the given synonyms and antonyms, students will better understand the denotational family of words of which each key word is part, and by comparing specific usages of key words and their synonyms, students can better appreciate appropriate contexts for, and nuances in meaning and connotation represented by, these words.

Note that the lists of synonyms and antonyms are not meant to be exhaustive. Grade-level parameters have been taken into account; and obscure, archaic, and slang synonyms and antonyms have generally been avoided.

ILLUSTRATIVE SENTENCE

Concluding each key entry is an illustrative sentence including a blank space in which students must write the taught word. These sentences, although necessarily brief, provide a context that clarifies the meaning of each word and points up its idiomatic usage. By writing the word in such contextual settings, students begin to see how it can be used effectively in their own writing. Furthermore, the act of writing is in itself a form of reinforcement, and by writing the word the student must focus attention on its spelling as well.

2. COMPLETING THE SENTENCE

The next activity, Completing the Sentence, is a simple completion exercise in which students are asked to choose and write the word that logically and meaningfully fits into a blank in a given sentence.

When using this activity in the classroom, the teacher should bear in mind the following considerations:

- The sentences in this activity call for the literal or direct (as opposed to the metaphorical or extended) meaning of the words involved. This is an easier usage for students to grasp and provides a good foundation for the more sophisticated contexts that appear in Choosing the Right Word.
- The sentences are designed so that one and only one of the words fits in the given blank. Selection of the proper word has been facilitated by the introduction of context clues into each sentence.
- The words are to be used as the part of speech given in Definitions. The only exceptions are: Nouns given in the singular in Definitions may be plural in the sentences; verbs given in the base form in Definitions may be used in any tense or form (including participial) required by the sentence.

3. SYNONYMS AND ANTONYMS

In this section students are given phrases that include synonyms or antonyms as presented in the Definitions section, then must choose the appropriate key word for each phrase. Each of the 20 key Unit words is covered once either in the Synonyms or Antonyms part of the section. Besides reinforcing meanings, this exercise provides students with further examples of usage and context.

4. Choosing the Right Word

The fourth activity in each Unit is called Choosing the Right Word. In it students are asked to choose the member of a pair of words that more satisfactorily completes the sentence. At first appearance, this exercise may seem an easier activity than Completing the Sentence. In fact, however:

- sentences in this final activity are more mature linguistically and in subject matter;
- in many cases the words covered are used in a more figurative, extended, or abstract meaning;
- the part of speech or form of the key word has been changed (for example, from an adjective to an adverb) whenever convenient.

Accordingly, this activity is in reality more difficult than Completing the Sentence and requires real effort and a thorough understanding of the range of a word to complete successfully.

5. Vocabulary in Context

The fifth, and last, section of each Unit is an activity titled Vocabulary in Context. The activity is presented in the form of a reading passage, approximating a standardized-test format, into which five or six of the key Unit words have been woven. Its purpose is threefold:

- to give further examples of usage for the selected words;
- to offer an opportunity to derive meaning from context;
- to provide practice in the sort of vocabulary exercises found on standardized tests.

With this activity, it may prove helpful to refer students, if necessary, to the section of Vocabulary of Vocabulary (see Student Text pages 7–17) that serves as an introduction to the strategies involved in studying vocabulary in context.

Follow-Up Activities

Once the work of the Unit is completed, you may find it useful to give a writing exercise in which students may apply and illustrate what they have learned about the words introduced in the Unit.

Writing Essays or Stories

Students might be invited to create their own brief essays or short stories, and encouraged to use as many of the Unit's key words as is practical. (Students should, however, be discouraged from trying to "force" key words into their essays or stories indiscriminately, just for the sake of number alone. It is essential that students get in the habit of using these words correctly.) If they are to write essays, students might refer to the Vocabulary in Context passages as models.

WRITING SENTENCES

Depending on the ability level of individual students or of classes, you may prefer instead to administer a short writing exercise (5–10 items) such as the one shown below. This exercise is not so challenging as writing a story or essay but will give students an opportunity to "try out" some of the words they have learned, and provide the teacher with a means of assessing how well students have mastered the meaning and usage of these words.

Sample Writing Exercise (Level F)

Framing Sentences — On the lines provided, write an **original** sentence that illustrates the meaning and use of each of the following words. Do **not** merely copy one of the sentences given in the Student Text.

1. expostulate

2. coalition

3. jaded

4. umbrage

5. prerogative

The Reviews

A Review follows every three Units. Every effort has been made to include all of the 60 key words at least once in the Review for the three corresponding Units.

Structure of the Review
1. Analogies
2. Word Associations
3. Vocabulary in Context
4. Choosing the Right Meaning
5. Antonyms
6. Word Families
7. Two-Word Completions
8. Building with Classical Roots
9. Writer's Challenge

SAT I SECTIONS

Four parts of each Review have been specially designed to meet the needs of students seriously preparing for the verbal part of the SAT I and similar standardized tests.

ANALOGIES (PART 1)

The first of these special SAT sections involves analogies.

- Analogies are valuable and revealing, not merely as a kind of mental gymnastics, but also as a means of pinning down the exact meanings of words and of remedying misconceptions or uncertainties about how those words are used.

- Analogies provide an excellent means for testing and refining the critical-thinking skills used on the college level.

- Words that receive the attention necessary to complete an analogy successfully are much more likely to become part of the student's active daily-use vocabulary.

It is impossible, of course, to catalog all the relationships that may be embodied in analogy questions. They are as open-ended as the mental capacity to manipulate ideas and terms. However, the analogies illustrated and discussed in Student Text pages 11–14 will be helpful in reviewing with the students a few of the general "types" that occur in the Reviews and Cumulative Reviews.

Note: In the Supplemental Answer Key on pages T38–T48, you will find explanations for the correct answers to all analogy exercises in the Student Text.

VOCABULARY IN CONTEXT (PART 3)

Like the Unit exercises that bear the same name, this activity is meant primarily as preparation for the vocabulary questions that appear in the SAT I and other standardized tests. Its format is changed in the Reviews, however, to more closely reflect the columnar format of standardized tests.

CHOOSING THE RIGHT MEANING (PART 4)

Focusing on usage-discrimination skills, this part of the Review challenges students to choose, from among two or more taught meanings of a word, the only one that the specific context will reasonably allow. This activity gives students useful practice in determining a word's meaning by careful attention to the context in which it appears, a skill assessed in the critical reading section of the SAT I.

Note: Explanations for the correct answers to the Choosing the Right Meaning exercises can be found in the Supplemental Answer Key on pages T38–T48.

TWO-WORD COMPLETIONS (PART 7)

This part of the Reviews has been designed to familiarize students with the type of word-omission (cloze) exercise that appears on typical standardized tests, including the SAT I. Again the aim here is to refine students' critical-thinking skills. Context clues are embedded within the passages to guide students to the correct choice.

Note: Explanations for the correct answers to Two-Word Completion exercises can be found in the Supplemental Answer Key on pages T38–T48.

OTHER SECTIONS OF THE REVIEW

WORD ASSOCIATIONS (PART 2)

The purpose of this activity is to reinforce and extend understanding of the meanings of key words with brief definitions or examples, situations, or allusions that in some way suggest key words.

ANTONYMS (PART 5)

As it requires of students that they recall the meaning of a key word in order to determine its opposite, this activity helps students "situate" a word within the cluster of words of related meanings.

WORD FAMILIES (PART 6)

This part extends the work of the Units by showing students that by learning one English word they often are acquiring a whole family of related words. It also provides practice in classifying words by part of speech.

BUILDING WITH CLASSICAL ROOTS (PART 8)

Building on the foundation laid down in the Vocabulary of Vocabulary section titled Studying Word Structure (Student Text pages 15–16), this part of the Reviews introduces students to English words derived from common Latin and Greek stems, and gives practice in the strategy of finding meaning by analyzing the parts of a word.

WRITER'S CHALLENGE (PART 9)

The concluding part of each Review provides an opportunity for students to apply to the writing and revising process what they have learned about word meanings and usage. Note that it is important that students understand that, apart from the conventions of Standard English (when applicable), there are no "rights" or "wrongs" in writing, and that this activity is meant to make them more aware of ways in which the choice of words affects the tone, clarity, and coherence of their written work.

The Cumulative Reviews

Once students have completed the Reviews (and any follow-up activities), they may turn to the Cumulative Reviews.

Of the four parts of the Cumulative Reviews, three mirror activities presented in the Reviews: Analogies, Choosing the Right Meaning, and Two-Word Completions. These are presented in the same format and serve the same purpose as their counterparts in the Reviews, primarily to give students practice in types of questions they will encounter on the SAT I and other standardized tests.

The fourth part of the Cumulative Review, Enriching Your Vocabulary, is designed to broaden and enhance student knowledge of the interesting origins, history, and relationships of the words that make up the English language.

The Final Mastery Test

The Final Mastery Test in the Student Text of Levels A–H is designed as a practice test of 100 items that gives students and teachers reasonably good insight into how much progress has been made during the year and what kind of additional work is in order.

The purpose of the Final Mastery Test is fourfold.

- It can serve as a dry run in preparation for the more formal (and "secure") tests available as optional components.
- It can serve as an informal evaluation of achievement to date.
- It can serve as a reinforcement activity.
- It can serve as a before-and-after comparison when used in conjunction with the Diagnostic Test.

For whichever purpose the test is used, it is both a testing and a teaching device, the culminating step in a process involving many class periods and, therefore, should be given careful attention.

Supplemental Assessment Components (Optional)

Test Generator CD-ROM (Levels A–F)

New to this edition, the Vocabulary Workshop Test Generator CD-ROM provides an array of secure student tests that support the Student Texts for Levels A–F. With the Test Generator, teachers may create countless unique vocabulary tests with a variety of question formats, all within seconds. With a database of more than 3,000 questions per Level, teachers never have to administer the same test twice.

The Test Generator CD-ROM provides:

- new and secure Unit Tests, Mastery Tests, Cumulative Tests, Diagnostic Tests, Mid-Year Tests, and Final Mastery Tests
- a wide assortment of question types to choose from: pronunciation, part of speech, spelling, definitions, synonyms and antonyms, sentence completions, sentence framing
- the ability to customize tests to include any number of questions and to assess any Unit in the Student Text
- a method of flagging questions so that they will not appear on other tests
- the option to save a test for future use
- an on-screen Help program
- a printed Teacher's Manual
- technical support

The Test Generator provides a convenient and secure source of assessment and/or extra practice. With the Test Generator CD-ROM, teachers may tailor tests to suit the specific needs of either individual students or an entire class.

The flexibility of the Test Generator makes it easy to use either as-needed or more systematically, as an integral part of the VOCABULARY WORKSHOP series. See pages T22–25 for recommendations on how it may be used in conjunction with the Student Text and other components of the program.

Test Booklets (Levels A–H)

Two Test Booklets (Form A and Form B) are available for each of Levels A–H. These Test Booklets have been designed to be used in alternating years, thereby reducing the risk of answers being passed on. Each Test Booklet contains a full set of testing materials and is designed to cover the work of one entire Level of the Student Text. Though the formats of the Test Booklets are the same, the items tested in any given section are completely different. The contents of the Test Booklets have been organized to reflect that of the Student Text, and include the following:

- preparatory test-taking tips for students
- a Warm-Up Test (corresponding to the Diagnostic Test in the Student Text)
- 15 Unit Tests, each consisting of 25 items focusing on pronunciation, part of speech, spelling, definitions, synonyms, antonyms, and sentence completions
- 5 Cumulative Tests of 50 items each (plus 2 optional items)

The Warm-Up Test may serve either as an introduction to the Test Booklet as a whole or as an effective follow-up to the Diagnostic Test in the Student Text.

Each Unit Test has been designed for use as soon as the students have completed work on the Unit to which it corresponds or at any point thereafter.

Each Cumulative Test, including the Final Cumulative Test, covers all of the work of the Student Text to the point at which it occurs and is designed to be used after the corresponding Review in the Student Text.

Note that these tests may also serve as effective "lead-ins" to the SAT-oriented Cumulative Reviews in the Student Texts and to the SAT-oriented PREP Worksheets in the corresponding TEST PREP Blackline Masters.

For recommendations on how to employ the Test Booklets as part of the complete VOCABULARY WORKSHOP program, see pages T22–T29.

TEST PREP Blackline Masters (Levels A-H)

For further assessment options, a booklet of reproducible TEST PREP Blackline Masters is available for each Level A–H. The TEST PREP component is designed to provide both practice in working with SAT I type test questions and formats *and* review tests covering the entire content of the corresponding Student Text.

- Prep Tests approximate as closely as possible, given the vocabulary that is to be covered, the analogy and word-omission sections of the SAT I, and provide practice in the vocabulary-in-context strand with brief reading passages as well.
- Answer sheets provide an SAT I type test format to develop student ease and familiarity with standardized testing materials.

- Mastery Tests are meant to be used when students have completed the corresponding group of three Units in the Student Text. Each test covers basic meanings, synonyms, antonyms, sentence completions, and analogies.
- Answer keys, including selected answer rationales, are provided for all tests.

For recommendations on the implementation of the TEST PREP Blackline Masters as part of the complete VOCABULARY WORKSHOP program, see pages T23–T25.

Interactive Audio Pronunciation Program (Levels A–F)

Now available in CD format as well as cassette, the Interactive Audio Pronunciation Program provides teachers and students with a convenient and effective means of teaching and learning the recommended pronunciations of all key words introduced in the Student Texts for Levels A–F. It is designed to be used either by the teacher in a classroom setting or by the student (either individually or in small groups) in a language laboratory or at home.

- Ideal for English Language Learners of all cultures and backgrounds, and for use in ESL classrooms.
- Students hear the recommended pronunciation of each word at least 6 times, both alone and in context.
- Full coverage is given to words with more than one recommended pronunciation.
- Students are provided with two opportunities to pronounce each word themselves.
- Pronunciations are followed by brief definitions based on those given in the Student Text.
- Usage examples in complete-sentence form extend student knowledge of how to use a word correctly in their speech and writing.
- Teacher's notes for the program are provided in Spanish as well as English.

For recommendations on when to use the program, see the chart on pages T22–25.

IMPLEMENTING THE PROGRAM

The format of the VOCABULARY WORKSHOP program allows for great flexibility. The teacher can easily adjust the activity assignments to conform to the special needs of an entire class, of groups within the class, or of individual students.

Schedule for the Year (28 Weeks)

The chart on pages T23–T25 shows how the various components of the VOCABULARY WORKSHOP program for Levels A–H can be scheduled effectively over an academic year lasting 28 weeks.

The following notes should prove helpful when adapting the chart to individual needs:

- Though the chart shows a disposition of material over 28 weeks, the time period can be extended to as many as 34 weeks simply by increasing to two weeks the time allotment for the items under weeks 6, 11, 16, 21, 26, and 28.

- It is not to be supposed that every item listed under Follow-Up Activities is meant to be covered during the week specified. The listings here are designed to offer teacher options from which to choose in order to tailor the VOCABULARY WORKSHOP program to the specific needs of a particular class. This is also true of the sections or subsections into which some of the Follow-Up components are divided.

KEY

IAPP = Interactive Audio Pronunciation Program, Levels A–F only

TB A/B = Test Booklet Form A/Form B

BLM = *TEST PREP Blackline Masters*

TG = Test Generator CD-ROM

Using the Program Over the Year (28 Weeks)

Note: "Framing Sentences" and "Story/Essay Writing" are to be supplied by the teacher.

Week	Student Text	Follow-Up Activities
1	Vocabulary of Vocabulary	
2	Diagnostic Test	Warm-Up Test (TB A/B) Warm-Up Prep Test (BLM)
3	Unit 1 IAPP	Framing Sentences Story/Essay Writing Unit Test 1 (TB A/B) Unit Test 1 (TG)
4	Unit 2 IAPP	Framing Sentences Story/Essay Writing Unit Test 2 (TB A/B) Unit Test 2 (TG)
5	Unit 3 IAPP	Framing Sentences Story/Essay Writing Unit Test 3 (TB A/B) Unit Test 3 (TG)
6	Review 1–3	Mastery Test 1–3 (BLM) Mastery Test (TG)
7	—	Cumulative Test 1–3 (TB A/B) Prep Worksheet 1–3 (BLM)
8	Unit 4 IAPP	Framing Sentences Story/Essay Writing Unit Test 4 (TB A/B) Unit Test 4 (TG)
9	Unit 5 IAPP	Framing Sentences Story/Essay Writing Unit Test 5 (TB A/B) Unit Test 5 (TG)
10	Unit 6 IAPP	Framing Sentences Story/Essay Writing Unit Test 6 (TB A/B) Unit Test 6 (TG)

(Continued on pg. T24)

(Continued from pg. T23)

Week	Student Text	Follow-Up Activities
11	Review 4–6	Mastery Test 4–6 (BLM) Mastery Test (TG)
12	Cumulative Review 1–6	Cumulative Test 1–6 (TB A/B) Prep Worksheet 4–6 (BLM)
13	Unit 7 IAPP	Framing Sentences Story/Essay Writing Unit Test 7 (TB A/B) Unit Test 7 (TG)
14	Unit 8 IAPP	Framing Sentences Story/Essay Writing Unit Test 8 (TB A/B) Unit Test 8 (TG)
15	Unit 9 IAPP	Framing Sentences Story/Essay Writing Unit Test 9 (TB A/B) Unit Test 9 (TG)
16	Review 7–9	Mastery Test 7–9 (BLM) Mastery Test (TG) Mid-Year Test (TG)
17	Cumulative Review 1–9	Cumulative Test 1–9 (TB A/B) Prep Worksheet 7–9 (BLM) Cumulative Test (TG)
18	Unit 10 IAPP	Framing Sentences Story/Essay Writing Unit Test 10 (TB A/B) Unit Test 10 (TG)
19	Unit 11 IAPP	Framing Sentences Story/Essay Writing Unit Test 11 (TB A/B) Unit Test 11 (TG)
20	Unit 12 IAPP	Framing Sentences Story/Essay Writing Unit Test 12 (TB A/B) Unit Test 12 (TG)

Week	Student Text	Follow-Up Activities
21	Review 10–12	Mastery Test 10–12 (BLM) Mastery Test (TG)
22	Cumulative Review 1–12	Cumulative Test 1–12 (TB A/B) Prep Worksheet 10–12 (BLM) Cumulative Test (TG)
23	Unit 13 IAPP	Framing Sentences Story/Essay Writing Unit Test 13 (TB A/B) Unit Test 13 (TG)
24	Unit Test 14 IAPP	Framing Sentences Story/Essay Writing Unit Test 14 (TB A/B) Unit Test 14 (TG)
25	Unit 15 IAPP	Framing Sentences Story/Essay Writing Unit Test 15 (TB A/B) Unit Test 15 (TG)
26	Review 13–15	Mastery Test 13–15 (BLM) Mastery Test (TG)
27	Cumulative Review 1–15	Cumulative Test 1–15 (TB A/B) Prep Worksheet 13–15 (BLM) Cumulative Test (TG)
28	Final Mastery Test	Cumulative Mastery Test (BLM) Cumulative Prep Test (BLM) Final Test (TG)

Using the Units

On the top of these 2 pages the teacher will find 2 models for using the Units effectively on a weekly basis. Though there is no single formula or plan that will be sure to yield optimum results all the time, the models presented here and on the next 2 pages are designed to get the teacher thinking about how best to adapt the program to the needs of individual classes.

KEY: IAPP = Interactive Audio Pronunciation Program
TB = Test Booklet Form A or B
TG = Test Generator CD-ROM
** Item to be supplied by teacher/student

Assignment
Classwork
Homework

MODEL B: 5 Sessions/Periods (20 Minutes)		
Assignment	**Day 1**	**Day 2**
Classwork	1. Collect Framing Sentences 2. Review Unit Test 3. Present Definitions	Review Completing the Sentences
Homework	1. Completing the Sentence 2. IAPP	Synonyms and Antonyms

Using the Reviews

On the bottom of these 2 pages the teacher will find 2 models for using the Reviews effectively on a weekly basis.

Assignment
Classwork
Homework

MODEL B: 5 Sessions/Periods (20 Minutes)		
Assignment	**Day 1**	**Day 2**
Classwork	Present Analogies	1. Review homework 2. Present Choosing the Right Meaning
Homework	1. Word Associations 2. Antonyms	Vocabulary in Context

Weekly Lesson Plans

MODEL A: 3 Sessions/Periods (35–40 Minutes)

Day 1	Day 2	Day 3
1. Collect Framing Sentences** **2.** Present Definitions	**1.** Review Completing the Sentence, Synonyms and Antonyms **2.** Present Choosing the Right Word and Vocabulary in Context	**1.** Unit Test (TB or TG) **2.** Review last week's Framing Sentences**
1. Completing the Sentence, Synonyms and Antonyms **2.** IAPP	Test Study	Framing Sentences**

Day 3	Day 4	Day 5
Review Synonyms and Antonyms	**1.** Review Choosing the Right Word **2.** Review Vocabulary in Context	**1.** Unit Test (TB or TG) **2.** Review last week's Framing Sentences
Choosing the Right Word	Test Study	Framing Sentences**

MODEL A: 3 Sessions/Periods (35–40 Minutes)

Day 1	Day 2	Day 3
Present: Word Associations Vocabulary in Context Word Families	Review homework Present: Antonyms Building with Classical Roots Choosing the Right Meaning	**1.** Mastery Test (TB or TG) **2.** Review homework
1. Analogies **2.** Two-Word Completions	**1.** Test Study **2.** Writer's Challenge	Remedial work as required

Day 3	Day 4	Day 5
1. Review homework **2.** Present Two-Word Completions	Mastery Test (TB or TG)	**1.** Review Mastery Test **2.** Review homework
1. Test Study **2.** Word Families	**1.** Building with Classical Roots **2.** Writer's Challenge	Remedial work as required

Using the Cumulative Reviews

On the top of these 2 pages the teacher will find 2 models for using the Cumulative Reviews effectively on a weekly basis.

Assignment
Classwork
Homework

MODEL B: 5 Sessions/Periods (20 Minutes)		
Assignment	**Day 1**	**Day 2**
Classwork	Present Cumulative Review	Cumulative Test Parts 1–4 (TB)
Homework	Test Study	Test Study

Implementing the Weekly Schedules

The following may prove helpful when adapting the foregoing schedules to specific situations.

- The models shown are, as their designation suggests, purely models—that is, starting points. Accordingly, the teacher is expected to adapt them to the particular situation at hand.

- The models make only minimal use of the Follow-Up Activities suggested earlier and no use whatsoever of the Alternative Approaches to Using the Program suggested on the following pages. The teacher should in all cases feel free to introduce such alternative approaches as convenient.

- Place assignments and timings are to some extent hypothetical. Teachers should switch items around and adjust timings as needed. Similarly, items may be modified or deleted and new items inserted as the teacher sees fit.

- Multiple listings in a Day's entry for either Classwork or Homework are to be seen as options from which the teacher should select appropriate material. It is unlikely that the teacher could cover all the suggested material in the indicated time allotment.

- With some adjustment, the allotments for each Day can accommodate a 2- or 4-day arrangement. There is usually too much material to cover in 1 day, and a 1-day approach is, therefore, not suggested.

MODEL A: 3 Sessions/Periods (35–40 Minutes)		
Day 1	**Day 2**	**Day 3**
Present Cumulative Review	Cumulative Test (TB or TG)	**1.** Review Cumulative Test **2.** Review Prep Worksheet
Test Study	Prep Worksheet	Remedial Work as Required

Day 3	**Day 4**	**Day 5**
Cumulative Test Parts 5–6 (TB)	Review Cumulative Test	Review Prep Worksheet
—	Prep Worksheet	Remedial Work as Required

Alternative Approaches to Using the Program

Writing Approach

Research has shown that vocabulary acquisition is maximized when learning is authentically contextualized—when learners have a "real-life" purpose for acquiring and using a new word. Activities such as the following can provide these authentic contexts.

- Students can create journals or logs in which they use the key words to express experiences, thoughts, or feelings that are personally meaningful. They are free to keep these entries for their eyes only or to share them with others.

- Students can use the key words in personal letters to friends and relatives or in letters to the editor of the school or local newspaper. Students should write about subjects of real interest and concern to them.

- Students can use the key words to write descriptions of people they know or characters they are interested in. These character sketches or personality profiles may be written for a class yearbook, for a book report, or as a reference for a friend.

Literature-Based Approach

The VOCABULARY WORKSHOP program can be combined with some of the items listed below to form a *literature-based* approach to vocabulary study. Each of the items listed has been surveyed for use of some of the key words presented in the specified level of VOCABULARY WORKSHOP. Seeing the words they are studying in classic world literature will reinforce student appreciation of the value of possessing a good active-use vocabulary.

Classic Literature To Use With The Program

Levels D and E

Louisa May Alcott *Little Women*

Maya Angelou *I know Why the Caged Bird Sings*

Ray Bradbury *Fahrenheit 451*

Charlotte Brontë *Jane Eyre*

Emily Brontë *Wuthering Heights*

Pearl S. Buck *The Good Earth*

Lewis Carroll *Alice's Adventures in Wonderland*

Willa Cather *My Antonia*

Sandra Cisneros *The House on Mango Street*

Daniel Defoe *Robinson Crusoe*

Charles Dickens *A Tale of Two Cities*

Arthur Conan Doyle *The Hound of the Baskervilles*

George Eliot *Silas Marner*

William Golding *Lord of the Flies*

Frank Herbert *Dune*

Harper Lee *To Kill a Mockingbird*

Carson McCullers *Member of the Wedding*

Nicholasa Mohr *El Bronx Remembered*

Walter Dean Myers *Fallen Angels*

George Orwell *Animal Farm*

Alan Paton *Cry, the Beloved Country*

John Steinbeck *The Pearl*

Level F

Sherwood Anderson *Winesburg, Ohio*

James Baldwin *Go Tell It on the Mountain*

Stephen Crane *The Red Badge of Courage*

Kate Chopin *The Awakening*

Ralph Ellison *Invisible Man*

Louise Erdrich *Love Medicine*

Jack Finney *Time and Again*

F. Scott Fitzgerald *The Great Gatsby*

Joseph Heller *Catch-22*

Ernest Hemingway *A Farewell to Arms*

Zora Neale Hurston *Their Eyes Were Watching God*

Nathaniel Hawthorne *The Scarlet Letter*

Henry James *Washington Square*

Maxine Hong Kingston *Woman Warrior*

N. Scott Momaday *The Way to Rainy Mountain*

Toni Morrison *Beloved*

John Steinbeck *The Grapes of Wrath*

Amy Tan *The Joy Luck Club*

Mark Twain *The Adventures of Huckleberry Finn*

Kurt Vonnegut, Jr. *Slaughterhouse Five*

Alice Walker *The Color Purple*

Edith Wharton *The House of Mirth* and *The Age of Innocence*

Richard Wright *Black Boy*

Levels G and H

Margaret Atwood *The Handmaid's Tale*

Chinua Achebe *Things Fall Apart*

Jane Austen *Pride and Prejudice*

Joseph Conrad *Lord Jim* and *Heart of Darkness*

Charles Dickens *David Copperfield*

Isak Dinesen *Out of Africa*

George Eliot *The Mill on the Floss*

Thomas Hardy *The Return of the Native*

Aldous Huxley *Brave New World*

James Joyce *A Portrait of the Artist as a Young Man*

Gabriel Garcia Marquez *One Hundred Years of Solitude*

Mark Mathabane *Kaffir Boy*

V.S. Naipaul *A House for Mr. Biswas*

Mary Shelley *Frankenstein*

Muriel Spark *The Prime of Miss Jean Brodie*

Jonathan Swift *Gulliver's Travels*

Virginia Woolf *A Room of One's Own* and *To the Lighthouse*

To coordinate reading and vocabulary study, the following may prove helpful:

- Instruct students to devote a special notebook to vocabulary. As they come across key words in their reading, they should head a page of the notebook with the word; copy the title of the work; and then indicate (a) the definition of the word used in that sentence, (b) its part of speech, and (c) whether it is used in a literal or figurative sense.

- Students may then be instructed to check *Bartlett's Familiar Quotations* for other famous examples of the use of the key word in question. These may be copied into the notebook and shared with others in the class.

Content-Area Approach

VOCABULARY WORKSHOP can be used to enhance student understanding and use of vocabulary in subjects such as social studies and history, science and health, and other curriculum areas.

In the following list of nonfiction print and video titles you will find works that relate in content to Vocabulary in Context exercises appearing in specific Units and Reviews of the VOCABULARY WORKSHOP Student Texts for Levels D–H. Students may wish to read or view some of these works and report on the topics and issues that they treat. In their reports, whether oral or written, students should be encouraged to use words they have come to know through their Student Texts.

Author & Title	Level & Unit
Lisa Aldred, *Thurgood Marshall*	Level G, U6; H, U6
Catherine Allgor, *Parlor Politics*	Level G, Unit 7
Isaac Asimov, "The Eureka Phenomenon" from *Left Hand of the Election*	Level E, Review 13–15
Russell Baker, *Growing Up*	Level E, U15; H, U4
Rachel Carson, *Silent Spring*	Level G, Unit 2
Agnes DeMille, "The Kosloff School" from *Dance to the Piper*	Level E, Unit 10
Benjamin Franklin, *The Autobiography*	Level E, Unit 3
James Herriot, *All Creatures Great and Small*	Level D, Unit 12
J. S. Holliday, *The World Rushed In*	Level E, Review 7–9
Washington Irving, *Dietrich Knickerbocker's A History of New York*	Level H, Review 10–12
Charles Kuralt, "Noah Webster's Dictionary" from *Dateline America*	Level H, Unit 2
Brian Lanker, "Daisy Bates," in *I Dream a World: Portraits of Black Women Who Changed America*	Level H, Unit 6
Patricia Lauber, *Volcano: The Eruption and Healing of Mt. St. Helens*	Level D, Unit 15
Bill Littlefield, *Champions*	F, Rev 4–6; H, U5, 12
John McPhee, "The Loch Ness Monster" from *Pieces of the Frame*	Level F, Unit 8
Tsuneo Nakamura, *Gentle Giant*	Level D, Unit 13
Ann Petry, *Harriet Tubman: Conductor on the Underground Railroad*	Level E, Unit 6
Franklin D. Roosevelt, *War Message to Congress, December 8, 1941*	Level F, Units 10, 11
Amy Tan, *The Joy Luck Club*	Level D, Unit 2
Ellen Harkins Wheat, *Jacob Lawrence, American Painter*	Level H, Unit 8

Title & Distributor Videos	Level & Unit
American Cinema (Discovery Channel Video)	Level F, Unit 1
American Photography (PBS Home Video)	Level F, Unit 7
American Visions (PBS Home Video)	E, U9; F, U3; G, U5; H, Rev. 1–3
Baseball: A Film by Ken Burns (PBS Home Video)	Level F, U5; Level H, U5
Bridges, Skyscrapers and Tunnels (Discovery Channel Video)	Level G, Unit 8
Cold War (PBS Home Video)	Level D, Unit 5
Flyers (PBS Home Video)	Level F, Review 1–3
Frank Lloyd Wright (PBS Home Video)	Level F, Unit 3
Gold Fever (PBS Home Video)	Level E, Review 7–9
The Great Depression (History Channel Video)	Level E, Unit 15
The Great Ships: Sailing Collection (History Channel Video)	Level E, Unit 7
John Ringling: Master of the Big Top (PBS Home Video)	Level E, Unit 1
Ken Burns' America: Statue of Liberty (PBS Home Video)	Level D, Unit 7
Liberty! The American Revolution (PBS Home Video)	D, U1, E, U3; F, U13; G, U4; H, U9
Not for Ourselves Alone (PBS Home Video)	Level H, Unit 7
Reflections on Elephants (National Geographic Video)	Level F, Review 7–9
Surviving the Dust Bowl (PBS Home Video)	Level H., Unit 14
Trains Unlimited (History Channel Video)	Level F, Unit 14
The Ultimate Guide: Birds of Prey (Discovery Channel Video)	Level E, Unit 12

Other content-related activities to which students might apply vocabulary study are:

- Working in pairs or small groups, they can choose sentences from Completing the Sentence or Choosing the Right Word and discuss a larger context in which these sentences could have appeared, such as a history or mathematics textbook, a daily newspaper, a book review, a personal letter, or a scientific article.
- Students can work together to link individual vocabulary words to a particular content area. Then working in pairs, they can find "real-world" examples of the words used in context in that content area.
- Students can work cooperatively to create sentence and paragraph contexts that illustrate the meaning of the content-area words that they have identified.

Useful Classroom Techniques

Classroom experience and research have shown that some students learn more readily when they can exercise a great deal of personal choice and can interact with others. VOCABULARY WORKSHOP can be adapted in the following ways to accommodate such students.

Cooperative Activities

Working cooperatively does not just mean working in proximity to other students or dividing an assignment or project into discrete tasks. Rather it means that students take individual and collective responsibility for the learning of all members of the group and for the successful completion of the group goal. Students who cooperate to develop their vocabulary should maintain an ongoing dialog to monitor the comprehension of all group members.

Oral and Kinesthetic

- One student can write the key words in a given unit on the chalkboard while the rest of the class is divided into pairs or small groups. A member of each group will read a numbered item from the Unit aloud. The rest of the group will confer and then supply the required vocabulary word. The student reader will evaluate each answer and give reasons why it is correct or incorrect based on the word's definition and any context clues.
- Students in groups can discuss the shades of meaning or connotations among selected synonyms and antonyms for a given Unit and among the alternative answers in Choosing the Right Meaning.
- Students can work together to create puns, riddles, Tom Swifties, and limericks to illustrate the multiple meanings of appropriate vocabulary words. They may want to collect and publish their creations in illustrated books or an audio-anthology.
- Members of a group can work together to improvise stories, skits, or pantomimes that illustrate the meaning of a key word in a given Unit, while other group members guess the word being illustrated.

Written

- Students can work cooperatively to brainstorm their own vocabulary word lists, based on their current reading and writing in all areas of the curriculum and on their personal reading and writing experiences.
- The class can collaborate to create their own Unit, covering vocabulary words they have chosen. Different groups can be assigned to develop each of the unit activities.
- Students may want to create their own mini-dictionaries, based on the word lists in VOCABULARY WORKSHOP or on categories of words that are especially meaningful or useful to them, such as sports, fashion, music, and career terms.
- Students can make use of semantic mapping and other graphic devices, such as flow charts, to generate new vocabulary or to demonstrate understanding of word relationships. Semantic mapping, or webbing, can be used to illustrate word families, synonyms, and antonyms. Flow charts can illustrate etymological and grammatical relationships.

Alternative Types of Assessment

The following types of assessment may be used in addition to or in lieu of the objective-scoring materials provided in the VOCABULARY WORKSHOP, Levels A–H. The emphasis here is on monitoring understanding rather than on ranking students.

Self-Evaluation

Students can use their journals to reflect on their own process of learning and use of new words. They may consider, for example, which words from VOCABULARY WORKSHOP they understood quickly and used frequently and why. They may want to use these insights to design their own vocabulary-acquisition strategies.

Teacher-Student Conferencing

Meetings take place at every stage of the vocabulary-acquisition process. Meeting over time allows teachers to assess students' developing understanding of words as used in specific contexts.

Observation

Using a checklist of 2 or 3 important criteria, the teacher can observe and evaluate students while they are interacting in groups or engaging in other oral activities. Teachers can also probe for deeper levels of comprehension by asking students to clarify or give reasons for their choice of word or context.

Peer Evaluation

Students meet in pairs or small groups to develop standards or criteria to evaluate their vocabulary acquisition. They then apply their standards to their peers' oral or written expression, giving positive feedback and concrete suggestions for improvement.

Portfolio Assessment

By having students collect and save self-selected samples of their writing over a period of time, teachers have an ongoing record of students' vocabulary development and of their facility in using words in context.

Multimodal Assessment

Students with strong nonverbal competencies can be given the opportunity to demonstrate in nonverbal media their understanding of new vocabulary. For example, they can draw, paint, model, dance, compose music, or construct objects to communicate their comprehension of a word and its definition.

TEACHER RESOURCES

The following lists have been compiled to assist the teacher in the effective presentation of the VOCABULARY WORKSHOP program, Levels A–H.

I. DICTIONARIES

Recommended

Merriam-Webster *Collegiate Dictionary* [Tenth Edition] (Springfield, MA: Merriam-Webster, 2000)

Webster's *Third New International Dictionary* (Springfield, MA: G. & C. Merriam, 1993)

American Heritage Dictionary (Boston; Houghton Mifflin, 2000)

Oxford English Dictionary [Compact Edition] (Oxford: Oxford University Press, 1971)

Skeat, W. *A. Concise Etymological Dictionary of the English Language* (NY: G.P. Putnam, 1980)

Supplemental

12,000 Words [A Supplement to Webster's *Third International Dictionary*] (Springfield, MA: Merriam-Webster, 1993)

The Random House Dictionary of the English Language [Unabridged Edition] (NY: Random House, 1987)

II. THESAURI

Recommended

Roget's II The New Thesaurus (Boston: Houghton Mifflin, 1995)

Random House Roget's Thesaurus (NY: Random House, 2001)

Rodale, J. [Revised by Urdang, L. and La Roche, N.] The Synonym Finder (Emmaus, PA: Rodale Press, 1979)

Supplemental

Chapman, R.L. (Ed.). *Roget A to Z* (NY: Harper Perennial, 1994)

Laird, C. *Webster's New World Thesaurus* (NY: Warner Books, 1990)

Roget's International Thesaurus [Fifth Edition] (NY: HarperCollins, 1992)

Abate, F. *The Oxford Dictionary and Thesaurus: The Ultimate Language Reference for American Readers* (NY: Oxford University Press, 1996)

III. OTHER REFERENCE WORKS

Recommended

Carroll, J., Davies, P., and Richman, B. *Word Frequency Book* (Boston: Houghton Mifflin, 1971)

Dale, E. and O'Rourke, J. *The Living Word Vocabulary* (Chicago: Scott & Fetzer, 1981)

Supplemental

Harris, A. and Jackson, M. *Basic Reading Vocabularies* (NY: Macmillan, 1982)

Thorndike, E. and Lorge, I. *The Teacher's Book of 30,000 Words* (NY: Teachers College Press, Columbia University, 1968)

IV. HISTORY

General

Baugh, A.C. and Cable, T. *A History of the English Language* [Third Edition] (Englewood Cliffs, NJ: Prentice-Hall, 1992)

Carver, C. *A History of English in Its Own Words* (NY: HarperCollins, 1991)

Jespersen, O. *Growth and Structure of the English Language* (University of Chicago Press, 1982)

McCrum, R., Cran, W., and MacNeil, R. *The Story of English* (NY: Penguin, 1993)

Myers, L.M. *The Roots of Modern English* (Boston: Little, Brown, 1961)

Pyles, T. *The Origins and Development of the English Language* [Fourth Edition] (NY: Harcourt, Brace, Jovanovich, 1993)

Robinson, O. *Old English and Its Closest Relatives* (Stanford, CA, 1993)

American English

Dillard, J.L. *All-American English* (NY: Random House, 1975)

Dillard, J.L. *American Talk* (NY: Random House, 1976)

Flexner, S.B. *I Hear America Talking* (NY: Simon & Schuster, 1976)

Mencken, H.L. *The American Language* (NY: Alfred A. Knopf, 1979)

V. OTHER USEFUL RESOURCES

A Dictionary of American Idioms (Woodbury, NY: Barron's Educational Series, Inc., 1995)

Bryson, B. *A Dictionary of Troublesome Words* (NY: Viking Penguin, 1988)

Carroll, D. *Dictionary of Foreign Terms in The English Language* (NY: Hawthorn Books, 1973)

Dixson, R. *Essential Idioms in English* (Englewood Cliffs, NJ: Pearson ESL, 1993)

Evans, I.H. (Ed.) *Brewer's Dictionary of Phrase & Fable* (NY: Harper & Row, 2000)

Harrison, G. *Vocabulary Dynamics* (NY: Warner Books, 1992)

Hendrickson, R. *The Dictionary of Eponyms* (NY: Stein and Day, 1985)

Morris, W. and M. *Morris Dictionary of Word & Phrase Origins* (NY: Harper & Row, 1988)

Orgel, J.R. *Building an Enriched Vocabulary* (NY: William H. Sadlier, Inc., 1999)

Paxson, W. *New American Dictionary of Confusing Words* (NY: NAL-Dutton, 1990)

Room, A. *Dictionary of Contrasting Pairs* (NY: Routledge Educational Series Inc., (1988)

Room, A. *The Penguin Dictionary of Confusibles* (NY: Penguin Books, 1989)

Shipley, J. *Dictionary of Word Origins* (Glenville, IL: Greenwood Press, 1988)

Smith, R. *Dictionary of English Word-Roots* (Totowa, NJ: Littlefield, Adams & Co., 1980)

Spears, R. *Slang and Euphemisms* (NY: NAL-Dutton, 1991)

Webster's Word Histories (Springfield, MA: Merriam Webster, 1989)

Answers To Exercises In Reviews And Cumulative Reviews

Review Units 1–3

Analogies (page 42)

1. (a). A means the same as B.
2. (b). In one A there are 10 Bs.
3. (a). Someone who is going to A against something would probably use B to achieve his or her ends.
4. (c). If you take A at something, you B it.
5. (c). A means the opposite of B.
6. (a). Someone who is A may justly be characterized as full of B.
7. (d). Someone who is A lacks B.
8. (c). Someone who As could justly be characterized as B.
9. (d). Someone who is about to A would be likely to use B to achieve his or her aim.
10. (c). An A is a person who by definition would be likely to B.
11. (b). An act that is A would be likely to receive or deserve B.
12. (d). A means the opposite of B.
13. (a). A means the opposite of B.
14. (b). B can be characterized by A.
15. (b). Something that is A lacks B.
16. (b). A lacks B.
17. (c). Someone who is A would lack B.
18. (b). A means the opposite of B.

Choosing the Right Meaning (page 45)

1. (d). (Inference clue: "disappearance") (a), (b), (c): irrelevant meaning of word (ir).
2. (a). (Inference clue: What might happen to a TV series after only six episodes?) (b), (c), (d): wrong sense of word (ws).
3. (b). (Contrast clues: "British," "native") (c): ws; (a), (d): ir.
4. (c). (Contrast clue: "survive intact") (b): ws; (a), (d): ir.
5. (c). (Contrast clue: "congenital") (d): ws; (a), (b): ir.

Two-Word Completions (page 47)

1. (b). approbation (Contrast clue: "severest censure"; Inference clue: What kind of reaction do death-defying feats of gallantry deserve from the general public?) . . . merit (Restatement clue: "deserve")
2. (a). prerogatives (Inference clue: What would you call a teacher's right to use school equipment, etc?) . . . hiatus (Restatement clue: "break")
3. (c). nominal (Contrast clue: "actually") . . . ex officio (Restatement clue: "by virtue of that position")

4. (b). lassitude (Contrast clue: "vigorous and aggressive," "however"; Inference clue: In what sort of state would people who were feeble be likely to be?) . . . decadent (Restatement clue: "feeble and")

5. (d). coalition (Restatement clue: "partnership") . . . transcend (Contrast clue: "become entangled in")

6. (c). exhorted (Inference clue: What would a Senator who strongly favored a certain proposal suggest that other Senators do?) . . . inveigh (Inference clue: What would a Senator who equally strongly opposed the bill suggest that other Senators do?)

Review Units 4–6

Analogies (page 72)

1. (c). Something that is A is difficult to B.
2. (a). If you felt A, you would be B.
3. (c). The tone of A is B.
4. (d). A is a drink that is by nature a B.
5. (d). Someone who is A has a great deal of B.
6. (b). An A is used to B.
7. (b). The prevailing mood of A can aptly be described as B.
8. (b). A person deals in A if his or her occupation is B.
9. (b). An A is a person who would be likely to B something.
10. (c). Something that is A is readily able to B.
11. (d). A means the opposite of B.
12. (a). Someone who can be described as A would be characterized by B.
13. (d). Something that is A is not subject to B.
14. (a). Something that is A is by definition of inferior (poor) B.
15. (c). Something that is A lacks B.
16. (b). A means the opposite of B.
17. (c). A means the opposite of B.
18. (c). An A would by definition be B.

Choosing the Right Meaning (page 75)

1. (a). (Restatement clue: "chain gang") (c), (d): ws (too abstract); (b): ws (inappropriate to context).

2. (c). (Contrast clue: "long-term visitors") (a), (b): ws (too specific); (d): ws (inappropriate to context).

3. (a). (Inference clue: What type of punishment was usual on a 19th-century naval vessel?) (c): ws (too general); (b), (d): ir.

4. (b). (Inference clue: What happens when one mirror is put in front of another?) (a), (c): ws; (d): ir.

5. (d). (Inference clue: Why would officials halt traffic when there was a fog?) (a), (c): ws; (b): ir.

Two-Word Completions (page 77)

1. (b). propensity (Inference clue: What does rubber possess in regard to its original shape?) . . . resilient (Inference clue: What would you call something that can resume its original shape?)
2. (c). reverberating (Inference clue: What sort of sound can be heard when you walk along an empty corridor?) . . . sepulchral (Inference clue: "It's . . . night")
3. (d). surreptitiously (Inference clue: How would a sneak thief move about?) . . . filch (Inference clue: What would a sneak thief attempt to do?)
4. (c). immutable (Inference clue: If something changes and develops over time, what wouldn't it be?) . . . irrevocable (Inference clue: same question)
5. (a). affable (Restatement clue: "courteous and"; Contrast clue: "surly") . . . brusque (Restatement clue: "and surly"; Contrast clue: "courteous")
6. (b). sedulous (Restatement clue: "worked . . . dog") . . . extricate (Contrast clue: "would . . . water")

Cumulative Review I

Analogies (page 81)

1. (c). If you A something, you make it B than it was.
2. (d). A means the opposite of B.
3. (a). You would use an A to B.
4. (b). A means the same as B.
5. (c). A means the same as B.
6. (c). A indicates that a person is feeling very B.
7. (b). Something that is A lacks B.
8. (a). A means the same as B.
9. (b). Someone who is A is very likely to B.
10. (c). Something that is A lacks B.

Choosing the Right Meaning (pages 81–82)

1. (c). (Inference clue: "degenerated") (d): ws; (a), (b): ir.
2. (d). (Contrast clue: "less malleable") (a), (c): ws; (b): ir.
3. (a). (Inference clue: Why might it be inadvisable to test missiles near populated areas?) (c): ws; (b), (d): ir.
4. (b). (Inference clue: "eclectic") (c): ws; (a), (d): ir.
5. (b). (Inference clue: How might a group of explorers look at one another when they had finally discovered what they were looking for?) (a), (c), (d): ir.

Two-Word Completions (page 82)

1. (b). lurid (Context clue: "flames") . . . permeated (Inference clue: What would the stench of burning rubber do to the air around a fire?)
2. (a). reverberated (Inference clue: How would you describe how the notes of an organ react in a cathedral?) . . . sepulchral (Restatement clue: "cavernous")
3. (b). millennia (Inference clue: How long traditionally has it been since Moses came down from Mt. Sinai with the Ten Commandments?) . . . precepts (Context clue: "the Ten Commandments")
4. (d). transgressions (Restatement clue: "sins") . . . expiate (Inference clue: What was the death of a sacrificial victim in an ancient religion intended to do?)
5. (c). sinecure (Inference clue: What kind of job *don't* you have to be talented to do?) . . . sedulous (Inference clue: What *don't* you have to be to perform a sinecure?)

REVIEW UNITS 7–9

Analogies (page 105)

1. (a). An A is a person who is by definition B.
2. (b). Something that is A lacks B.
3. (b). A would make a person B.
4. (c). A means the opposite of B.
5. (a). Something or someone who is A would inspire B in others.
6. (d). An A is by definition a person who would be guilty of B.
7. (c). If you felt A at something, B would aptly describe your reaction.
8. (d). A means the same as B.
9. (d). A mistake that is A is as big as a B.
10. (c). A means the opposite of B.
11. (d). Someone who is A lacks B.
12. (b). A means the same as B.
13. (d). Someone who was known for his or her A might aptly be described as B.
14. (a). An A would be the recipient (or object) of public B.
15. (c). Someone who is A is seriously deficient in B.
16. (b). An A is a piece of protective armor for the B.
17. (a). Someone who is A lacks B.
18. (c). Living in an A would indicate that a person's life style is B.

Choosing the Right Meaning (page 108)

1. (b). (Inference clue: What kind of a liquid does one usually get when mixing a powder with water?) (a), (c), (d): ws.
2. (d). (Contrast clue: "smooth") (a), (b), (c): ws.
3. (a). (Contrast clue: "cravens") (b), (c): ws; (d): ir.
4. (a). (Inference clue: How was Hathor usually represented?) (c): ws; (b), (d): ir.
5. (c). (Inference clue: What effect does Aurora [the dawn] have on the black skies of night?) (a), (b), (d): ws.

Two-Word Completions (page 110)

1. (d). grandiose (Inference clue: On what kind of scale would a few lucky "haves" be able to live?) . . . penury (Inference clue: In what state would a pauper be likely to live?)
2. (a). culpable (Inference clue: "the . . . offense") . . . mitigated (Inference clue: "the . . . committed")
3. (b). infraction (Restatement clue: "violation") . . . relegated (Restatement clue: "put there")
4. (c). cadavers (Inference clue: In what do morgues and funeral parlors deal?) . . . squeamish (Contrast clue: "has . . . stomach")
5. (b). odium (Inference clue: With what would history be likely to regard a traitor like Benedict Arnold?) . . . perfidy (Inference clue: What is Benedict Arnold's villainous act an example of?)
6. (c). pillaged (Inference clue: What would barbarians do to a civilized town they raided?) . . . desecrated (Inference clue: What would they do to its temples?)

CUMULATIVE REVIEW II

Analogies (page 114)

1. (a). An A is by definition B.
2. (c). A means the same as B.
3. (b). An A is a person who would by definition be likely to B.
4. (c). A means the opposite of B.
5. (a). An A is by definition B.
6. (c). A means the same as B.
7. (d). Someone who is A would possess a great deal of B.
8. (c). Someone who is A pays a great deal of attention to (is concerned about) B.
9. (c). Someone who is A would by definition exhibit B.
10. (c). If you A something, you make it B.

Choosing the Right Meaning (pages 114–115)

1. (c). (Inference clue: What do industrial waste and other contaminants do to water?) (a), (d): ws; (b): ir.
2. (b). (Inference clue: "Sweeps . . . along") (c): ws; (a), (d): ir.
3. (d). (Inference clue: "distilled") (c): ws; (a), (b): ir.
4. (a). (Inference clue: "concrete") (b), (c), (d): ws.

Two-Word Completions (page 115)

1. (b). straitlaced (Inference clue: How would most people characterize the typical Victorian mentality?) . . . expurgated (Inference clue: What did Thomas Bowdler do to the plays of Shakespeare?)
2. (c). anathema (Inference clue: How would you describe a practice that was abhorrent to you?) . . . inveighed (Inference clue: What did the Old Testament prophets do in regard to practices they considered abhorrent?)
3. (d). compensation (Restatement clue: "salary or") . . . prerogative (Restatement clue: "privilege")
4. (b). abates (Inference clue: Does a summer thundershower last a long time?) . . . transient (Inference clue: What adjective would describe something that didn't last long?)
5. (a). Scourge (Inference clue: What would you call the instrument of divine retribution?) . . . transgressions (Inference clue: Why would a deity visit divine retribution on human beings?)

REVIEW UNITS 10–12

Analogies (page 138)

1. (a). If something is A, you can B it.
2. (b). A properly refers to B in an unflattering way.
3. (a). An A is a person who would by definition be B.
4. (b). An A is a kind of address that would by definition be filled with B.
5. (d). A means the opposite of B.
6. (d). A is by definition something that is B.
7. (a). A indicates a burlesque kind of B.
8. (c). If you A something, you make B of it than there was originally.
9. (b). Something that is A has an extraordinary ability to B.
10. (d). The characteristic attire of an A is B, or an A is a person who would be likely to wear B.
11. (b). A means the opposite of B.
12. (c). The tone of A is B.

(Continued on pg. T44)

(Continued from pg. T43)

13. (b). An A is a person who would by definition exemplify B.
14. (d). Someone who is A would by definition possess a great deal of B.
15. (c). If you A something, you put it B; if you C something, you take it D.
16. (c). A properly refers to a B that is highly colored or decorated.
17. (b). An A is by definition B.
18. (a). If you had been A, you would probably feel B.

Choosing the Right Meaning (page 141)

1. (a). (Inference clue: What figure is produced by the troop movements indicated?) (b), (c), (d): ir.
2. (b). (Inference clue: What kind of person would the speaker regret having made himself?) (a), (c), (d): ws.
3. (c). (Inference clue: "The funeral . . . tables") (b), (d): ws; (a): ir.
4. (d). (Contrast clue: "sedentary") (b), (c): ws; (a): ir.

Two-Word Completions (page 143)

1. (c). sedentary (Restatement clue: "desk jockey"; Inference clue: What is the nature of an office worker's job?) . . . efficacious (Inference clue: Why is it important for an office worker to make frequent use of a gym?)
2. (d). ostentatious (Restatement clue: "flamboyant") . . . dowdy (Restatement clue: "drab and")
3. (c). searing (Restatement clue: "withering") . . . invective (Inference clue: What would a withering political attack be likely to contain?)
4. (b). enthralled (Contrast clue: "find . . . bore") . . . satiated (Contrast clue: "had . . . enough")
5. (a). denizens (Restatement clue: "crew") . . . motley (Restatement clue: "come . . . life")
6. (a). procrastinate (Inference clue: What *aren't* you doing when you take immediate steps to stop something from happening?) . . . pernicious (Inference clue: What kind of effect would a highly dangerous development be likely to have?)

CUMULATIVE REVIEW III

Analogies (pages 147–148)

1. (d). A means the same as B.
2. (b). A means the opposite of B.
3. (c). You would use an A in order to B.
4. (d). A means the opposite of B.
5. (a). An A is a person who would *not* be B.
6. (c). Something that was in a state of A would be full of B.
7. (a). A means the opposite of B.
8. (c). A refers to a B that is slow-moving.
9. (d). A means the same as B.
10. (c). If a person has great A, he or she is very B.
11. (c). Someone who is A would be guilty of B.
12. (a). A means the same as B.
13. (d). Something that would A your appetite would be likely to make you feel B.
14. (d). A means the same as B.
15. (a). A means the opposite of B.
16. (b). Someone who performed something with A would *not* be described as B.
17. (b). An A is someone who by definition would be B.
18. (a). You A something with B.
19. (a). An A is a person who by definition would be B.
20. (c). A means the same as B.

Choosing the Right Meaning (pages 148–149)

1. (d). (Inference clue: In what might a bed of flowers lie snugly?) (a), (b), (c): ws.

2. (b). (Inference clue: "pall," "see not"; restatement clue: "dark") (c): ws; (a), (d): ir.

3. (c). (Inference clue: "meaningless") (a): ws; (b), (d): ir.

4. (b). (Inference clue: "A true . . . Prison") (a): ws; (c), (d): ir.

5. (a). (Inference clue: What would one need to do to the environment after a major oil spill?) (b), (c), (d): ws.

6. (c). (Inference clue: What would one do if one wanted to protect the confidentiality of one's sources?) (a), (b), (d): ws.

■ *T45*

Two-Word Completions (page 149)

1. (a). specious (Restatement clue: "faulty") . . . transmute (Inference clue: What did the medieval alchemists attempt to do to base metals?)

2. (a). contraband (Inference clue: What do smugglers deal in?) . . . corroborates (Inference clue: What would incriminating evidence do to a charge brought against a suspect?)

3. (d). astute (Inference clue: What kind of comments would be made by a person of notable intelligence and common sense?) . . . redoubtable (Inference clue: More than what amount of common sense would you need to make astute comments?)

4. (c). repudiate (Inference clue: In the old days what were people forced to do if they did not hold orthodox beliefs?) . . . heresy (Inference clue: If they didn't, what would they be charged with?)

5. (d). epitome (Inference clue: What is the lead paragraph in a newspaper article supposed to do?) . . . salient (Inference clue: What kind of ideas would an epitome by likely to contain?)

6. (b). erudition (Inference clue: What would scholarly notes and comments indicate about the person who wrote them?) . . . annotated (Inference clue: What kind of edition contains scholarly notes and comments?)

Review Units 13–15

Analogies (page 172)

1. (c). An A is something that by definition would B a person.
2. (c). The tone of A is B.
3. (d). An A is an animal that is proverbially B.
4. (a). Someone who is A will not B.
5. (b). Someone who is A is likely to B.
6. (d). An A is someone who would by definition tend to B money.
7. (a). Something that is A has no B.
8. (b). If something is A, a person cannot B it.
9. (c). An A is something that by definition would B a person.
10. (c). Too much of a good thing would A the B.
11. (a). A means the opposite of B.
12. (a). A indicates that something has great B.
13. (d). A means the same as B.
14. (d). A indicates that something is excessive in B.
15. (d). An A is used to B something.
16. (b). A matters are within the purview of a B.
17. (c). It is difficult to A someone who is B.
18. (b). A means the opposite of B.

Choosing the Right Meaning (page 175)

1. (a). (Inference clue: The sense of the sentence and the book it comes from suggest that the context deals with a ship.) (b), (c): ws; (d): ir.
2. (d). (Inference clue: What does a magnet usually do to a piece of electrically charged material?) (a), (b), (c): ws.
3. (c). (Inference clue: What kind of medicine might make one gag?) (a), (b), (d): ws.
4. (b). (Inference clue: What might be sitting on a sideboard?) (d), (a), (c): ir.

Two-Word Completions (page 177)

1. (a). precocious (Inference clue: How would a person characterize a youngster who had written his first opera at the age of eleven?) . . . prolific (Contrast clue: "negligible")
2. (c). supplications (Restatement clue: "entreaties") . . . adamantly (Inference clue: How would you describe a refusal to yield to entreaty, however piteous?)
3. (d). blatant (Inference clue: What adjective would you use for a display of emotion that was not restrained?) . . . impassivity (Inference clue: With what was a true stoic supposed to react to bad news?)
4. (c). carnage (Restatement clue: "bodies," "the dead") . . . grisly (Inference clue: What sort of task would burying dead soldiers be?)
5. (b). curtail (Inference from "Once . . . forever") . . . depleted (Inference clue: "Once . . . forever")
6. (b). thwart (Inference clue: What is protective consumer legislation designed to do in regard to swindlers and con artists?) . . . credulous (Inference clue: On what sort of people do swindlers and con artists prey?)

CUMULATIVE REVIEW IV

Analogies (pages 181–182)

1. (c). A means the opposite of B.
2. (d). By definition B is characterized by A.
3. (c). It is easy to A someone who is B.
4. (b). An A is a statement that is by definition B.
5. (a). An A is a person who would by definition be B.
6. (d). An A is an animal that is proverbially B.
7. (d). Someone who is A would be likely to B.
8. (a). Something that would A would make a person feel B.
9. (c). An A would by definition make a person feel B.
10. (b). If you A something, you add B to it.

(Continued from pg. T47)

11. (b). If something is A, you cannot B it.
12. (c). A means the same as B.
13. (c). A means the same as B.
14. (d). An A is someone who is by nature B.
15. (b). Something that is A lacks B.
16. (a). A means the same as B.
17. (c). A means the same as B.
18. (d). Someone who is A is suffering from B.
19. (b). A indicates that something is decidedly reminiscent of a B.
20. (d). A indicates that there is an excess of B in something.

Choosing the Right Meaning (page 182)

1. (c). (Inference clue: "bloody") (a), (b), (d): ws.
2. (b). (Inference clue: "bars," "captive") (d): ws; (a), (c): ir.
3. (c). (Inference clue: What would a feast do to hunger?) (b), (d): ws (too weak); (a): ir.
4. (b). (Inference clue: What effect would he rocking of a ship have on a person?) (a), (c), (d): ws.
5. (a). (Inference clue: The meaning here must apply to birds.) (c): ws; (b), (d): ir.

Two-Word Completions (page 183)

1. (c). abet (Restatement clue: "aid and") . . . culpable (Inference clue: How would you describe someone who had committed a crime?)
2. (d). potpourri (Restatement clue: "assortment") . . . motley (Inference clue: How would you describe the assortment of acts that used to be presented at a vaudeville house?)
3. (b). Contingents (Inference clue: Into what are crack troops usually organized?) . . . foment (Inference clue: What would malcontent firebrands be likely to do in regard to a riot and similar disorders?)
4. (d). sartorial (Inference clue: What kind of splendor would a dapper person be likely to have?) . . . slovenly (Contrast clue: "dapper"; Inference clue: How would a person who appeared to have slept in his or her clothes probably look?)
5. (b). nebulous (Restatement clue: "shapeless") . . . dissipated (Restatement clue: "and vanished")
6. (a). rejoinder (Inference clue: What wouldn't it be possible to make in regard to an airtight case?) . . . incontrovertible (Inference clue: What kind of evidence would an airtight case be likely to contain?)

Vocabulary Workshop

Level F

Jerome Shostak

Senior Series Consultant

Alex Cameron, Ph.D.
Department of English
University of Dayton
Dayton, Ohio

Series Consultants

Sylvia A. Rendón, Ph.D.
Coord., Secondary Language Arts
  and Reading
Cypress-Fairbanks I.S.D.
Houston, Texas

Mel H. Farberman
Supervisor of Instruction
Brooklyn High Schools
New York City Board of Education
Brooklyn, New York

John Heath, Ph.D.
Department of Classics
Santa Clara University
Santa Clara, California

Sadlier-Oxford
A Division of William H. Sadlier, Inc.

Reviewers

The publisher wishes to thank for their comments and suggestions the following teachers and administrators, who read portions of the series prior to publication.

Anne S. Crane
Clinician, English Education
Georgia State University
Atlanta, GA

Susan W. Keogh
Curriculum Coordinator
Lake Highland Preparatory
Orlando, FL

Mary Louise Ellena-Wygonik
English Teacher
Hampton High School
Allison Park, PA

Lisa Anne Pomi
Language Arts Chairperson
Woodside High School
Woodside, CA

Arlene A. Oraby
Dept. Chair (Ret.), English 6–12
Briarcliff Public Schools
Briarcliff Manor, NY

Susan Cotter McDonough
English Department Chair
Wakefield High School
Wakefield, MA

Sr. M. Francis Regis Trojano
Sisters of St. Joseph (CSJ)
Educational Consultant
Boston, MA

Keith Yost
Director of Humanities
Tomball Ind. School District
Tomball, TX

Patricia M. Stack
English Teacher
South Park School District
South Park, PA

Joy Vander Vliet
English Teacher
Council Rock High School
Newtown, PA

Karen Christine Solheim
English Teacher
Jefferson High School
Jefferson, GA

Photo Credits

Jack Anthony: 71. *Archive*: 27, 123. *Corbis*/Bettmann: 57, 104; Walker Evans: 90; Owen Franken: 137; Christel Gerstenberg: 157; Morton Beebe: 164. *FPG*: Jim Cummins: 64. *Hulton Getty*: 97. *The Kobal Collection*: 83. *Image Works*/Dick Blume: 34; Mark Gibson: 41; Sean Cayton: 184. *Library of Congress*: 130. *Stone*/Chad Slattery: 171; David E. Myers: 116; 150.

NOTE: ALL RIGHTS RESERVED. NO PART OF THIS BOOK MAY BE REPRODUCED, STORED IN A DATABASE OR RETRIEVAL SYSTEM, OR TRANSMITTED IN ANY FORM BY ANY MEANS, ELECTRONIC, MECHANICAL, PHOTOCOPYING, RECORDING, OR OTHERWISE, WITHOUT THE PRIOR WRITTEN PERMISSION OF WILLIAM H. SADLIER, INC. COPYRIGHT INFRINGERS WILL BE PROSECUTED TO THE FULL EXTENT OF THE LAW AND MAY BE LIABLE FOR DAMAGES OF UP TO $150,000. REPORT ALL VIOLATIONS, IN CONFIDENCE, TO THE PUBLISHER AT THE ADDRESS SHOWN BELOW.

Copyright © 2002 by William H. Sadlier, Inc. All rights reserved.

This publication, or any part thereof, may not be reproduced in any form, or by any means, including electronic, photographic, or mechanical, or by any sound recording system, or by any device for storage or retrieval of information, without the written permission of the publisher. Address inquiries to Permissions Department, William H. Sadlier, Inc., 9 Pine Street, New York, New York 10005-1002.

S is a registered trademark of William H. Sadlier, Inc.

Printed in the United States of America.
ISBN: 0-8215-7611-9
456789/05 04 03

PREFACE

For over five decades, VOCABULARY WORKSHOP has proven a highly successful tool for guiding systematic vocabulary growth. It has also been a valuable help to students preparing for the vocabulary-related parts of standardized tests. In this, the latest edition of the series, many new features have been added to make VOCABULARY WORKSHOP even more effective in increasing vocabulary and improving vocabulary skills.

The **Definitions** sections in the fifteen Units, for example, have been expanded to include synonyms and antonyms and for each taught word an illustrative sentence for each part of speech.

In the **Synonyms** and **Antonyms** sections, exercise items are now presented in the form of phrases, the better to familiarize you with the range of contexts and distinctions of usage for the Unit words.

New to this edition is **Vocabulary in Context**, an exercise that appears at the end of each Unit and in the Reviews. In this exercise, you will read an expository passage containing a selection of Unit words. In addition to furnishing you with further examples of how and in what contexts Unit words are used, this exercise will also provide you with practice with vocabulary questions in standardized-test formats.

In the five Reviews, you will find two important new features, in addition to Analogies, Two-Word Completions, and other exercises designed to help you prepare for standardized tests. One of these new features, **Building with Classical Roots**, will acquaint you with Latin and Greek roots from which many English words stem and will provide you with a strategy that may help you find the meaning of an unknown or unfamiliar word.

Another new feature, **Writer's Challenge**, is designed to do just that—challenge you to improve your writing skills by applying what you have learned about meanings and proper usage of selected Unit words.

Finally, another new feature has been introduced in the four Cumulative Reviews. **Enriching Your Vocabulary** is meant to broaden and enhance your knowledge and understanding of the relationships, history, and origins of the words that make up our rich and dynamic language.

In this Level of VOCABULARY WORKSHOP, you will study three hundred key words, and you will be introduced to hundreds of other words in the form of synonyms, antonyms, and other relatives. Mastery of these words will make you a better reader, a better writer and speaker, and better prepared for the vocabulary parts of standardized tests.

Contents

Pronunciation Key 6
The Vocabulary of Vocabulary 7
    Denotation and Connotation 7
    Literal and Figurative Usage 7
    Synonyms and Antonyms 8
Vocabulary Strategy: Using Context 9
Working with Analogies 11
Vocabulary Strategy: Word Structure 15
Vocabulary and Writing 17
Diagnostic Test 18
Unit One 21
Unit Two 28
Unit Three 35
Review (Units One–Three)
    Analogies 42
    Word Associations 43
    Vocabulary in Context 44
    Choosing the Right Meaning 45
    Antonyms 45
    Word Families 46
    Two-Word Completions 47
    Building with Classical Roots 48
    Writer's Challenge 50
Unit Four 51
Unit Five 58
Unit Six 65
Review (Units Four–Six)
    Analogies 72
    Word Associations 73
    Vocabulary in Context 74
    Choosing the Right Meaning 75
    Antonyms 75
    Word Families 76
    Two-Word Completions 77
    Building with Classical Roots 78
    Writer's Challenge 80
Cumulative Review I (Units One–Six)
    Analogies 81
    Choosing the Right Meaning 81
    Two-Word Completions 82
    Enriching Your Vocabulary 83
Unit Seven 84
Unit Eight 91
Unit Nine 98
Review (Units Seven–Nine)
    Analogies 105
    Word Associations 106
    Vocabulary in Context 107

Choosing the Right Meaning	108
Antonyms	108
Word Families	109
Two-Word Completions	110
Building with Classical Roots	111
Writer's Challenge	113

Cumulative Review II (Units One–Nine)

Analogies	114
Choosing the Right Meaning	114
Two-Word Completions	115
Enriching Your Vocabulary	116

Unit Ten . . . 117
Unit Eleven . . . 124
Unit Twelve . . . 131

Review (Units Ten–Twelve)

Analogies	138
Word Associations	139
Vocabulary in Context	140
Choosing the Right Meaning	141
Antonyms	141
Word Families	142
Two-Word Completions	143
Building with Classical Roots	144
Writer's Challenge	146

Cumulative Review III (Units One–Twelve)

Analogies	147
Choosing the Right Meaning	148
Two-Word Completions	149
Enriching Your Vocabulary	150

Unit Thirteen . . . 151
Unit Fourteen . . . 158
Unit Fifteen . . . 165

Review (Units Thirteen–Fifteen)

Analogies	172
Word Associations	173
Vocabulary in Context	174
Choosing the Right Meaning	175
Antonyms	175
Word Families	176
Two-Word Completions	177
Building with Classical Roots	178
Writer's Challenge	180

Cumulative Review IV (Units One–Fifteen)

Analogies	181
Choosing the Right Meaning	182
Two-Word Completions	183
Enriching Your Vocabulary	184

Final Mastery Test . . . 185
Index . . . 190

PRONUNCIATION KEY

The pronunciation is indicated for every basic word introduced in this book. The symbols used for this purpose, as listed below, are similar to those appearing in most standard dictionaries of recent vintage. The author has consulted a large number of dictionaries for this purpose but has relied primarily on *Webster's Third New International Dictionary* and *The Random House Dictionary of the English Language (Unabridged)*.

There are, of course, many English words for which two (or more) pronunciations are commonly accepted. In virtually all cases where such words occur in this book, the author has sought to make things easier for the student by giving just one pronunciation. The only significant exception occurs when the pronunciation changes in accordance with a shift in the part of speech. Thus we would indicate that *project* in the verb form is pronounced prə jekt′, and in the noun form, präj′ ekt.

It is believed that these relatively simple pronunciation guides will be readily usable by the student. It should be emphasized, however, that the *best* way to learn the pronunciation of a word is to listen to and imitate an educated speaker.

Vowels	ā	lake	e	str*e*ss	ü	l*oo*t, n*ew*
	a	m*a*t	ī	kn*i*fe	ủ	f*oo*t, p*u*ll
	â	c*a*re	i	s*i*t	ə	r*u*g, brok*e*n
	ä	b*a*rk, b*o*ttle	ō	fl*o*w	ər	b*ir*d, bett*er*
	aủ	d*ou*bt	ô	*a*ll, c*o*rd		
	ē	b*ea*t, word*y*	oi	*oi*l		

Consonants	ch	*ch*ild, lec*t*ure	s	*s*ellar	wh	*wh*at
	g	*g*ive	sh	*sh*un	y	*y*earn
	j	*g*entle, bri*dge*	th	*th*ank	z	i*s*
	ŋ	si*ng*	<u>th</u>	*th*ose	zh	mea*s*ure
	All other consonants are sounded as in the alphabet.					

Stress	The accent mark *follows* the syllable receiving the major stress: en rich′

Abbreviations	*adj.* adjective	*n.* noun	*prep.* preposition
	adv. adverb	*part.* participle	*v.* verb
	int. interjection	*pl.* plural	

See page T21 for information about the
Interactive Audio Pronunciation Program.

The Vocabulary of Vocabulary

There are some interesting and useful words that are employed to describe and identify words. The exercises that follow will help you to check and strengthen your knowledge of this "vocabulary of vocabulary."

Denotation and Connotation

The **denotation** of a word is its specific dictionary meaning. Here are a few examples:

Word	Denotation
eminent	distinguished or noteworthy
cumbersome	hard to handle or manage
remember	call to mind

The **connotation** of a word is its **tone**—that is, the emotions or associations it normally arouses in people using, hearing, or reading it. Depending on what these feelings are, the connotation of a word may be *favorable* (*positive*) or *unfavorable* (*negative, pejorative*). A word that does not normally arouse strong feelings of any kind has a *neutral* connotation. Here are some examples of words with different connotations:

Word	Connotation
eminent	favorable
cumbersome	unfavorable
remember	neutral

Exercises *In the space provided, label the connotation of each of the following words* ***F*** *for "favorable,"* ***U*** *for "unfavorable," or* ***N*** *for "neutral."*

__U__ 1. perverse   __F__ 3. lucrative   __F__ 5. savory

__U__ 2. liability   __N__ 4. adieu   __F__ 6. magnanimous

Literal and Figurative Usage

When a word is used in a **literal** sense, it is being employed in its strict (or primary) dictionary meaning in a situation (or context) that "makes sense" from a purely logical or realistic point of view. For example:

> Yesterday I read an old tale about a knight who slew a *fire-breathing* dragon.

In this sentence, *fire-breathing* is employed literally. The dragon is pictured as breathing real fire.

Sometimes words are used in a symbolic or nonliteral way in situations that do not "make sense" from a purely logical or realistic point of view. We call this nonliteral application of a word a **figurative** or **metaphorical** usage. For example:

> Suddenly my boss rushed into my office *breathing fire*.

In this sentence *breathing fire* is not being used in a literal sense. That is, the boss was not actually breathing fire out of his nostrils. Rather, the expression is intended to convey graphically that the boss was very angry.

Exercises In the space provided, write **L** for "literal" or **F** for "figurative" next to each of the following sentences to show how the italicized expression is being used.

   F **1.** The years of silence allowed resentment to silently *creep* into their relationship.

   L **2.** The ivy vines *crept* over the trestle.

   F **3.** "It was *easy as cake*," she said of the math exam.

Synonyms

A **synonym** is a word that has *the same* or *almost the same* meaning as another word. Here are some examples:

eat—consume
hurt—injure
big—large

clash—conflict
fire—discharge
slim—slender

Exercises In each of the following groups, circle the word that is most nearly the **synonym** of the word in **boldface** type.

1. opaque
a. sturdy
b. cubic
c. ionic
d. murky *(circled)*

2. salvage
a. garner
b. save *(circled)*
c. requisition
d. surrender

3. dilate
a. soften
b. enrich
c. enlarge *(circled)*
d. dissolve

4. rectify
a. corroborate
b. subscribe
c. usurp
d. correct *(circled)*

Antonyms

An **antonym** is a word that means *the opposite* of or *almost the opposite* of another word. Here are some examples:

enter—leave
wild—tame
buy—sell

happy—sad
leader—follower
war—peace

Exercises In each of the following groups, circle the word that is most nearly the **antonym** of the word in **boldface** type.

1. candid
a. dishonest *(circled)*
b. alien
c. new
d. accepted

2. embroil
a. embargo
b. extricate *(circled)*
c. entangle
d. enigma

3. chaos
a. science
b. entropy
c. order *(circled)*
d. imposition

4. immunity
a. untenable
b. eminence
c. susceptibility *(circled)*
d. boorishness

VOCABULARY STRATEGY: USING CONTEXT

How do you go about finding the meaning of an unknown or unfamiliar word that you come across in your reading? You might look the word up in a dictionary, of course, provided one is at hand. But there are two other useful strategies that you might employ to find the meaning of a word that you do not know at all or that is used in a way that you do not recognize. One strategy is to analyze the **structure** or parts of the word. (See pages 15 and 16 for more on this strategy.) The other strategy is to try to figure out the meaning of the word by reference to context.

When we speak of the **context** of a word, we mean the printed text of which that word is part. By studying the context, we may find **clues** that lead us to its meaning. We might find a clue in the immediate sentence or phrase in which the word appears (and sometimes in adjoining sentences or phrases, too); or we might find a clue in the topic or subject matter of the passage in which the word appears; or we might even find a clue in the physical features of a page itself. (Photographs, illustrations, charts, graphs, captions, and headings are some examples of such features.)

One way to use context as a strategy is to ask yourself what you know already about the topic or subject matter in question. By applying what you have learned before about deserts, for example, you would probably be able to figure out that the word *arid* in the phrase "the arid climate of the desert" means "dry."

The **Vocabulary in Context** exercises that appear in the Units and the **Choosing the Right Meaning** exercises that appear in the Reviews and Cumulative Reviews both provide practice in using subject matter or topic to determine the meaning of given words.

When you do the various word-omission exercises in this book, look for **context clues** built into the sentence or passage to guide you to the correct answer. Three types of context clues appear in the exercises in this book.

A **restatement clue** consists of a *synonym* for, or a *definition* of, the missing word. For example:

"I'm willing to tell what I know about the matter," the reporter said, "but I can't _____ my sources."
a. conceal   b. defend   c. find   (d. reveal)

In this sentence, *tell* is a synonym of the missing word, *reveal*, and acts as a restatement clue for it.

A **contrast clue** consists of an *antonym* for, or a phrase that means the *opposite* of, the missing word. For example:

"I'm trying to help you, not (**assist, hinder**) you!" she exclaimed in annoyance.

In this sentence, *help* is an antonym of the missing word, *hinder*. This is confirmed by the presence of the word *not*. *Help* thus functions as a contrast clue for *hinder*.

Using Context ■ 9

An **inference clue** implies but does not directly state the meaning of the missing word or words. For example:

> A utility infielder has to be a very _____ player because he is a veritable jack-of-all-trades on the _____ diamond.
>
> a. veteran . . . football
> (b. versatile . . . baseball)
> c. experienced . . . hockey
> d. energetic . . . golf

In this sentence, there are several inference clues: (a) the term *jack-of-all-trades* suggests the word *versatile* because a jack-of-all-trades is by definition versatile; the word *utility* in the term *utility infielder* suggests the same thing; (b) the words *infielder* and *diamond* suggest *baseball* because they are terms employed regularly in that sport. Accordingly, all these words are inference clues because they suggest or imply, but do not directly state, the missing word or words.

Exercises Use context clues to choose the word or words that complete each of the following sentences or sets of sentences.

1. If I don't understand the lesson now, I certainly won't _____ it after I go home.
   (a. comprehend)
   b. deliver
   c. disregard
   d. enumerate

2. At our picnic, the neighbor's dog got into the _____ basket and managed to _____ all the sandwiches.
   a. silver . . . devour
   (b. food . . . eat)
   c. egg . . . hide
   d. treasure . . . steal

3. If you provide the car, I will (**pay,** **look**) for the gas.

Working with Analogies

Today practically every standardized examination involving vocabulary, especially the SAT-I, employs the **analogy** as a testing device. For that reason, it is an excellent idea to learn how to read, understand, and solve such verbal puzzles.

What Is an Analogy?

An analogy is a kind of equation using words rather than numbers or mathematical symbols and quantities. Normally, an analogy contains two pairs of words linked by a word or symbol that stands for an equal sign (=). A complete analogy compares the two pairs of words and makes a statement about them. It asserts that the logical relationship between the members of the first pair of words is *the same as* the logical relationship between the members of the second pair of words. This is the only statement a valid analogy ever makes.

Here is an example of a complete analogy. It is presented in two different formats.

Format 1
maple is to tree as rose is to flower

Format 2
maple : tree :: rose : flower

Reading and Interpreting Analogies

As our sample indicates, analogies are customarily presented in formats that need some deciphering in order to be read and understood correctly. There are a number of these formats, but you need concern yourself with only the two shown.

Format 1: Let's begin with the format that uses all words:

maple is to tree as rose is to flower

Because this is the simplest format to read and understand, it is the one used in the student texts of Vocabulary Workshop. It is to be read exactly as printed. Allowing for the fact that the word pairs change from analogy to analogy, this is how to read every analogy, no matter what the format is.

Now you know how to read an analogy. Still, it is not clear exactly what the somewhat cryptic statement "maple is to tree as rose is to flower" means. To discover this, you must understand what the two linking expressions *as* and *is to* signify.

- The word *as* links the two word pairs in the complete analogy. It stands for an equal sign (=) and means "is the same as."

- The expression *is to* links the two members of each word pair, so it appears twice in a complete analogy. In our sample, *is to* links *maple* and *tree* (the two words in the first pair) and also *rose* and *flower* (the two words in the second word pair). Accordingly, the expression *is to* means "the logical relationship between" the two words it links.

Putting all this information together, we can say that our sample analogy means:

> The logical relationship between a *maple* and a *tree* is *the same as* (=) the logical relationship between a *rose* and a *flower*.

Now you know what our sample analogy means. This is what every analogy means, allowing for the fact that the word pairs will vary from one analogy to another.

Format 2: Our second format uses symbols, rather than words, to link its four members.

> maple : tree :: rose : flower

This is the format used on the SAT-I and in the *TEST PREP Blackline Masters* that accompany each Level of VOCABULARY WORKSHOP. In this format, a single colon (:) replaces the expression *is to*, and a double colon (::) replaces the word *as*. Otherwise, format 2 is the same as format 1; that is, it is read in exactly the same way ("maple is to tree as rose is to flower"), and it means exactly the same thing ("the logical relationship between a *maple* and a *tree* is the same as the logical relationship between a *rose* and a *flower*").

Completing Analogies

So far we've looked at complete analogies. However, standardized examinations do not provide the test taker with a complete analogy. Instead, the test taker is given the first, or key, pair of words and then asked to *complete* the analogy by selecting the second pair from a given group of four or five choices, usually lettered *a* through *d* or *e*.

Here's how our sample analogy would look on such a test:

1. maple is to tree as
a. acorn is to oak
b. hen is to rooster
c. rose is to flower
d. shrub is to lilac

or

1. maple : tree ::
a. acorn : oak
b. hen : rooster
c. rose : flower
d. shrub : lilac

It is up to the test taker to complete the analogy correctly.

Here's how to do that in just four easy steps!

Step 1: Look at the two words in the key (given) pair, and determine the logical relationship between them.

In our sample analogy, *maple* and *tree* form the key (given) pair of words. They indicate the key (given) relationship. Think about these two words for a moment. What is the relationship of a maple to a tree? Well, a maple is a particular kind, or type, of tree.

Step 2: *Make up a short sentence stating the relationship that you have discovered for the first pair of words.*

For our model analogy, we can use this sentence: "A maple is a particular kind (type) of tree."

Step 3: *Extend the sentence you have written to cover the rest of the analogy, even though you haven't completed it yet.*

The easiest way to do this is to repeat the key relationship after the words *just as*, leaving blanks for the two words you don't yet have. The sentence will now read something like this:

A maple is a kind (type) of tree, just as a ? is a kind of ? .

Step 4: *Look at each of the lettered pairs of words from which you are to choose your answer. Determine which lettered pair illustrates the same relationship as the key pair.*

The easiest and most effective way to carry out step 4 is to substitute each pair of words into the blanks in the sentence you made up to see which sentence makes sense. Only one will.

Doing this for our sample analogy, we get:

a. A maple is a kind of tree, just as an acorn is a kind of oak.
b. A maple is a kind of tree, just as a hen is a kind of rooster.
c. A maple is a kind of tree, just as a rose is a kind of flower.
d. A maple is a kind of tree, just as a shrub is a kind of lilac.

Look at these sentences. Only *one* of them makes any sense. Choice *a* is clearly wrong because an acorn is *not* a kind of oak. Choice *b* is also wrong because a hen is *not* a kind of rooster. Similarly, choice *d* is incorrect because a shrub is *not* a kind of lilac, though a *lilac* is a kind of shrub. In other words, the two words are in the wrong order. That leaves us with choice *c*, which says that a rose is a kind of flower. Well, that makes sense; a rose is indeed a kind of flower. So, choice *c* must be the pair of words that completes the analogy correctly.

Determining the Key Relationship

Clearly, determining the nature of the key relationship is the most important and the most difficult part of completing an analogy. Since there are literally thousands of key relationships possible, you cannot simply memorize a list of them. The table on page 14, however, outlines some of the most common key relationships. Study the table carefully.

Working with Analogies ■ *13*

Table of Key Relationships

Complete Analogy	Key Relationship
big is to **large** as **little** is to **small**	**Big** means the same thing as **large**, just as **little** means the same thing as **small**.
tall is to **short** as **thin** is to **fat**	**Tall** means the opposite of **short**, just as **thin** means the opposite of **fat**.
brave is to **favorable** as **cowardly** is to **unfavorable**	The tone of **brave** is **favorable**, just as the tone of **cowardly** is **unfavorable**.
busybody is to **nosy** as **klutz** is to **clumsy**	A **busybody** is by definition someone who is **nosy**, just as a **klutz** is by definition someone who is **clumsy**.
cowardly is to **courage** as **awkward** is to **grace**	Someone who is **cowardly** lacks **courage**, just as someone who is **awkward** lacks **grace**.
visible is to **see** as **audible** is to **hear**	If something is **visible**, you can by definition **see** it, just as if something is **audible**, you can by definition **hear** it.
invisible is to **see** as **inaudible** is to **hear**	If something is **invisible**, you cannot **see** it, just as if something is **inaudible**, you cannot **hear** it.
frigid is to **cold** as **blistering** is to **hot**	**Frigid** is the extreme of **cold**, just as **blistering** is the extreme of **hot**.
chef is to **cooking** as **tailor** is to **clothing**	A **chef** is concerned with **cooking**, just as a **tailor** is concerned with **clothing**.
liar is to **truthful** as **bigot** is to **fair-minded**	A **liar** is by definition not likely to be **truthful**, just as a **bigot** is by definition not likely to be **fair-minded**.
starvation is to **emaciation** as **overindulgence** is to **corpulence**	**Starvation** will cause **emaciation**, just as **overindulgence** will cause **corpulence**.
practice is to **proficient** as **study** is to **knowledgeable**	**Practice** will make a person **proficient**, just as **study** will make a person **knowledgeable**.
eyes are to **see** as **ears** are to **hear**	You use your **eyes** to **see** with, just as you use your **ears** to **hear** with.
sloppy is to **appearance** as **rude** is to **manner**	The word **sloppy** can refer to one's **appearance**, just as the word **rude** can refer to one's **manner**.
learned is to **knowledge** as **wealthy** is to **money**	Someone who is **learned** has a great deal of **knowledge**, just as someone who is **wealthy** has a great deal of **money**.

Exercises   In each of the following, circle the item that best completes the analogy. Then explain the key relationship involved.

1. **greed** is to **unfavorable** as
   a. anger is to favorable
   b. generosity is to unfavorable
   c. contentment is to unfavorable
   (d. generosity is to favorable)

2. **apple** is to **fruit** as
   a. fruit is to plum
   b. dog is to fur
   (c. carrot is to vegetable)
   d. star is to constellation

3. **silent** is to **hear** as
   a. loud is to hear
   b. restful is to dream
   c. quiet is to touch
   (d. hidden is to see)

4. **shoes** are to **feet** as
   a. glasses are to pocket
   b. fingers are to rings
   (c. gloves are to hands)
   d. hats are to brims

Vocabulary Strategy: Word Structure

One important way to build your vocabulary is to learn the meaning of word parts that make up many English words. These word parts consist of **prefixes**, **suffixes**, and **roots**, or **bases**. A useful strategy for determining the meaning of an unknown word is to "take apart" the word and think about the parts. For example, when you look at the word parts in the word *invisible,* you find the prefix *in-* ("not") + the root *-vis-* ("see") + the suffix *-ible* ("capable of"). From knowing the meanings of the parts of this word, you can figure out that *invisible* means "not capable of being seen."

Following is a list of common prefixes. Knowing the meaning of a prefix can help you determine the meaning of a word in which the prefix appears.

Prefix	Meaning	Sample Words
bi-	two	bicycle
com-, con-	together, with	compatriot, contact
de-, dis-	lower, opposite	devalue, disloyal
fore-, pre-	before, ahead of time	forewarn, preplan
il-, im-, in-, ir, non-, un-	not	illegal, impossible, inactive, irregular, nonsense, unable
in-, im-	in, into	inhale, import
mid-	middle	midway
mis-	wrongly, badly	mistake, misbehave
re-	again, back	redo, repay
sub-	under, less than	submarine, subzero
super-	above, greater than	superimpose, superstar
tri-	three	triangle

Following is a list of common suffixes. Knowing the meaning and grammatical function of a suffix can help you determine the meaning of a word.

Noun Suffix	Meaning	Sample Nouns
-acy, -ance, -ence, -hood, -ity, -ment, -ness, -ship	state, quality, or condition of, act or process of	adequacy, attendance, persistence, neighborhood, activity, judgment, brightness, friendship
-ant, -eer, -ent, -er, -ian, -ier, -ist, -or	one who does or makes something	contestant, auctioneer, resident, banker, comedian, financier, dentist, doctor
-ation, -ition, -ion	act or result of	organization, imposition, election

Verb Suffix	Meaning	Sample Verbs
-ate	to become, produce, or treat	validate, salivate, chlorinate
-en	to make, cause to be	weaken
-fy, -ify, -ize	to cause, make	liquefy, glorify, legalize

Adjective Suffix	Meaning	Sample Adjectives
-able, -ible	able, capable of	believable, incredible
-al, -ic	relating to, characteristic of	natural, romantic
-ful, -ive, -ous	full of, given to, marked by	beautiful, protective, poisonous
-ish, -like	like, resembling	foolish, childlike
-less	lacking, without	careless

A **base** or **root** is the main part of a word to which prefixes and suffixes may be added. Many roots come to English from Latin, such as *-socio-,* meaning "society," or from Greek, such as *-logy-,* meaning "the study of." Knowing Greek and Latin roots can help you determine the meaning of a word such as *sociology,* which means "the study of society."

In the **Building with Classical Roots** sections of this book you will learn more about some of these Latin and Greek roots and about English words that derive from them. The lists that follow may help you figure out the meaning of new or unfamiliar words that you encounter in your reading.

Greek Root	Meaning	Sample Word
-astr-, -aster-, -astro-	star	astral, asteroid, astronaut
-auto-	self	autograph
-bio-	life	biography
-chron-, chrono-	time	chronic, chronological
-cosm-, -cosmo-	universe, order	microcosm, cosmopolitan
-cryph-, -crypt-	hidden, secret	apocryphal, cryptographer
-dem-, -demo-	people	epidemic, democracy
-dia-	through, across, between	diameter
-dog-, -dox-	opinion, teaching	dogmatic, orthodox
-gen-	race, kind, origin, birth	generation
-gnos-	know	diagnostic
-graph-, -graphy-, -gram-	write	graphite, autobiography, telegram
-log-, -logue-	speech, word, reasoning	logic, dialogue
-lys-	break down	analysis
-metr-, -meter-	measure	metric, kilometer
-micro-	small	microchip
-morph-	form, shape	amorphous
-naut-	sailor	cosmonaut
-phon-, -phone-, -phono-	sound, voice	phonics, telephone, phonograph
-pol-, -polis-	city, state	police, metropolis
-scop-, -scope-	watch, look at	microscope, telescope
-tele-	far off, distant	television
-the-	put or place	parentheses

Latin Root	Meaning	Sample Word
-cap-, -capt-, -cept-, -cip-	take	capitulate, captive, concept, recipient
-cede-, -ceed-, -ceas-, -cess-	happen, yield, go	precede, proceed, decease, cessation
-cred-	believe	incredible
-dic-, -dict-	speak, say, tell	indicate, diction
-duc-, -duct-, -duit-	lead, conduct, draw	educate, conduct, conduit
-fac-, -fact-, -fect-, -fic-, -fy-	make	faculty, artifact, defect, beneficial, clarify
-ject-	throw	eject
-mis-, -miss-, -mit-, -mitt-	send	promise, missile, transmit, intermittent
-note-, -not-	know, recognize	denote, notion
-pel-, -puls-	drive	expel, compulsive
-pend-, -pens-	hang, weight, set aside	pendulum, pension
-pon-, -pos-	put, place	component, position
-port-	carry	portable
-rupt-	break	bankrupt
-scrib-, -scribe-, -script-	write	scribble, describe, inscription
-spec-, -spic-	look, see	spectator, conspicuous
-tac-, -tag-, -tang-, -teg-	touch	contact, contagious, tangible, integral
-tain-, -ten-, -tin-	hold, keep	contain, tenure, retinue
-temp-	time	tempo
-ven-, -vent-	come	intervene, convention
-vers-, -vert-	turn	reverse, invert
-voc-, -vok-	call	vocal, invoke

Vocabulary and Writing

When you study vocabulary, you make yourself not only a better reader but also a better writer. The greater the number of words at your disposal, the better you will be able to express your thoughts. Good writers are always adding new words to their personal vocabularies, the pool of words that they understand *and* know how to use properly. They use these words both when they write and when they revise.

There are several factors to consider when choosing words and setting the tone of your writing. First, your choice of words should suit your purpose and your audience. If you are writing an essay for your history teacher, you will probably want to choose words that are formal in tone and precise in meaning. If you are writing a letter to a friend, however, you will probably choose words that are more informal in tone and freer in meaning. Your **audience** is the person or people who will be reading what you write, and your **purpose** is the reason why you are writing. Your purpose, for example, might be to explain; or it might be to describe, inform, or entertain.

Almost any kind of writing—whether a school essay, a story, or a letter to a friend—can be improved by careful attention to vocabulary. Sometimes you will find, for example, that one word can be used to replace a phrase of five or six words. This is not to say that a shorter sentence is always better. However, readers usually prefer and appreciate **economy** of expression. They grow impatient with sentences that plod along with vague, unnecessary words rather than race along with fewer, carefully chosen ones. Writing can also be improved by attention to **diction** (word choice). Many writers use words that might make sense in terms of *general* meaning but that are not precise enough to convey *nuances* of meaning. In the **Writer's Challenge** sections of this book, you will have an opportunity to make word choices that will more clearly and precisely convey the meaning you intend.

Exercises *Read the following sentences, paying special attention to the words and phrases underlined. From the words in the box, find better choices for the underlined words and phrases.*

1. It was discovered in the late 18th century that people who had cowpox were <u>unavailable</u> to smallpox.

liable	(immune)	prone	repulsed

2. Nathaniel Hawthorne, author of *The Scarlet Letter*, was <u>linked by birth</u> to one of the presiding judges in the Salem witch trials.

(related)	cuffed	unnecessary	friendly

3. Impressionist painter Mary Cassatt was one of the few American artists who <u>made great efforts on behalf of</u> the avant-garde movement.

(advocated for)	consisted of	withdrew from	listened to

4. Greek philosopher Diogenes was said to have <u>roamed aimlessly about</u> the streets of Athens with a lantern, searching for an honest man.

inspected	(wandered)	studied	peripatetic

5. His enthusiasm was <u>so strong I could almost feel it</u>.

vitriolic	segmented	ecstatic	(palpable)

Diagnostic Test

This test contains a sampling of the words that are to be found in the exercises in this Level of VOCABULARY WORKSHOP. It will give you an idea of the types of words to be studied and their level of difficulty. When you have completed all the units, the Final Mastery Test at the end of this book will assess what you have learned. By comparing your results on the Final Mastery Test with your results on the Diagnostic Test below, you will be able to judge your progress.

Synonyms

In each of the following groups, circle the word or phrase that *most nearly* expresses the meaning of the word in **boldface** type in the given phrase.

1. a state of **bedlam**
   a. discipline   b. dreaminess   **c. disorder**   d. peace
2. an **erudite** study
   a. breezy   b. prestigious   c. dull   **d. scholarly**
3. **concoct** a story
   a. listen to   b. expose   **c. make up**   d. confirm
4. **transient** interests
   a. long-lasting   b. ardent   c. scholarly   **d. temporary**
5. **scurrilous** rumors
   a. abusive   b. well-informed   c. false   d. interesting
6. **unwieldy** packages
   a. valuable   **b. bulky**   c. light   d. unidentified
7. suffer from **ennui**
   a. boredom   b. fever   c. tension   d. fear
8. an **infraction** of a regulation
   a. violation   b. enactment   c. enforcement   d. author
9. **impugn** my sincerity
   a. praise   **b. question**   c. describe   d. imitate
10. a **propensity** for dangerous pursuits
    a. desire   **b. inclination**   c. distaste   d. dream
11. his **torpid** reactions
    a. logical   b. erratic   c. quick   **d. sluggish**
12. **commiserate** with us
    a. sympathize   b. eat   c. discuss   d. travel
13. **precipitated** a crisis in the government
    a. foresaw   b. prevented   c. analyzed   **d. caused**
14. nothing but **drivel**
    a. nonsense   b. light rain   c. soil   d. pollution
15. **abominate** all forms of injustice
    a. study   **b. loathe**   c. abolish   d. fear

18 ■ *Diagnostic Test*

DIAGNOSTIC TEST

16. an **anomalous** situation
   a. safe   b. dangerous   c. embarrassing   (d. abnormal)
17. heinous deeds
   a. charitable   (b. wicked)   c. childish   d. effective
18. a **motley** crew
   a. frightened   b. musical   (c. variegated)   d. incompetent
19. remain **irresolute**
   (a. wavering)   b. determined   c. uncontrolled   d. alert
20. the **epitome** of the scholarly professor
   (a. embodiment) b. career   c. prestige   d. knowledge
21. omit the **lurid** details
   a. unimportant   b. repetitious   c. complicated   (d. sensational)
22. simulate interest
   a. destroy   (b. pretend)   c. create   d. ignore
23. anonymous rumors and **innuendoes**
   (a. insinuations) b. lawsuits   c. editorials   d. compliments
24. elicit a response
   a. reject   b. deny   c. explain   (d. draw out)
25. flout her expressed wishes
   (a. ignore)   b. obey   c. back up   d. dislike
26. the **soporific** effect of the drug
   (a. narcotic)   b. hallucinogenic   c. stimulant   d. laxative
27. castigate the students
   a. address   b. appeal to   c. listen   (d. rebuke)
28. assuage her feelings
   a. arouse   b. redirect   (c. allay)   d. hide
29. an **equitable** arrangement
   (a. fair)   b. uncomfortable   c. lucrative   d. tiresome
30. expurgate a play
   a. analyze   (b. censor)   c. produce   d. develop

Antonyms

*In each of the following groups, circle the word that is **most nearly opposite** in meaning to the word in **boldface** type in the given phrase.*

31. the **grisly** scene that met our eyes
   a. curious   (b. delightful)   c. bloody   d. unexpected
32. had a **deleterious** effect on his health
   a. harmful   b. puzzling   c. minimal   (d. beneficial)
33. a decidedly **insular** upbringing
   a. foreign   b. narrow   (c. cosmopolitan)   d. inferior
34. will certainly **buttress** our case
   (a. undermine)   b. clarify   c. clinch   d. strengthen

35. a victim of his own **avarice**
    a. simplemindedness   b. greed   (c. generosity)   d. kindness
36. her rather **austere** taste in clothing
    a. dreadful   (b. flamboyant)   c. expensive   d. simple
37. **abet** the culprits
    (a. hinder)   b. assist   c. release   d. try
38. a **sleazy** hotel
    (a. elegant)   b. quaint   c. sordid   d. modern
39. a **gauche** remark
    (a. tactful)   b. silly   c. typical   d. pointed
40. **hypothetical** situations
    a. interesting   b. typical   c. puzzling   (d. actual)
41. a truly **inauspicious** beginning
    a. unpromising   b. belated   c. harrowing   (d. propitious)
42. **paraphrase** the passage
    a. consider   (b. quote)   c. edit   d. publish
43. a life of **penury**
    a. deprivation   (b. opulence)   c. sacrifice   d. self-denial
44. **pretentious** claims
    a. extravagant   b. meaningless   c. ancient   (d. modest)
45. **deplete** our grain reserves
    a. exhaust   b. commandeer   c. estimate   (d. replenish)
46. a truly **perceptive** critic
    (a. undiscriminating)   b. well-known   c. self-appointed   d. shrewd
47. **foment** an insurrection
    a. instigate   b. join   (c. suppress)   d. predict
48. **extraneous** data
    a. accurate   (b. relevant)   c. complete   d. new
49. **corroborate** their testimony
    a. report   b. confirm   c. collect   (d. refute)
50. **covert** meetings
    a. occasional   b. noisy   (c. public)   d. important

See page T21 for information.

UNIT 1

Definitions

Note carefully the spelling, pronunciation, part(s) of speech, and definition(s) of each of the following words. Then write the word in the blank space(s) in the illustrative sentence(s) following. Finally, study the lists of synonyms and antonyms given at the end of each entry.

1. approbation
(ap rə bā' shən)

(*n.*) the expression of approval or favorable opinion, praise; official approval

My broad hint that I had paid for the lessons myself brought smiles of _____**approbation**_____ from all the judges at the piano recital.

SYNONYMS: commendation, sanction
ANTONYMS: disapproval, condemnation, censure

2. assuage
(ə swāj')

(*v.*) to make easier or milder, relieve; to quiet, calm; to put an end to, appease, satisfy, quench

Her eyes told me that more than a few well-chosen words would be needed to _____**assuage**_____ her hurt feelings.

SYNONYMS: mitigate, alleviate, slake, allay
ANTONYMS: intensify, aggravate, exacerbate

3. coalition
(kō ə lish' ən)

(*n.*) a combination, union, or merger for some specific purpose

The various community organizations formed a _____**coalition**_____ to lobby against parking laws.

SYNONYMS: alliance, league, federation, combine
ANTONYM: splinter group

4. decadence
(de' kə dəns)

(*n.*) decline, decay, or deterioration; a condition or period of decline or decay; excessive self-indulgence

Some characterized her love of chocolate as ___**decadence**___ because she ate at least two candy bars a day.

SYNONYMS: degeneration, corruption
ANTONYMS: rise, growth, development, maturation

5. elicit
(ē lis' it)

(*v.*) to draw forth, bring out from some source (such as another person)

My attempt to _____**elicit**_____ information over the phone was met with a barrage of irrelevant recordings.

SYNONYMS: call forth, evoke, extract, educe
ANTONYMS: repress, quash, squelch, stifle

6. expostulate
(ik späs' chə lāt)

(*v.*) to attempt to dissuade someone from some course or decision by earnest reasoning

Shakespeare's Hamlet finds it useless to ___**expostulate**___ with his mother for siding with his stepfather.

SYNONYMS: protest, remonstrate, complain

7. hackneyed
(hak′ nēd)

(*adj.*) used so often as to lack freshness or originality
The Great Gatsby tells a universal story without being marred by _____**hackneyed**_____ prose.
SYNONYMS: banal, trite, commonplace, corny
ANTONYMS: new, fresh, novel, original

8. hiatus
(hī ā′ təs)

(*n.*) a gap, opening, break (in the sense of having an element missing)
I was awakened not by a sudden sound but by a _____**hiatus**_____ in the din of traffic.
SYNONYMS: pause, lacuna
ANTONYMS: continuity, continuation

9. innuendo
(in yü en′ dō)

(*n.*) a hint, indirect suggestion, or reference (often in a derogatory sense)
Those lacking the facts or afraid of reprisals often tarnish an enemy's reputation by use of _____**innuendo**_____.
SYNONYMS: insinuation, intimation
ANTONYM: direct statement

10. intercede
(in tər sēd′)

(*v.*) to plead on behalf of someone else; to serve as a third party or go-between in a disagreement
She will _____**intercede**_____ in the dispute between the two children, and soon they will be playing happily again.
SYNONYMS: intervene, mediate

11. jaded
(jā′ did)

(*adj.*) wearied, worn-out, dulled (in the sense of being satiated by excessive indulgence)
The wilted handclasp and the fast-melting smile mark the _____**jaded**_____ refugee from too many parties.
SYNONYMS: sated, surfeited, cloyed
ANTONYMS: unspoiled, uncloyed

12. lurid
(lür′ əd)

(*adj.*) causing shock, horror, or revulsion; sensational; pale or sallow in color; terrible or passionate in intensity or lack of restraint
Bright, sensational, and often _____**lurid**_____, some old-time movie posters make today's newspaper ads look tame.
SYNONYMS: gruesome, gory, grisly, baleful, ghastly
ANTONYMS: pleasant, attractive, appealing, wholesome

13. meritorious
(mer i tôr′ ē əs)

(*adj.*) worthy, deserving recognition and praise
Many years of _____**meritorious**_____ service could not dissuade him from feeling that he had not chosen work that he liked.
SYNONYMS: praiseworthy, laudable, commendable
ANTONYMS: blameworthy, reprehensible, discreditable

14. petulant
(pech' ə lənt)

(*adj.*) peevish, annoyed by trifles, easily irritated and upset
An overworked parent may be unlikely to indulge the complaints of a _____petulant_____ child.
SYNONYMS: irritable, testy, waspish
ANTONYMS: even-tempered, placid, serene, amiable

15. prerogative
(prē räg' ə tiv)

(*n.*) a special right or privilege; a special quality showing excellence
She seemed to feel that a snooze at her desk was not an annoying habit but the _____prerogative_____ of a veteran employee.
SYNONYMS: perquisite, perk

16. provincial
(prə vin' shəl)

(*adj.*) pertaining to an outlying area; local; narrow in mind or outlook, countrified in the sense of being limited and backward; of a simple, plain design that originated in the countryside; (*n.*) a person with a narrow point of view; a person from an outlying area; a soldier from a province or colony
The banjo, once thought to be a _____provincial_____ product of the Southern hills, actually came here from Africa.
At first, a _____provincial_____ may do well in the city using charm alone, but charm, like novelty, wears thin.
SYNONYMS: (*adj.*) narrow-minded, parochial, insular, naive
ANTONYMS: (*adj.*) cosmopolitan, catholic, broad-minded

17. simulate
(sim' yə lāt)

(*v.*) to make a pretense of, imitate; to show the outer signs of
Some skilled actors can _____simulate_____ emotions they might never have felt in life.
SYNONYMS: feign, pretend, affect

18. transcend
(tran send')

(*v.*) to rise above or beyond, exceed
A great work of art may be said to _____transcend_____ time, and it is remembered for decades, or even centuries.
SYNONYMS: surpass, outstrip

19. umbrage
(em' brəj)

(*n.*) shade cast by trees; foliage giving shade; an overshadowing influence or power; offense, resentment; a vague suspicion
She hesitated to offer her opinion, fearing that they would take _____umbrage_____ at her criticism.
SYNONYMS: irritation, pique, annoyance
ANTONYMS: pleasure, delight, satisfaction

20. unctuous
(əŋk' chü əs)

(*adj.*) excessively smooth or smug; trying too hard to give an impression of earnestness, sincerity, or piety; fatty, oily; pliable
Her constant inquiring about the health of my family at first seemed friendly, later merely _____unctuous_____.
SYNONYMS: mealymouthed, servile, fawning, greasy
ANTONYMS: gruff, blunt

Completing the Sentence

From the words for this unit, choose the one that best completes each of the following sentences. Write the word in the space provided.

1. I certainly appreciate your praise, but I must say that I can see nothing so remarkably **meritorious** in having done what any decent person would do.

2. Since I don't like people who play favorites in the office, I have frequently **expostulated** against such behavior with my superiors.

3. Various insects have a marvelous capacity to protect themselves by **simulating** the appearance of twigs and other objects in their environment.

4. In the question-and-answer session, we tried to **elicit** from the candidates some definite indication of how they proposed to reduce the national debt.

5. I feel that, as an old friend, I have the **prerogative** of criticizing your actions without arousing resentment.

6. The only way to defeat the party in power is for all the reform groups to form a(n) **coalition** and back a single slate of candidates.

7. Although we tried to express our sympathy, we knew that mere words could do nothing to **assuage** her grief.

8. Their tastes have been so **jaded** by luxurious living that they seem incapable of enjoying the simple pleasures of life.

9. Of course you have a right to ask the waiter for a glass of water, but is there any need to use the **petulant** tone of a spoiled child?

10. His confidence grew as he received clear signs of the **approbation** of his superiors.

11. During the brief **hiatus** in the music, someone's ringing cell phone split the air.

12. I take no **umbrage** at your personal remarks, but I feel you would have been better advised not to make them.

13. The midnight fire in our apartment building cast a(n) **lurid**, unearthly light on the faces of the firefighters struggling to put it out.

14. The issue of good faith that your conduct raises far **transcends** the specific question of whether or not you are responsible for the problem.

15. If you cannot meet the college's entrance requirements, it will be futile to have someone **intercede** on your behalf.

16. If you take pride in expressing yourself with force and originality, you should not use so many **hackneyed** phrases.

17. In an age when the United States has truly global responsibilities, we cannot afford to have leaders with **provincial** points of view.

18. The manager expressed her unfavorable opinion of the job applicant by ____innuendo____ rather than by direct statement.

19. Weakened militarily, and with a large part of the population living on free "bread and circuses," the once mighty Roman Empire now entered a period of ____decadence____.

20. Forever humbling himself and flattering others, Dickens' Uriah Heep is famously ____unctuous____.

Synonyms

*Choose the word from this unit that is **the same** or **most nearly the same** in meaning as the **boldface** word or expression in the given phrase. Write the word on the line provided.*

1. **pause** in the hectic workday — hiatus
2. **insinuation** not supported by fact — innuendo
3. **wearied** by too many compliments — jaded
4. impolite and **peevish** questions — petulant
5. a **perquisite** of her rank — prerogative
6. exploding in **annoyance** — umbrage
7. unceasing and **servile** modesty — unctuous
8. **feign** a reconciliation — simulate
9. **alleviate** his worst fears — assuage
10. seeking the boss's **commendation** — approbation
11. **gruesome** tales of grave robbers — lurid
12. **protest** against a course of action — expostulate
13. to **exceed** one's limitations — transcend
14. finding strength through an **alliance** — coalition
15. **mediate** in a dispute — intercede

Antonyms

*Choose the word from this unit that is **most nearly opposite** in meaning to the **boldface** word or expression in the given phrase. Write the word on the line provided.*

16. the **development** of a civilization — decadence
17. a **broad-minded** approach to education — provincial
18. trying to **squelch** suggestions — elicit
19. a record of **discreditable** actions — meritorious
20. a series of **novel** magic tricks — hackneyed

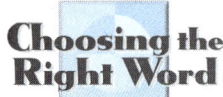

Choosing the Right Word Circle the **boldface** word that more satisfactorily completes each of the following sentences.

1. The magnificence of the scene far (**simulated, transcended**) my ability to describe it in words.
2. The most (**meritorious, lurid**) form of charity, according to the ancient Hebrew sages, is to help a poor person to become self-supporting.
3. The American two-party system almost always makes it unnecessary to form a (**hiatus, coalition**) of minority parties to carry on the government.
4. To impress her newly made friends, she (**simulated, assuaged**) an interest in modern art, of which she knew nothing.
5. Apparently mistaking us for the millionaire's children, the hotel manager overwhelmed us with his (**petulant, unctuous**) attentions.
6. I see no point in (**expostulating, simulating**) with a person who habitually refuses to listen to reason.
7. After watching four TV football games on New Year's Day, I was (**jaded, hackneyed**) with the pigskin sport for weeks to come.
8. Anyone who thinks that it is still a gentleman's (**prerogative, hiatus**) to ask a lady to dance didn't attend our Senior Prom.
9. We cannot know today what sort of accent Abraham Lincoln had, but it may well be that there was a decidedly (**meritorious, provincial**) twang in his speech.
10. Who would have thought he would take (**prerogative, umbrage**) at an e-mail from a friend who wanted only to help?
11. My teacher is so accomplished that she can (**simulate, elicit**) some degree of interest and attention from even the most withdrawn children.
12. When the (**umbrage, hiatus**) in the conversation became embarrassingly long, I decided that the time had come to serve the sandwiches.
13. His skillful use of academic jargon and fashionable catchphrases could not conceal the essentially (**hackneyed, meritorious**) quality of his ideas.
14. On the air the star seemed calm, but he privately sent (**petulant, jaded**) notes to those who gave him bad reviews.
15. I truly dislike the kind of sensational popular biography that focuses solely on the more (**lurid, hackneyed**) or scandalous aspects of a superstar's career.
16. How can you accuse me of employing (**umbrage, innuendo**) when I am saying in the plainest possible language that I think you're a crook?
17. If you try to (**elicit, intercede**) in a lovers' quarrel, the chances are that you will only make things worse.
18. Popularity polls seem to be based on the mistaken idea that the basic task of a political leader is to win immediate (**approbation, coalition**) from the people.
19. They try to "prove" the (**umbrage, decadence**) of modern youth by emphasizing everything that is bad and ignoring whatever is good.
20. Perhaps it will (**expostulate, assuage**) your fright if I remind you that everyone must have a first date at some time in his or her life.

Vocabulary in Context

*Read the following passage, in which some of the words you have studied in this unit appear in **boldface** type. Then complete each statement given below the passage by circling the letter of the item that is **the same** or **almost the same** in meaning as the highlighted word.*

Screen Time

(Line)

Americans' love of the movies goes back to the early years of the twentieth century, when shabby little theaters charged a nickel to see a film about a **lurid** crime, a **meritorious** deed, or a thrilling chase. These twenty-minute "flickers," as many called them, offered a short but exciting **hiatus** from everyday life. By the
(5) 1920s the movies had become big business, and cities bragged of cinema palaces three stories tall, their lobbies embellished with splendid carpeted stairways, plaster statues, and colorful lighting. Built in the center of town, these theaters showed brand-new, less **hackneyed**, and longer films, which were later shown
(10) at smaller neighborhood theaters and in **provincial** towns.

In the 1930s the Great Depression hit. Banks closed, businesses failed, and ten percent of Americans lost their jobs, while
(15) many others accepted wage cuts and feared they would be next. By now it cost twenty cents to go to the movies, which was more than the price of a loaf of bread. Why should frightened people short of
(20) cash spend money unnecessarily?

Movie-makers came up with clever answers. For many years they had made films in which poor people proved themselves smarter, kinder, or braver
(25) than the rich and **jaded**. To these they now

Hollywood Premiere of "The Robe," 1953

added movies made from novels set in faraway times and places unlike the alarming here and now. Theaters began showing two full-length films for the price of one, added a cartoon, gave away dishes, and awarded money to the holder of the lucky ticket on "bank night." Ticket sales climbed, and going to the movies
(30) every week became an American pastime.

---

1. The meaning of **lurid** (line 2) is
   a. unsolved
   b. ghastly ✓
   c. true
   d. ridiculous

2. Meritorious (line 3) most nearly means
   a. difficult
   b. praiseworthy ✓
   c. wicked
   d. unusual

3. Hiatus (line 4) is best defined as
   a. story
   b. excerpt
   c. pause ✓
   d. lesson

4. The meaning of **hackneyed** (line 8) is
   a. ragged
   b. exciting
   c. noisy
   d. trite ✓

5. Provincial (line 11) most nearly means
   a. outlying ✓
   b. prosperous
   c. deserving
   d. middle-size

6. Jaded (line 25) is best defined as
   a. famous
   b. notorious
   c. disappointed
   d. surfeited ✓

Unit 1 ■ 27

Unit 2

See page T21 for information.

Note carefully the spelling, pronunciation, part(s) of speech, and definition(s) of each of the following words. Then write the word in the blank space(s) in the illustrative sentence(s) following. Finally, study the lists of synonyms and antonyms given at the end of each entry.

1. **ameliorate**
   (ə mēl′ yə rāt)

   (*v.*) to improve, make better, correct a flaw or shortcoming

   A hot meal can __ameliorate__ the discomforts of even the coldest day.

   SYNONYMS: amend, better
   ANTONYMS: worsen, aggravate, exacerbate

2. **aplomb**
   (ə pläm′)

   (*n.*) poise, assurance, great self-confidence; perpendicularity

   Considering the family's tense mood, you handled the situation with __aplomb__.

   SYNONYMS: composure, self-possession, levelheadedness
   ANTONYMS: confusion, embarrassment, abashment

3. **bombastic**
   (bäm bas′ tik)

   (*adj.*) pompous or overblown in language; full of high-sounding words intended to conceal a lack of ideas

   He delivered a __bombastic__ speech that did not even address our problems.

   SYNONYMS: inflated, highfalutin, high-flown, pretentious
   ANTONYMS: unadorned, simple, plain, austere

4. **callow**
   (kal′ ō)

   (*adj.*) without experience; immature, not fully developed; lacking sophistication and poise; without feathers

   They entered the army as __callow__ recruits and left as seasoned veterans.

   SYNONYMS: green, raw, unfledged, inexperienced
   ANTONYMS: mature, grown-up, polished, sophisticated

5. **drivel**
   (driv′ əl)

   (*n.*) saliva or mucus flowing from the mouth or nose; foolish, aimless talk or thinking; nonsense; (*v.*) to let saliva flow from the mouth; to utter nonsense or childish twaddle; to waste or fritter away foolishly

   To me, my dream made perfect sense, but when I told it to my friend it sounded like __drivel__.

   Knowing that his time was nearly up, we kept silent and let him __drivel__ on.

   SYNONYMS: (*n.*) balderdash, hogwash, tommyrot, slaver

6. **epitome**
   (i pit′ ə mē)

   (*n.*) a summary, condensed account; an instance that represents a larger reality

   Admitting when you have been fairly defeated is the __epitome__ of sportsmanship.

   SYNONYMS: abstract, digest, model, archetype

7. exhort
(eg zôrt′)

(v.) to urge strongly, advise earnestly
With dramatic gestures, our fans vigorously __exhorted__ the team to play harder.
SYNONYMS: entreat, implore, adjure
ANTONYMS: discourage, advise against, deprecate

8. ex officio
(eks ə fish′ ē ō)

(adj., adv.) by virtue of holding a certain office
The President is the __ex officio__ commander-in-chief of the armed forces in time of war.

9. infringe
(in frinj′)

(v.) to violate, trespass, go beyond recognized bounds
If you continue to __infringe__ on my responsibilities, will you also take the blame for any mistakes?
SYNONYMS: encroach, impinge, intrude, poach
ANTONYM: stay in bounds

10. ingratiate
(in grā′ shē āt)

(v.) to make oneself agreeable and thus gain favor or acceptance by others (sometimes used in a critical or derogatory sense)
It is not a good idea to __ingratiate__ oneself by paying cloying compliments.
SYNONYMS: cozy up to, curry favor with
ANTONYMS: alienate, humiliate oneself, mortify oneself

11. interloper
(in′ tər lōp ər)

(n.) one who moves in where he or she is not wanted or has no right to be, an intruder
The crowd was so eager to see the band perform that they resented the opening singer as an __interloper__.
SYNONYMS: trespasser, meddler, buttinsky

12. intrinsic
(in trin′ sik)

(adj.) belonging to someone or something by its very nature, essential, inherent; originating in a bodily organ or part
It had been my father's favorite book when he was my age, but for me it held little __intrinsic__ interest.
SYNONYMS: immanent, organic
ANTONYMS: extrinsic, external, outward

13. inveigh
(in vā′)

(v.) to make a violent attack in words, express strong disapproval
You should not __inveigh__ against the plan with quite so much vigor until you have read it.
SYNONYMS: rail, harangue, fulminate, remonstrate
ANTONYMS: acclaim, glorify, extol

14. lassitude
(las′ ə tüd)

(n.) weariness of body or mind, lack of energy
On some days I am overcome by __lassitude__ at the thought of so many more years of schooling.
SYNONYMS: fatigue, lethargy, torpor, languor
ANTONYMS: energy, vitality, animation, liveliness

15. **millennium**
(*pl.*, **millennia**)
(mə len' ē əm)

(*n.*) a period of one thousand years; a period of great joy

In 1999 an argument raged over whether 2000 or 2001 would mark the beginning of the new __millennium__.

SYNONYMS: chiliad, golden age, prosperity, peace
ANTONYMS: doomsday, day of judgment

16. **occult**
(ə kəlt')

(*adj.*) mysterious, magical, supernatural; secret, hidden from view; not detectable by ordinary means; (*v.*) to hide, conceal; eclipse; (*n.*) matters involving the supernatural

One need not rely on __occult__ knowledge to grasp why things disappear in a house where two cats live.

Much of his talk about the __occult__ seems grounded in nothing but trick photography and folklore.

SYNONYMS: (*adj.*) supernatural, esoteric, abstruse, arcane
ANTONYMS: (*adj.*) mundane, common, public, exoteric

17. **permeate**
(pər' mē āt)

(*v.*) to spread through, penetrate, soak through

The rain __permeated__ all of my clothing and reduced the map in my pocket to a pulpy mass.

18. **precipitate**
(*v.*, pri sip' ə tāt; *adj.*, *n.*, pri sip' ət ət)

(*v.*) to fall as moisture; to cause or bring about suddenly; to hurl down from a great height; to give distinct form to; (*adj.*) characterized by excessive haste; (*n.*) moisture; the product of an action or process

Scholars often disagree over which event or events __precipitate__ an historic moment.

I admit that my outburst was __precipitate__.

Too many eggs in this particular pudding will leave a messy __precipitate__ in the baking pan.

SYNONYMS: (*v.*) provoke, produce; (*adj.*) reckless, impetuous
ANTONYMS: (*adj.*) wary, cautious, circumspect

19. **stringent**
(strin' jənt)

(*adj.*) strict, severe; rigorously or urgently binding or compelling; sharp or bitter to the taste

Some argue that more __stringent__ laws against speeding will make our streets safer.

SYNONYMS: stern, rigorous, tough, urgent, imperative
ANTONYMS: lenient, mild, lax, permissive

20. **surmise**
(sər mīz')

(*v.*) to think or believe without certain supporting evidence; to conjecture or guess; (*n.*) likely idea that lacks definite proof

I cannot be sure, but I __surmise__ that she would not accept my apology even if I made it on my knees.

The police had no proof, nothing to go on but a suspicion, a mere __surmise__.

SYNONYMS: (*v.*) infer, gather; (*n.*) inference, presumption

Completing the Sentence

From the words for this unit, choose the one that best completes each of the following sentences. Write the word in the space provided.

1. They have a great deal to say on the subject, but unfortunately most of it is meaningless __drivel__.

2. The Vice President of the United States, the Secretary of State, and the Secretary of Defense are __ex officio__ members of the National Security Council.

3. That dancer is very talented, but isn't it going rather far to call her "the very __epitome__ of feminine beauty and grace"?

4. Representing an organization of senior citizens, the rally's keynote speaker __inveighed__ vehemently against conditions that rob the elderly of their dignity and independence.

5. "The rash and __precipitate__ actions of that young hothead almost cost us the battle, to say nothing of the war," the general remarked sourly.

6. The mere fact that we cannot explain at the present time how she was hurt doesn't mean that she was the victim of some __occult__ power.

7. After completing those long, grueling exams, I was overwhelmed by a(n) __lassitude__ so great that I felt I would never be able to study again.

8. We do not know what her motives were, but we may __surmise__ that she was mainly concerned for the child's well-being.

9. A good definition of *freedom* is: "The right to do anything you wish as long as you do not __infringe__ on the rights of others."

10. Addressing the school assembly for the first time was a nerve-racking experience, but I managed to deliver my speech with a reasonable amount of __aplomb__.

11. "If you think my training rules are too __stringent__ and confining," the coach said, "then you probably shouldn't be a candidate for the team."

12. We looked up hungrily as the delightful odor of broiled steak and fried onions __permeated__ the room.

13. He tries to give the impression of being a true man of the world, but his conduct clearly shows him to be a(n) __callow__ and somewhat feckless youth.

14. The voters of this city are looking for practical answers to urgent questions and will not respond to that kind of __bombastic__ and pretentious claptrap.

15. Though fossils show that human beings have been on earth a very, very long time, the earliest written records of their activities date back only about five __millennia__.

16. I refuse to accept the idea that conditions in this slum have deteriorated so far that nothing can be done to __ameliorate__ them.

17. How can we have any respect for people who try to __ingratiate__ themselves with their superiors by flattery and favors?

18. This old necklace has little ____intrinsic____ value, but it means a great deal to me because it belonged to my mother.
19. The people trying to "crash" our dance may think of themselves as merry pranksters, but they are really ____interlopers____ who would prevent us all from having a good time.
20. The prophets of old fervently ____exhorted____ the people to amend their lives.

Synonyms

Choose the word from this unit that is **the same** or **most nearly the same** in meaning as the **boldface** word or expression in the given phrase. Write the word on the line provided.

1. a **buttinsky** at their reunion — interloper
2. a stain that **spread through** — permeated
3. overdramatic, **high-flown** language — bombastic
4. the **model** of what not to wear — epitome
5. a smile meant to **curry** favor — ingratiate
6. to **rail** against a harmless mistake — inveigh
7. a line delivered with **composure** — aplomb
8. thought the idea to be **hogwash** — drivel
9. a **strict** requirement — stringent
10. seemed to be a logical **presumption** — surmise
11. to **encroach** on their rights — infringe
12. to **entreat** the people to resist — exhort
13. an **inexperienced** trainee — callow
14. tonight's moderator **by virtue of her job** — ex officio
15. hints of a **supernatural** presence — occult

Antonyms

Choose the word from this unit that is **most nearly opposite** in meaning to the **boldface** word or expression in the given phrase. Write the word on the line provided.

16. **external** to the whole plan — intrinsic
17. a notable **energy** in her manner — lassitude
18. a **cautious** move on the chess board — precipitate
19. waiting for the **day of judgment** — millennium
20. swift action to **worsen** the situation — ameliorate

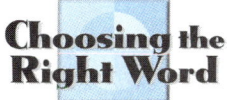

Choosing the Right Word

*Circle the **boldface** word that more satisfactorily completes each of the following sentences.*

1. I trust that we will have the will to improve what can now be improved and the patience to bear what cannot now be (**ameliorated,** surmised).
2. When the bridge suddenly collapsed in the high winds, the people on it at the time were (inveighed, **precipitated**) to their deaths in the watery abyss below.
3. "Long periods of intense boredom punctuated by short periods of intense fear"—in this famous definition a British general (**epitomized,** infringed) the nature of war.
4. We are all ready and willing to do what must be done; what we need is leadership—not (**exhortation,** aplomb)!
5. Must we continue to listen to all this childish (lassitude, **drivel**)!
6. A sour odor of decay, stale air, and generations of living (**permeated,** precipitated) every corner of the old tenement.
7. She handled a potentially embarrassing situation with cool (drivel, **aplomb**).
8. His message may seem (**bombastic,** callow), but there is a solid framework of practical ideas underlying the rather pompous language.
9. In this situation we cannot act on the basis of what may be (**surmised,** inveighed), but only in accordance with what is definitely known.
10. "I'm sure your every wish will be granted," I assured the demanding child, my tongue firmly in my check, "when and if the (exhortation, **millennium**) ever comes!"
11. It is easy to (**inveigh,** precipitate) against "dirty politics," but less easy to play a positive role, however small, in the political process.
12. In stating that "All men are created equal and endowed . . . with certain inalienable rights," the Declaration of Independence proclaims the (**intrinsic,** callow) value of every human being.
13. After years of fighting for social reforms, she experienced a sort of spiritual (**lassitude,** aplomb) that caused her to withdraw and let other people lead the struggle.
14. Do we need new laws to combat crime, or rather, more (ingratiating, **stringent**) enforcement of the laws we already have?
15. The publisher will take prompt legal action against anyone who (inveighs, **infringes**) on the copyright of this book.
16. I can usually forgive a(n) (**callow,** ex officio) display of feeble jokes and showing off—but not by someone who has passed his 40th birthday!
17. There is evidence that proves that many persons supposed to possess (**occult,** stringent) powers have either been clever frauds or the victims of self-deception.
18. After the unexpected defeat, the members of the team wanted to be alone and regarded anyone who entered the locker room as a(n) (**interloper,** lassitude).
19. The song had a pleasant, (stringent, **ingratiating**) melody that gained it quick popularity and then caused it to be forgotten just as quickly.
20. Because I believe in spreading governmental powers among several officials, I am opposed to having the Mayor serve as (occult, **ex officio**) head of the Board of Education.

Vocabulary in Context

Read the following passage, in which some of the words you have studied in this unit appear in **boldface** *type. Then complete each statement given below the passage by circling the letter of the item that is **the same** or **almost the same** in meaning as the highlighted word.*

Speaking Up

(Line)

Most people shiver at the prospect of making a speech, of facing a roomful of strangers and trying to persuade or inform them. Here are some tips that can help the inexperienced to do the job with **aplomb**.

First, remember that you and your audience are all in one room together. You are not an **interloper**, and your audience is not the enemy. The truth is that your listeners (5) will probably like you if you appear to like them. Try your best to put *them* at ease, for by doing so, you can **ameliorate** your own discomfort.

A student debater makes a point

How should you begin? Despite what you may have been told, do not start off with a joke. Telling jokes successfully to strangers takes practice (10) and skill. Besides, any joke you have recently heard is likely to be one that your listeners have also heard. In short, do not start by trying to **ingratiate** yourself. Instead, pay the audience the compliment of being yourself. Try to be (15) simple and direct. By all means smile if you say something funny, but bear in mind that only **callow** speakers laugh aloud at their own wit.

Should the speech be written out word for word? If you are to speak for as long as thirty (20) minutes, it probably should. (For so long a speech, keep the sentences fairly short; strings of long ones will end up sounding **bombastic**.) If your time is brief, you may need only notes you can scan as you move from point to point. (25) Either way, rehearse and rehearse—so you can look often at your audience. Nothing will increase your bravery and put *you* more at ease than looking into friendly faces.

---

1. The meaning of **aplomb** (line 3) is
 a. assistance c. applause
 b. poise ✓ d. victory

2. Interloper (line 5) most nearly means
 a. professional **c. intruder** ✓
 b. amateur d. fool

3. Ameliorate (line 7) is best defined as
 a. amend ✓ c. increase
 b. wipe out d. replace

4. The meaning of **ingratiate** (line 14) is
 a. curry favor for ✓ c. exaggerate
 b. disguise d. make fun of

5. Callow (line 18) most nearly means
 a. pale c. proud
 b. raw ✓ d. loud

6. Bombastic (line 23) is best defined as
 a. complicated c. silly
 b. odd **d. highfalutin** ✓

34 ■ Unit 2

See page T21 for information.

UNIT 3

Definitions

Note carefully the spelling, pronunciation, part(s) of speech, and definition(s) of each of the following words. Then write the word in the blank space(s) in the illustrative sentence(s) following. Finally, study the lists of synonyms and antonyms given at the end of each entry.

1. abominate
(ə bäm′ ə nāt)

(*v.*) to have an intense dislike or hatred for

I _____**abominate**_____ cruelty yet do not always notice when I have said something cruel without meaning to.

SYNONYMS: loathe, abhor, despise, detest
ANTONYMS: relish, savor, cherish, esteem

2. acculturation
(ə kəl chə rā′ shən)

(*n.*) the modification of the social patterns, traits, or structures of one group or society by contact with those of another; the resultant blend

Every immigrant group newly arrived in another country goes through a slow process of _____**acculturation**_____.

SYNONYM: adaptation

3. adventitious
(ad ven tish′ əs)

(*adj.*) resulting from chance rather than from an inherent cause or character; accidental, not essential; (*medicine*) acquired, not congenital

It was no _____**adventitious**_____ meeting that led to their writing songs together, for in fact they were cousins.

SYNONYMS: extrinsic, incidental, fortuitous
ANTONYMS: essential, intrinsic, inherent, congenital

4. ascribe
(ə skrīb′)

(*v.*) to assign or refer to (as a cause or source), attribute

You may _____**ascribe**_____ these holes to gophers or elves, but I blame the dog from next door.

SYNONYMS: impute, credit, attribute

5. circuitous
(sər kyü′ ə təs)

(*adj.*) roundabout, not direct

I followed a _____**circuitous**_____ path through the woods, not because I feared pursuit, but because I was lost.

SYNONYMS: indirect, meandering, winding
ANTONYMS: straight, direct, as the crow flies

6. commiserate
(kə miz′ ə rāt)

(*v.*) to sympathize with, have pity or sorrow for, share a feeling of distress

The family _____**commiserated**_____ with her after the loss of her old and faithful dog.

SYNONYMS: feel sorry for, empathize
ANTONYM: feel no sympathy for

7. enjoin
(en join′)

(*v.*) to direct or order; to prescribe a course of action in an authoritative way; to prohibit

I _____enjoined_____ them to stop spending so much money or to face the consequences.

SYNONYMS: bid, charge, command, adjure
ANTONYMS: allow, permit

8. expedite
(ek′ spə dīt)

(*v.*) to make easy, cause to progress faster

The pleasant background music did not _____expedite_____ my work but instead, distracted me.

SYNONYMS: accelerate, facilitate, speed up
ANTONYMS: hinder, hamper, impede, obstruct

9. expiate
(ek′ spē āt)

(*v.*) to make amends, make up for; to avert

They seemed more than willing to _____expiate_____ their guilt by whatever means necessary.

SYNONYMS: redeem, make amends for, atone, make reparation

10. ferment
(*n.*, fər′ ment;
v., fər ment′)

(*n.*) a state of great excitement, agitation, or turbulence; (*v.*) to be in or work into such a state; to produce alcohol by chemical action

Caught in the _____ferment_____ of revolution, the young men enlisted with the local militias.

If left for a time, cider will eventually _____ferment_____.

SYNONYMS: (*n.*) commotion, turmoil, unrest
ANTONYMS: (*n.*) peace and quiet, tranquility, placidity

11. inadvertent
(in əd vər′ tənt)

(*adj.*) resulting from or marked by lack of attention; unintentional, accidental

The poor fellow was stronger than he realized, and the damage he did was _____inadvertent_____.

SYNONYMS: accidental, unconsidered
ANTONYMS: deliberate, intentional, premeditated

12. nominal
(näm′ ə nəl)

(*adj.*) existing in name only, not real; too small to be considered or taken seriously

Because so many of its patients were having financial troubles, the health clinic charged only _____nominal_____ fees.

SYNONYMS: titular, token, trifling, inconsequential
ANTONYMS: real, actual, exorbitant, excessive

13. noncommittal
(nän kə mit′ əl)

(*adj.*) not decisive or definite; unwilling to take a clear position or to say yes or no

We questioned her quietly, carefully, and at length, but her answers remained _____noncommittal_____.

SYNONYMS: cagey, uninformative, playing it safe, playing it close to the vest
ANTONYMS: positive, definite, committed

14. peculate
(pek′ yü lāt)

(*v.*) to steal something that has been given into one's trust; to take improperly for one's own use

Investigators discovered that the clerk came up with a scheme to __peculate__ from the company.

SYNONYMS: embezzle, defraud, misappropriate

15. proclivity
(prō kliv′ ə tē)

(*n.*) a natural or habitual inclination or tendency (especially of human character or behavior)

Curious, patient, and fond of long walks outdoors, she soon displayed a __proclivity__ for nature study.

SYNONYMS: natural bent, penchant, propensity
ANTONYMS: inability or incapacity

16. sangfroid
(säŋ frwä′)

(*n.*) composure or coolness, especially in trying circumstances

An experienced actor can perform with what seems like limitless __sangfroid__, even when he forgets a line.

SYNONYMS: poise, self-assurance, equanimity
ANTONYMS: excitability, hysteria, flappability

17. seditious
(sə dish′ əs)

(*adj.*) resistant to lawful authority; having the purpose of overthrowing an established government

Dictators usually begin their reigns by searching out and silencing __seditious__ opinion.

SYNONYMS: mutinous, rebellious, subversive
ANTONYMS: supportive, loyal, faithful, allegiant

18. tenuous
(ten′ yü əs)

(*adj.*) thin, slender, not dense; lacking clarity or sharpness; of slight importance or significance; lacking a sound basis, poorly supported

My grasp of trigonometry was __tenuous__ until I attended the extra-help sessions.

SYNONYMS: flimsy, insubstantial, vague, hazy
ANTONYMS: strong, solid, substantial, valid

19. vitriolic
(vi trē äl′ ik)

(*adj.*) bitter, sarcastic; highly caustic or biting (like a strong acid)

Though hurt by his __vitriolic__ language, I had to admit that some of his points were valid.

SYNONYMS: withering, acerbic, mordant
ANTONYMS: bland, saccharine, honeyed, sugary

20. wheedle
(whēd′ əl)

(*v.*) to use coaxing or flattery to gain some desired end

The spy used charm and flattery in order to __wheedle__ the information from the diplomat.

SYNONYMS: cajole, inveigle, soft-soap, sweet-talk
ANTONYMS: coerce, browbeat, intimidate, strong-arm

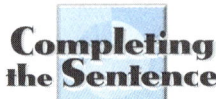

Completing the Sentence

From the words for this unit, choose the one that best completes each of the following sentences. Write the word in the space provided.

1. He _____**expiated**_____ the crime committed during his youth by a lifetime of service to humanity.

2. Since she seems to have a strong _____**proclivity**_____ both for science and for service to others, I think that she should plan to study medicine.

3. We Americans do not believe that honest criticism of our public officials, no matter how severe, should be regarded as _____**seditious**_____.

4. Declaring the boycott to be illegal, the judge _____**enjoined**_____ the labor union from applying it against the employing firm.

5. Wines from that part of France are produced by _____**fermenting**_____ the juice of the luscious grapes that grow on the hillsides.

6. No matter what their other likes or dislikes are, all Americans thoroughly _____**abominate**_____ slavery in all its forms.

7. Certain languages such as Afrikaans are the product of _____**acculturation**_____, and were created when two societies merged.

8. Some people say that they cannot understand her defeat in the election, but I _____**ascribe**_____ it to her failure to discuss the issues in simple, down-to-earth terms.

9. While he remained the _____**nominal**_____ leader of the group, the real power passed into the hands of his wily aide.

10. His line of questioning was so _____**circuitous**_____ that I began to suspect that he was not sure of what he was trying to prove.

11. He claims to be a close friend of the Senator, but I believe that the connection between them is extremely _____**tenuous**_____.

12. The new computerized referral system will greatly _____**expedite**_____ the processing of complaints by customers.

13. Only someone who has suffered from bursitis can fully _____**commiserate**_____ with me when I am in the throes of an acute attack.

14. Who in the world can hope to match the unshakable _____**sangfroid**_____ of the indestructible James Bond in moments of great peril?

15. We must distinguish between the truly basic policies of our political party and those that are _____**adventitious**_____ and have little connection with the essential program.

16. Much of the money that the "robber barons" _____**peculated**_____ from the public trust was never recovered—or even missed!

17. You could have indicated frankly what you thought was wrong without embittering them with such _____**vitriolic**_____ criticism.

18. As charming, clever, and persuasive as you may be, you will certainly not __wheedle__ me into lending you my tennis racquet.
19. We had hoped to learn his opinion of the new energy program, but he remained completely __noncommittal__ during the interview.
20. If, as you say, your slamming of the door on the way out was completely __inadvertent__, you should be more careful in the future.

Synonyms

*Choose the word from this unit that is **the same** or **most nearly the same** in meaning as the **boldface** word or expression in the given phrase. Write the word on the line provided.*

1. **charge** both sides to negotiate — enjoin
2. **speed up** the registration procedure — expedite
3. a motive **attributed** to me — ascribed
4. **embezzle** from the treasury — peculate
5. was **cajoled** into agreeing — wheedled
6. an **acerbic** tone of voice — vitriolic
7. the **adaptation** of American students in Spain — acculturation
8. to **atone** for her unkindness — expiate
9. only **trifling** objections raised — nominal
10. **empathize** with your disappointment — commiserate
11. the **turmoil** of opening night — ferment
12. arguing a **poorly supported** point — tenuous
13. their leader's **self-assurance** — sangfroid
14. a nasty **penchant** for lying — proclivity
15. a **fortuitous** sequence of events — adventitious

Antonyms

*Choose the word from this unit that is **most nearly opposite** in meaning to the **boldface** word or expression in the given phrase. Write the word on the line provided.*

16. **cherish** everything about her — abominate
17. a **deliberate** misuse of the money — inadvertent
18. a **definite** statement of intentions — noncommittal
19. a kingdom filled with **loyal** subjects — seditious
20. a **direct** way home — circuitous

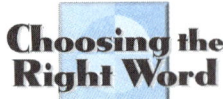

Choosing the Right Word

Circle the **boldface** word that more satisfactorily completes each of the following sentences.

1. I was simply unable to follow the (**circuitous**, **adventitious**) reasoning by which she "proved" that a straight line is not necessarily the shortest distance between two points.
2. Our military is prepared to deal with external aggression, but our best defense against (**sedition**, **peculation**) at home is the loyalty of the American people.
3. (**Commiseration**, **Proclivity**) is a noble human emotion, but in itself it is no substitute for vigorous efforts to help other people.
4. Since he has been able to (**expiate**, **wheedle**) almost anything he wants out of his parents, he is quite unprepared now to face the harsh realities of life.
5. An experienced politician always tries to avoid making (**fermented**, **inadvertent**) remarks that may offend some voters.
6. Although the Queen is the (**nominal**, **adventitious**) head of state, the Prime Minister is the real leader of the British government.
7. (**Peculation**, **Sedition**) was such a common offense among Roman provincial governors that, when asked how they made their fortunes, most simply replied, "In the provinces."
8. His investments proved to be profitable, but they were (**adventitious**, **nominal**) rather than the result of knowledge and planning.
9. The Biblical prophets (**abominated**, **acculturated**) idol worship of any kind and railed vehemently against such practices.
10. You are following an all too familiar pattern in (**ascribing**, **expediting**) your failures to anyone and everyone—except yourself.
11. Although that critic is feared for (**noncommittal**, **vitriolic**) reviews, I have learned that there is usually a sound basis for her unfavorable judgments.
12. I learned that I would have to make a choice between my strong aversion to hard work and my equally strong (**proclivity**, **wheedle**) for eating.
13. It is only in my fantasies that I display the (**ferment**, **sangfroid**) associated with movie heroes who are "as cool as a cucumber."
14. After he had seen the error of his ways, the villain attempted to (**expiate**, **enjoin**) the dark deeds of his past by acts of kindness and mercy.
15. Experienced lawyers know that the line between literal truth and slight but significant distortion of the facts is often a (**seditious**, **tenuous**) one.
16. With the deadline fast approaching, the local newspaper office was in a (**ferment**, **sedition**) of last-minute activity and preparation.
17. They are conscientious objectors to military service because they are (**enjoined**, **ascribed**) by a deep religious conviction not to take a human life.
18. When I spoke to Mother about going on the Easter trip to Washington, her only reply was a (**nominal**, **noncommittal**) "We'll see."
19. Modern American society can justly be said to be the end point of the (**commiseration**, **acculturation**) of diverse groups of immigrants.
20. The worst way I can think of to (**expedite**, **ascribe**) this program would be to set up a new Committee on (**Expediting**, **Ascribing**) Programs.

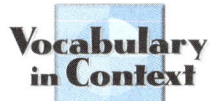

Vocabulary in Context

*Read the following passage, in which some of the words you have studied in this unit appear in **boldface** type. Then complete each statement given below the passage by circling the letter of the item that is **the same** or **almost the same** in meaning as the highlighted word.*

Building in Place

(Line)

Frank Lloyd Wright (1867–1959) is widely considered the greatest American architect in history. Few had a greater vision for how Americans should live or a harder time, despite handling professional obstacles with **sangfroid**, in getting others to further that vision by erecting the buildings he had designed. After college,
(5) where he studied engineering, he worked in Chicago for Louis Sullivan, a great architect who shared Wright's belief that American structures should suit the splendid and varied American landscape in which they were built. Wright
(10) **abominated** and eschewed the classical European designs that formed only a **tenuous** connection to the actual lives his clients lived. He loved nature in general and was inspired by the American plains in particular. He designed
(15) Midwestern "prairie houses" that were long and low. Their shapes and surfaces showed that they were a part of the land on which they stood, and this style became known as "organic architecture." Later, when he was asked to
(20) design larger buildings such as churches and offices, he used concrete for its thriftiness and glass ceilings for their natural and brilliant sunshine.

Country club designed by Wright in Maui

Branching out to Nevada, California, Pennsylvania, and elsewhere, he designed hundreds of buildings, and about 500 of them were built. A man of strong opinions, he stuck by his designs and could be **vitriolic** about preserving their integrity. Wright
(25) later went on to design the Imperial Hotel in Tokyo. Determined to match the building to its place, he made it resistant to the **adventitious** menace of earthquakes, a common danger in Japan. Sure enough, a terrible quake destroyed much of Tokyo, but the Imperial Hotel remained standing.

Toward the end of his career, Wright built a school for architects, and though its
(30) **nominal** purpose was design, its real impetus was his vision of life. Of his work he once said, "The mother of art is architecture. Without an architecture of our own we have no soul of our own civilization."

---

1. The meaning of **sangfroid** (line 3) is
  a. menace   c. bank account
  b. investment   **d. composure** ✓

2. Abominated (line 10) most nearly means
  a. loathed ✓   c. made fun of
  b. destroyed   d. tried out

3. Tenuous (line 11) is best defined as
  a. permanent   c. expensive
  b. vague ✓   d. pretty

4. The meaning of **vitriolic** (line 24) is
  a. acerbic ✓   c. confusing
  b. loud   d. tricky

5. Adventitious (line 26) most nearly means
  a. frequent   **c. accidental** ✓
  b. destructive   d. massive

6. Nominal (line 30) is best defined as
  a. popular   c. freshman
  b. easy   **d. token** ✓

Unit 3 ■ 41

Review Units 1–3

Visit us at www.sadlier-oxford.com
for interactive puzzles and games.

Analogies — In each of the following, circle the item that best completes the comparison.

See pages T38–T48 for explanations of answers.

1. **hiatus** is to **gap** as
   a. **epitome is to synopsis**
   b. ferment is to tranquility
   c. umbrage is to pleasure
   d. proclivity is to dislike

2. **millennium** is to **century** as
   a. ton is to pound
   b. **dollar is to dime**
   c. hour is to minute
   d. meter is to centimeter

3. **expostulate** is to **reason** as
   a. **inveigh is to invective**
   b. exhort is to compliment
   c. permeate is to warning
   d. transcend is to argument

4. **umbrage** is to **resent** as
   a. interest is to ascribe
   b. notice is to abominate
   c. **delight is to relish**
   d. pity is to enjoin

5. **nominal** is to **exorbitant** as
   a. provincial is to parochial
   b. bombastic is to occult
   c. **tenuous is to substantial**
   d. lurid is to sensational

6. **unctuous** is to **oil** as
   a. **vitriolic is to acid**
   b. decadent is to water
   c. petulant is to wine
   d. seditious is to milk

7. **callow** is to **experience** as
   a. self-assured is to aplomb
   b. exhausted is to lassitude
   c. petulant is to imagination
   d. **provincial is to sophistication**

8. **rant** is to **bombastic** as
   a. exhort is to jaded
   b. whine is to inadvertent
   c. **inveigh is to vitriolic**
   d. advocate is to noncommittal

9. **wheedle** is to **flattery** as
   a. ingratiate is to threats
   b. transcend is to prerogatives
   c. simulate is to surmises
   d. **insinuate is to innuendoes**

10. **embezzler** is to **peculate** as
    a. sovereign is to precipitate
    b. critic is to expiate
    c. **interloper is to infringe**
    d. engineer is to simulate

11. **meritorious** is to **approbation** as
    a. noncommittal is to consent
    b. **reprehensible is to condemnation**
    c. seditious is to commiseration
    d. laudable is to abomination

12. **inadvertent** is to **deliberate** as
    a. meritorious is to commendable
    b. unctuous is to occult
    c. petulant is to peevish
    d. **adventitious is to intrinsic**

13. **lax** is to **stringent** as
    a. **circuitous is to straight**
    b. hackneyed is to trite
    c. seditious is to subversive
    d. occult is to arcane

14. **lassitude** is to **fatigue** as
    a. ingratiation is to senility
    b. **decadence is to decay**
    c. acculturation is to paralysis
    d. sedation is to decrepitude

15. **hackneyed** is to **originality** as
    a. circuitous is to meandering
    b. **tenuous is to soundness**
    c. adventitious is to chance
    d. intrinsic is to value

16. **drivel** is to **substance** as
    a. criticism is to simplicity
    b. **gibberish is to meaning**
    c. reply is to thoroughness
    d. adage is to coherence

17. **awkward** is to **aplomb** as
    a. jaded is to decadence
    b. brazen is to temerity
    c. **excitable is to sangfroid**
    d. militant is to activity

18. **assuage** is to **irritate** as
    a. intercede is to meditate
    b. **expedite is to hamper**
    c. surmise is to verify
    d. ameliorate is to improve

REVIEW UNITS 1–3

Word Associations

In each of the following groups, circle the word that is best defined or suggested by the given phrase.

1. argue with the referee
   a. expostulate · b. expiate · c. confer · d. wheedle

2. sensational account of the tragedy
   a. circuitous · **b. lurid** · c. adventitious · d. vitriolic

3. encroach on my territory
   a. occult · **b. infringe** · c. intercede · d. precipitate

4. inclination for foreign languages
   a. aversion · **b. proclivity** · c. genius · d. prerogative

5. commanded our attendance
   a. enjoined · b. occulted · c. precipitated · d. ameliorated

6. A weary expression
   a. nominal · **b. jaded** · c. lurid · d. bombastic

7. plead on her friend's behalf
   a. commiserate · b. assuage · c. abominate · **d. intercede**

8. fill the air
   a. defray · b. stagnate · c. usurp · **d. permeate**

9. during the last 1000 years
   a. famine · b. war · **c. millennium** · d. revolution

10. adopt strict rules
    a. jaded · b. inadvertent · c. hackneyed · **d. stringent**

11. stolen from company funds
    a. simulated · **b. peculated** · c. cleaved · d. exploited

12. took offense at my remark
    a. sangfroid · **b. umbrage** · c. innuendo · d. deliberation

13. urge them to cooperate
    a. assuage · **b. exhort** · c. ascribe · d. wheedle

14. the right to change one's mind
    a. aplomb · b. proclivity · **c. prerogative** · d. approbation

15. surpass limitations
    a. transcend · b. permeate · c. salvage · d. ameliorate

16. cutting words
    a. decadent · **b. vitriolic** · c. meritorious · d. nominal

17. the result of low standards
    a. decadence · b. innuendo · c. millennium · d. sedition

18. imitate his diction
    a. simulate · b. abominate · c. callow · d. belittle

19. drew forth our applause
    a. expiated · b. transcended · c. wheedled · **d. elicited**

20. credit the painting to Picasso
    a. elicit · **b. ascribe** · c. enjoin · d. expedite

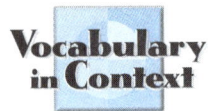

Vocabulary in Context

Read the following passage, in which some of the words you have studied in Units 1–3 appear in **boldface** type. Then complete each statement given below the passage by circling the item that is **the same** or **almost the same** in meaning as the highlighted word.

"Wrong-way" Corrigan

(Line)

Readers of American history know that in 1927 Charles A. Lindbergh made the first solo flight across the Atlantic Ocean in a plane called the
(5) *Spirit of St. Louis*. But how many people know that in 1938 Douglas Corrigan achieved what might be called the first transatlantic spoof?

At 31, Corrigan, a native Texan, was
(10) an airplane mechanic and flight instructor who longed to fly across the Atlantic. To **assuage** this itch, he prepared his 1929 Curtis-Robin monoplane for the journey but
(15) because of its age and poor condition, federal aviation authorities refused to certify the plane for a transoceanic flight. Even so, Corrigan flew his patched-up plane from California to
(20) New York in the summer of 1938. He then **elicited** permission from the aviation authorities to fly back home to California. Like Lindbergh, Corrigan took off from Long Island. Since his
(25) flight plan showed a return trip to California, his departure **precipitated** no suspicion. As he took off he must have seemed the very **epitome** of an innocent amateur, for the flight staff at
(30) the Long Island airfield noted that he headed eastward into clouds instead of turning west. This seemed a **circuitous** way to begin a trip to Los Angeles!
(35) Twenty-eight hours and thirteen minutes later, an odd-looking plane landed at an airfield in Dublin, Ireland. "I'm Douglas Corrigan," said the pilot. "Just got in from New York.
(40) Where am I?" (The outrage of the American officials, when they heard, can be imagined, but Corrigan continued to play the part of a cheerful, well-meaning amateur.) He
(45) **ascribed** his "mistake" in direction to a remarkably faulty compass and said that the clouds below him had kept him from seeing that he was flying over an ocean rather than the
(50) continental United States.

Within hours of his landing the story of "Wrong-way" Corrigan circled the world. Though his flight license was suspended for a short time, he was
(55) given a ticker-tape parade upon his return to New York. During a time of economic depression, Corrigan, who thwarted authority with a grin and a wink, captured Americans' hearts. He
(60) stuck by his story, that he had gotten lost on his way to California, for the rest of his life.

1. The meaning of **assuage** (line 12) is
   a. pay for   c. increase
   b. begin   (d. allay)

2. **Elicited** (line 21) most nearly means
   (a. extracted)   c. pleaded for
   b. ignored   d. faked

3. **Precipitated** (line 26) is best defined as
   a. got rid of   (b. provoked)
   b. suggested   d. described

4. The meaning of **epitome** (line 28) is
   (a. model)   c. imitation
   b. opposite   d. inspiration

5. **Circuitous** (line 33) most nearly means
   a. silly   c. dangerous
   b. mysterious   (d. indirect)

6. **Ascribed** (line 45) is best defined as
   a. denied   c. described
   b. concealed   (d. imputed)

44 ■ Review Units 1–3

REVIEW UNITS 1–3

Choosing the Right Meaning

Read each sentence carefully. Then circle the item that best completes the statement below the sentence.

See pages T38–T48 for explanations of answers.

"Planets like stars may be occulted; but as a planet shows a disk and does not appear as a mere point, the disappearance is gradual." (Patrick Moore) (2)

1. The best definition for the word **occulted** in line 1 is
a. discovered   b. observed   c. photographed   (**d. eclipsed**)

I thoroughly enjoyed that particular TV series and was saddened to discover that it was going on hiatus after only six episodes. (2)

2. The best meaning of the word **hiatus** in line 2 is
(**a. a break**)   b. an opening   c. a passage   d. a gap

Contingents of provincial militiamen regularly fought side by side with British regulars and their native allies in each of the four great wars France and England waged for (2) control of North America.

3. The word **provincial** in line 1 is used to mean
a. Italian local   (**b. American colonial**)   c. French rural   d. British parochial

Of the one hundred forty-two books of Livy's great *History of Rome* only thirty-five survive intact; the rest are known solely from epitomes by later writers. (2)

4. In line 2 the word **epitomes** can best be defined as
a. quotations   b. archetypes   (**c. summaries**)   d. explanations

"Her family has such a long history of deafness that I am forced to regard her difficulties in that area as congenital, not adventitious," the specialist replied. (2)

5. The word **adventitious** in line 2 most nearly means
a. fatal   b. inherent   (**c. acquired**)   d. fortuitous

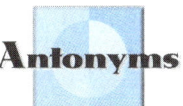

Antonyms

In each of the following groups, circle the word or expression that is most nearly the **opposite** of the word in **boldface** type.

1. commiserate
a. empathize
b. liberate
c. shackle
(**d. feel no sympathy**)

2. circuitous
a. dangerous
(**b. direct**)
c. unusual
d. confusing

3. abominate
a. avoid
b. encourage
c. loathe
(**d. relish**)

4. ferment
a. passion
(**b. tranquility**)
c. solitude
d. turmoil

5. ingratiate
a. curry favor
(**b. alienate**)
c. ungrateful
d. grateful

6. noncommittal
(**a. positive**)
b. reliable
c. irregular
d. nominal

7. surmise
a. dusk
b. inference
c. indifference
(**d. certainty**)

8. petulant
a. unruly
(**b. even-tempered**)
c. beautiful
d. brilliant

Review Units 1–3 ■ 45

9. bombastic
a. peaceful *(circled)*
b. illiterate
c. boring
d. unpretentious

10. assuage
a. sense
b. record
c. inflame *(circled)*
d. soothe

11. aplomb
a. skill
b. awkwardness *(circled)*
c. assurance
d. nobility

12. sangfroid
a. composure
b. bravery
c. speed
d. anxiety *(circled)*

13. provincial
a. selfish
b. unreasonable
c. worldly *(circled)*
d. local

14. seditious
a. violent
b. loyal *(circled)*
c. planned
d. subtle

15. tenuous
a. logical
b. remote
c. strong *(circled)*
d. nonexistent

16. hackneyed
a. amiable
b. blunt
c. original *(circled)*
d. essential

Word Families

A. On the line provided, write the word you have learned in Units 1–3 that is related to each of the following nouns.
EXAMPLE: sedition—**seditious**

1. province, provincialism, provinciality — provincial
2. simulation, simulator — simulate
3. amelioration, ameliorant, ameliorator — ameliorate
4. exhortation, exhorter — exhort
5. vitriol, vitriolization — vitriolic
6. infringement, infringer — infringe
7. bombast — bombastic
8. interceder, intercession — intercede
9. abomination — abominate
10. fermentation, fermenting — ferment
11. petulance — petulant
12. callowness — callow
13. expostulation — expostulate
14. precipitation — precipitate
15. millennia — millennium

B. On the line provided, write the word you have learned in Units 1–3 that is related to each of the following verbs.
EXAMPLE: approbate—**approbation**

16. decay — decadence
17. coalesce — coalition
18. acculturate — acculturation
19. merit — meritorious
20. epitomize — epitome

REVIEW UNITS 1-3

Two-Word Completions

Circle the pair of words that best complete the meaning of each of the following passages.

See pages T38–T48 for explanations of answers.

1. "The general's death-defying feats of gallantry in the recent war certainly deserve our _____," the article declared. "But, by the same token, his wanton acts of cruelty _____ our severest censure."
   a. umbrage . . . enjoin
   b. approbation . . . merit
   c. aplomb . . . expiate
   d. sangfroid . . . elicit

2. Though my teaching job entails numerous responsibilities, it also brings with it certain _____, one of which is the right to use school equipment, services, and facilities during the _____ between semesters or the summer break.
   a. prerogatives . . . hiatus
   b. surmises . . . innuendoes
   c. simulations . . . millennia
   d. ameliorations . . . proclivities

3. Though the Prime Minister actually directs the British government, the reigning monarch is the _____ head of state and, by virtue of that position, also the _____ leader of the Anglican Church.
   a. intrinsic . . . occult
   b. tenuous . . . inadvertent
   c. nominal . . . ex officio
   d. adventitious . . . noncommittal

4. While the Roman people remained vigorous and aggressive, their empire flourished. Once they began to sink into a sort of physical and spiritual _____, however, it became feeble and _____.
   a. umbrage . . . petulant
   b. lassitude . . . decadent
   c. aplomb . . . jaded
   d. ferment . . . adventitious

5. "A(n) _____ government will prove workable only so long as its members are able to _____ party differences," the professor remarked. "As soon as they become entangled in factional disputes, the partnership will begin to collapse."
   a. provincial . . . surmise
   b. ex officio . . . abominate
   c. seditious . . . ameliorate
   d. coalition . . . transcend

6. Some Senators favored the new budget proposal and in the warmest terms _____ their colleagues to pass the measure. Others disliked the idea and just as vehemently _____ against its adoption.
   a. wheedled . . . enjoined
   b. assuaged . . . interceded
   c. exhorted . . . inveighed
   d. elicited . . . infringed

Review Units 1–3 ■ 47

Building with Classical Roots

cede, cess, ceas—to happen, yield, go

This root appears in **intercede** (page 22), literally "to go between." The word now means "to ask a favor from one person for another." Other words based on the same root are listed below.

| accede | cessation | decease | predecessor |
| accessory | concession | precedence | recession |

From the list of words above, choose the one that corresponds to each of the brief definitions below. Write the word in the blank space in the illustrative sentence below the definition.

1. someone or something that comes before another in time, especially in an office or position ("one who leaves before")
   Starting today, I will take over from my ____**predecessor**____.

2. death ("*going away*")
   Marcia will inherit the estate after her aunt's ____**decease**____.

3. priority in order, rank, or importance
   Studying for finals must take ____**precedence**____ over everything else.

4. to give in, agree; to attain ("*to yield to*")
   The King's subjects are expected to ____**accede**____ to all his requests.

5. an admission, anything yielded, a compromise; a franchise
   There is always a line at the food ____**concession**____.

6. something added, a finishing touch; a helper in a crime
   Her sister was held by the police as a(n) ____**accessory**____.

7. a stopping, ceasing
   The ambassador called for a ____**cessation**____ of hostilities.

8. a withdrawal, departure; a period of economic slump
   Millions of workers were unemployed during the ____**recession**____.

From the list of words above, choose the one that best completes each of the following sentences. Write the word in the space provided.

1. This stern new measure will call for a(n) ____**cessation**____ of all economic assistance to both nations involved in the dispute.

2. In order to reach an agreement, both sides in the dispute will have to make important ____**concessions**____.

REVIEW UNITS 1–3

3. The new gymnasium will be an essential part of the community center, not just a(n) __accessory__.

4. The ultramodern office building that now occupies the site in no way resembles its stately old __predecessor__.

5. A provision was made for the maintenance of the family estate in the event that the __decease__ of the mother occurred before that of her husband.

6. In a monarchy, the oldest son usually __accedes__ to the throne on the death of the king.

7. The authorities declared that deliveries of such essentials as food and medical supplies would be given __precedence__ over all other shipments into the disaster area.

8. After four years of record-high unemployment, the economists admitted that the __recession__ was more serious than they had anticipated.

---

*Circle the **boldface** word that more satisfactorily completes each of the following sentences.*

1. No matter how vehemently that mother coaxed her child, the stubborn little boy would not (**accede**, **precede**) to her wishes.

2. The terrified public waited forty-eight hours for a (**concession**, **cessation**) in the tremors that followed the major earthquake.

3. The couple agreed that saving for their children's education would have to take (**precedence**, **predecessor**) over vacation spending.

4. With the (**recession**, **decease**) of the last member of the family, the house and property were taken over by a private foundation.

5. Congress narrowly passed a tax reduction bill designed to head off a likely (**cessation**, **recession**).

6. Because the current director has no respect for her (**predecessor**, **accessory**), she has reversed all his policies and replaced them with her own.

7. In order to reach a compromise, both sides in the dispute have to be willing to make some major (**concessions**, **recessions**).

8. In the 1940s and 1950s, hats and gloves were considered essential (**accessories**, **predecessors**) for well-dressed women.

Read the following sentences, paying special attention to the words and phrases underlined. From the words in the box below, find better choices for these underlined words and phrases. Then use these choices to rewrite the sentences.

WORD BANK				
acculturation	drivel	expiate	proclivity	stringent
bombastic	elicit	expostulate	provincial	surmise
coalition	enjoin	lurid	seditious	transcend
commiserate	epitome	occult	simulate	wheedle

Civil War Reenactors

1. People who possess an interest in the American Civil War (1861–1865) and a(n) innate inclination for imagining history may choose to become Civil War reenactors.
proclivity

2. Short of injury or death, reenactors go to great lengths to make a pretense of as many of the actual conditions of the Civil War experience as possible.
simulate

3. Depending on the rules of a unit, a reenactor's uniform, gear, and food may have to meet confining guidelines for realism.
stringent

4. Some reenactors consider surviving on stale foods, sleeping in scratchy woolen uniforms in bug-infested sleeping rolls, and brewing "coffee" from chicory to be the consummation of authenticity.
epitome

5. Reenactors get a feel for the life and hardships of a 19th century soldier and in doing so, share some of the feelings of distress and fear with their historical counterparts.
commiserate

6 "Hardcore" reenactors preclude themselves from using any objects or knowledge that would have been unavailable in the 1860s.
enjoin

7. For the 1993 film *Gettysburg*, the director brought together a fusion of several groups of reenactors to serve as extras in the battle scenes.
coalition

UNIT 4

See page T21 for information.

Definitions

Note carefully the spelling, pronunciation, part(s) of speech, and definition(s) of each of the following words. Then write the word in the blank space(s) in the illustrative sentence(s) following. Finally, study the lists of synonyms and antonyms given at the end of each entry.

1. affable
(af′ ə bəl)

(*adj.*) courteous and pleasant, sociable, easy to speak to
We spent a pleasant afternoon with our __affable__ neighbors.
SYNONYMS: genial, amicable, agreeable, cordial
ANTONYMS: surly, cantankerous, dour, inhospitable

2. aggrandize
(ə gran′ dīz)

(*v.*) to increase in greatness, power, or wealth; to build up or intensify; to make appear greater
John D. Rockefeller worked to __aggrandize__ his empire by purchasing oil wells, refineries, and pipelines.
SYNONYMS: augment, amplify, enhance, exalt
ANTONYMS: reduce, decrease, diminish

3. amorphous
(ə môr′ fəs)

(*adj.*) shapeless, without definite form; of no particular type or character; without organization, unity, or cohesion
The __amorphous__ body of the amoeba was fascinating to watch under the microscope.
SYNONYMS: formless, unstructured, nebulous, inchoate
ANTONYMS: definite, well-defined, clear-cut

4. aura
(ôr′ ə)

(*n.*) that which surrounds (as an atmosphere); a distinctive air or personal quality
What people thought was her __aura__ of mystery was actually a mask for her shyness.
SYNONYMS: ambience, atmosphere

5. contraband
(kän′ trə band)

(*n.*) illegal traffic, smuggled goods; (*adj.*) illegal, prohibited
Three jeweled combs from the 17th century were among the __contraband__ seized by the police.
SYNONYMS: (*adj.*) illicit, bootleg, unlawful
ANTONYMS: (*adj.*) legal, lawful, licit

6. erudite
(er′ yü dīt)

(*adj.*) scholarly, learned, bookish, pedantic
For my paper, I would like to find an __erudite__ history of the subject written in a clear and unbiased manner.
SYNONYMS: profoundly educated, well-read
ANTONYMS: ignorant, uneducated, illiterate

7. **gossamer**
   (gäs' ə mər)

   (*adj.*) thin, light, delicate, insubstantial; (*n.*) a very thin, light cloth
   Ghosts are often depicted in literature as wearing _____**gossamer**_____ clothing that makes them seem all the more ethereal.
   The book was so old that each finely printed page seemed only the weight of _____**gossamer**_____ .
   SYNONYMS: (*adj.*) filmy, diaphanous, sheer, airy, feathery, gauzy
   ANTONYMS: (*adj.*) thick, dense, solid, massive

8. **infer**
   (in fər')

   (*v.*) to find out by reasoning; to arrive at a conclusion on the basis of thought; to hint, suggest, imply
   I can _____**infer**_____ nothing from his odd behavior.
   SYNONYMS: gather, deduce, presume, guess, speculate

9. **inscrutable**
   (in skrü' tə bəl)

   (*adj.*) incapable of being understood; impossible to see through physically
   I could not tell by her _____**inscrutable**_____ smile whether she was pleased or only amused with me.
   SYNONYMS: impenetrable, incomprehensible, enigmatic
   ANTONYMS: comprehensible, intelligible, penetrable

10. **insular**
    (in' syə lər)

    (*adj.*) relating to, characteristic of, or situated on an island; narrow or isolated in outlook or experience
    You seem too sophisticated to hold such _____**insular**_____ opinions.
    SYNONYMS: narrow-minded, parochial, provincial
    ANTONYMS: catholic, cosmopolitan, liberal

11. **irrevocable**
    (i rev' ə kə bəl)

    (*adj.*) incapable of being changed or called back
    We tend to think of court verdicts as _____**irrevocable**_____, but they are often overturned by higher courts.
    SYNONYMS: irreversible, unrecallable, unalterable
    ANTONYMS: reversible, changeable

12. **propensity**
    (prə pen' sə tē)

    (*n.*) a natural inclination or predilection toward
    Queen Elizabeth I showed a strong _____**propensity**_____ for putting off decisions in the hopes that they would resolve themselves.
    SYNONYMS: natural bent, proclivity, penchant
    ANTONYMS: natural incapacity or inability

13. **querulous**
    (kwer' ə ləs)

    (*adj.*) peevish, complaining, fretful
    Some flight attendants dread a _____**querulous**_____ airline passenger more than they do rough weather.
    SYNONYMS: petulant, touchy, cranky, irritable
    ANTONYMS: uncomplaining, stoical, serene, placid

14. remonstrate
(ri män′ strāt)

(*v.*) to argue or plead with someone against something, protest against, object to

Slowly, carefully, keeping his voice down, he argued with the caller as one might ____**remonstrate**____ with a child.

SYNONYMS: reason against, expostulate

15. repudiate
(ri pyü′ dē āt)

(*v.*) to disown, reject, or deny the validity of

He was forced to ____**repudiate**____ a statement he had made before he'd had all the information.

SYNONYMS: disavow, abjure, renounce
ANTONYMS: avow, affirm, aver, avouch

16. resilient
(ri zil′ yənt)

(*adj.*) able to return to an original shape or form; able to recover quickly

The development of lightweight, ____**resilient**____ plastics revolutionized the design of many durable goods.

SYNONYMS: springy, elastic, buoyant, bouncy
ANTONYMS: rigid, stiff, inflexible, unyielding

17. reverberate
(ri vər′ bə rāt)

(*v.*) to re-echo, resound; to reflect or be reflected repeatedly

From the construction site, the noise of bulldozers and dump trucks ____**reverberated**____ across the valley.

SYNONYMS: rumble, thunder, boom, echo

18. scurrilous
(skər′ ə ləs)

(*adj.*) coarsely abusive, vulgar or low (especially in language), foul-mouthed

Days passed and unrest grew, and soon the rebels began a ____**scurrilous**____ attack on their absent leader.

SYNONYMS: obscene, filthy, abusive, vituperative
ANTONYMS: decorous, seemly, tasteful, dignified

19. sedulous
(sej′ ə ləs)

(*adj.*) persistent, showing industry and determination

No one could say that he was lazy, for he was a careful, ____**sedulous**____ copier of other people's work.

SYNONYMS: assiduous, tireless, indefatigable
ANTONYMS: lackadaisical, listless, indolent, otiose

20. sleazy
(slē′ zē)

(*adj.*) thin or flimsy in texture; cheap; shoddy or inferior in quality or character; ethically low, mean, or disreputable

The old lady made her clothes at home in order to avoid the ____**sleazy**____ goods sold in the general store.

SYNONYMS: inferior, cheesy, tawdry, tatty
ANTONYMS: superior, first-rate, quality, sturdy

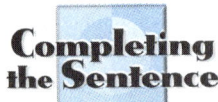
Completing the Sentence

From the words for this unit, choose the one that best completes each of the following sentences. Write the word in the space provided.

1. The program he suggested was so barren of guiding ideas and specific proposals that I felt justified in referring to it as __amorphous__.

2. This jacket is made of a material so __resilient__ that it sheds wrinkles and keeps its shape even when one has worn it for days.

3. Under the latest regulations, any shipment of arms to those countries is illegal and may be seized as __contraband__.

4. His attempts to discredit her by belittling her ability and character were nothing more than __scurrilous__ abuse.

5. The commitment you have made is __irrevocable__ without the consent of the other party to the agreement.

6. The sharp crack of the rifle shot __reverberated__ through the hills.

7. On his combat uniform he wore absolutely no insignia of rank, but he was surrounded with an unmistakable __aura__ of authority.

8. He used his admittedly remarkable talents only to __aggrandize__ himself, not to benefit the society that was so kind to him.

9. I am not going to __repudiate__ the ideas and standards by which I have guided my life just because they have become unpopular.

10. As my opponent cited facts and figures without once referring to notes, I became aware of how __erudite__ she was.

11. The drops of dew sparkled like diamonds on the __gossamer__ threads of the spider web.

12. Since our efforts to __remonstrate__ with the factory managers about pollution of the lake have been ineffective, we are now considering legal action.

13. He is really insufferable when he gets into one of those __querulous__ moods in which nothing in the world pleases him.

14. If you happen to have a(n) __affable__ seatmate on a long airplane flight, you may find yourself talking more freely about personal matters than you would under other circumstances.

15. He tried in vain to guess what surprise he might expect next from that __inscrutable__ power, Lady Luck.

16. Am I to __infer__ from what you just said that you were not present at the scene of the accident?

17. While tsarist Russia's vast territories were almost purely continental, the British Empire included numerous __insular__ possessions.

18. Because of his __propensity__ for gossiping, we tried not to let him learn anything about our personal affairs.
19. __Sleazy__ dives full of disreputable and dangerous-looking characters have given the waterfront areas of many cities a bad reputation.
20. Perhaps she had less native ability than some of her classmates, but her powers of concentration and __sedulous__ study program enabled her to finish first in the class.

Synonyms

Choose the word from this unit that is **the same** or **most nearly the same** in meaning as the **boldface** word or expression in the given phrase. Write the word on the line provided.

1. **expostulate** with a noisy neighbor — remonstrate
2. had a festive **ambience** — aura
3. said her decision was **irreversible** — irrevocable
4. **resound** from wall to wall — reverberate
5. answer with an **enigmatic** smile — inscrutable
6. only a **nebulous** idea of his future — amorphous
7. **disavow** an earlier promise — repudiate
8. a relaxed, **agreeable** companion — affable
9. to **surmise** from her expression — infer
10. **scholarly** study of the topic — erudite
11. a **tawdry** appearance — sleazy
12. prevailed due to **assiduous** preparation — sedulous
13. **springy** as a trampoline — resilient
14. smuggling **illicit** drugs — contraband

Antonyms

Choose the word from this unit that is **most nearly opposite** in meaning to the **boldface** word or expression in the given phrase. Write the word on the line provided.

15. a **serene** little boy of four — querulous
16. a **cosmopolitan** awareness of culture — insular
17. a **tasteful** account of her private life — scurrilous
18. his natural **incapacity** for meanness — propensity
19. a **thick** morning mist on the garden — gossamer
20. intended to **diminish** her fame — aggrandize

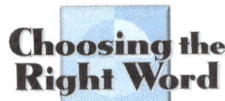

Choosing the Right Word

Circle the **boldface** word that more satisfactorily completes each of the following sentences.

1. The musical composition, with no melodic pattern and no well-defined structure of development, seemed (**amorphous**, **querulous**) to my ear.
2. The minister said that Cain's question, "Am I my brother's keeper?" has continued to (**reverberate**, **infer**) through the ages.
3. What we really resent is not sensible criticism but nagging that is petty, capricious, and (**querulous**, **affable**).
4. Since he seems to have no moral standards whatsoever, it would probably be futile to (**infer**, **remonstrate**) with him about his outrageous behavior.
5. The language he used in his bitter attack on us was so (**amorphous**, **scurrilous**) that I hesitate even to repeat it.
6. What a pleasure to talk about old times with so (**affable**, **erudite**) a companion!
7. The pitiful derelict's only protection against the elements was a cheap overcoat made out of some kind of (**resilient**, **sleazy**) material that wouldn't keep the cold out in a heat wave.
8. I think that nothing in Shakespeare is lighter or more delightful than the (**gossamer**, **aggrandized**) wit and fancy of *A Midsummer Night's Dream*.
9. I tried to make some sense out of the strange orders he had given us, but his plan and purpose remained utterly (**erudite**, **inscrutable**).
10. Your (**propensity**, **repudiation**) for spending more than you can afford will lead to only one result—bankruptcy!
11. Throughout his career, the man has emphasized the (**aggrandizement**, **inscrutability**) of wealth and power at the expense of other values.
12. Am I to (**remonstrate**, **infer**) from your statement that there would be no point in further negotiations?
13. Lucy finally completed her (**querulous**, **erudite**) term paper, in which she quoted from more than a hundred sources.
14. Carefully avoiding any attempt at originality, he has fashioned his style on (**sedulous**, **scurrilous**) mimicry of other, more talented writers.
15. On the Sabbath, the entire village is immersed in a(n) (**propensity**, **aura**) of religious devotion that is difficult to convey to outsiders.
16. When we arrived home we were tired and depressed, but the (**gossamer**, **resilient**) spirit of youth made things look brighter the next morning.
17. Our determination never to yield to force or the threat of force is firm and (**amorphous**, **irrevocable**)!
18. We cannot bar foreign influences from our shores, and we cannot treat unfamiliar ideas as (**aura**, **contraband**)!
19. To limit the free expression of unpopular ideas is to (**repudiate**, **infer**) the basic spirit of the Bill of Rights.
20. In an age when the world has become a "global village," we cannot afford leaders with (**insular**, **sedulous**) outlooks.

Vocabulary in Context

*Read the following passage, in which some of the words you have studied in this unit appear in **boldface** type. Then complete each statement given below the passage by circling the letter of the item that is **the same** or **almost the same** in meaning as the highlighted word.*

Fast Talk

(Line)
   Slang is a set of informal words or phrases used mainly for speaking rather than writing. Some slang terms are original and unique, while others are given the meaning of a word that already exists. Either way the chief point of slang is to amuse one's listeners with something new, odd, or clever.

(5) Slang perseveres because it makes us feel **affable** and at home. In its **aura** we know we belong to some group, large or small, that understands it. (In this way, **scurrilous** slang works all too well.) Those outside the group may regard such talk as a form of **contraband** language, a somewhat snobbish secret code. Still
(10) others become bored by it, for it lives by constant use, like other habits.

   Oddly enough, most slang words are not **resilient**. They change their meaning or go stale and are quietly forgotten. Above all,
(15) slang is a game that anyone can play at any time. For instance, *Money* has coined countless slang terms at various times, such as *lettuce, cabbage,* and *bread.* One who supports you with
(20) money can be called your *meal ticket.*
   In England in the 1740s the slang for *complete* happened to be *cool.* In the 1940s American jazz musicians such as Duke Ellington (right) took up *cool* to mean
(25) *relaxed, restrained,* or *not emotional.* Since then the word has been used at various times to mean *not* **reverberating** or *soft* or simply *good.*

   Every language has its slang, some of it unkind, most of it harmless. Not much of it is timeless, however, and some of this year's words will soon be showing their age.

Ellington (1899–1974) at the keyboard.

---

1. The meaning of **affable** (line 5) is
   a. amusing   c. genial
   b. careless   d. calm

2. **Aura** (line 5) most nearly means
   a. protection   c. sound
   b. atmosphere   d. spotlight

3. **Scurrilous** (line 7) is best defined as
   a. abusive   c. mysterious
   b. old-fashioned d. surprising

4. The meaning of **contraband** (line 8) is
   a. familiar   c. puzzling
   b. illicit   d. second

5. **Resilient** (line 13) most nearly means
   a. important   c. good
   b. likeable   d. elastic

6. **Reverberating** (line 26) is best defined as
   a. re-echoing   c. replaying
   b. repeating   d. listening

Unit 5

 See page T21 for information.

Definitions

Note carefully the spelling, pronunciation, part(s) of speech, and definition(s) of each of the following words. Then write the word in the blank space(s) in the illustrative sentence(s) following. Finally, study the lists of synonyms and antonyms given at the end of each entry.

1. amnesty
(am′ nə stē)

(*n.*) a general pardon for an offense against a government; in general, any act of forgiveness or absolution

Many political prisoners were freed under the __**amnesty**__ granted by the new regime.

2. autonomy
(ô tän′ ə mē)

(*n.*) self-government, political control

Even after the thirteen colonies gained __**autonomy**__ from England, many Americans clung to English traditions.
SYNONYM: home rule
ANTONYMS: dependence, subjection, colonial status

3. axiomatic
(ak sē ə mat′ ik)

(*adj.*) self-evident, expressing a universally accepted principle or rule

One should not accept the idea that the camera never lies as an __**axiomatic**__ truth.
SYNONYM: taken for granted
ANTONYMS: questionable, dubious, controversial

4. blazon
(blāz′ ən)

(*v.*) to adorn or embellish; to display conspicuously; to publish or proclaim widely

They will __**blazon**__ the results of the election across the Internet and every television set in the land.
SYNONYMS: broadcast, trumpet
ANTONYMS: hide, conceal, cover up, bury

5. caveat
(kav′ ē at)

(*n.*) a warning or caution to prevent misunderstanding or discourage behavior

The well known Latin phrase "__**caveat**__ emptor" means "Let the buyer beware."
SYNONYMS: admonition, word to the wise

6. equitable
(ek′ wə tə bəl)

(*adj.*) fair, just, embodying principles of justice

He did more work, so a sixty-forty split of the profits seemed an __**equitable**__ arrangement.
SYNONYMS: right, reasonable, evenhanded
ANTONYMS: unjust, unfair, one-sided, disproportionate

7. extricate
(ek′ strə kāt)

(*v.*) to free from entanglements or difficulties; to remove with effort

The ring must have slid off my finger as I was trying to __**extricate**__ the fish from the net.

SYNONYMS: disentangle, extract, disengage
ANTONYMS: enmesh, entangle, involve

8. filch
(filch)

(v.) to steal, especially in a sneaky way and in petty amounts

If you __**filch**__ pennies from the cash drawer, you are unlikely, after a while, to be satisfied with only pennies.

SYNONYMS: pilfer, purloin, swipe

9. flout
(flaut)

(v.) to mock, treat with contempt

She chose to ignore my advice, not because she wanted to __**flout**__ my beliefs, but because she had strong opinions of her own.

SYNONYMS: scoff at, sneer at, snicker at, scorn
ANTONYMS: obey, honor, revere, uphold

10. fractious
(frak' shəs)

(adj.) tending to be troublesome; unruly, quarrelsome, contrary; unpredictable

It seems as if even the smoothest-running organizations contain one or two __**fractious**__ elements.

SYNONYMS: refractory, recalcitrant, peevish
ANTONYMS: docile, tractable, cooperative

11. precept
(prē' sept)

(n.) a rule of conduct or action

Many religions follow the __**precept**__ that it is important to treat others as you, yourself, would like to be treated.

SYNONYMS: principle, maxim

12. salutary
(sal' yə ter ē)

(adj.) beneficial, helpful; healthful, wholesome

The cute new puppy had a __**salutary**__ effect on her health.

SYNONYMS: salubrious, curative
ANTONYMS: detrimental, deleterious, pernicious

13. scathing
(skā' thiŋ)

(adj.) bitterly severe, withering; causing great harm

Sometimes a carefully reasoned discussion does more to change people's minds than a __**scathing**__ attack.

SYNONYMS: searing, harsh, ferocious, savage
ANTONYMS: bland, mild

14. scourge
(skərj)

(v.) to whip, punish severely; (n.) a cause of affliction or suffering; a source of severe punishment or criticism

Jonathan Swift used wit to __**scourge**__ the British government for its cruel treatment of Ireland.

Competing teams consider my daughter the __**scourge**__ of the soccer field.

Unit 5 ■ 59

SYNONYMS: (v.) flog, beat; (n.) bane, plague, pestilence
ANTONYMS: (n.) godsend, boon, blessing

15. sepulchral
(sə pəl' krəl)

(adj.) funereal, typical of the tomb; extremely gloomy or dismal

My sister announced in a severe and _____sepulchral_____ tone of voice that we were out of cookies.

SYNONYMS: doleful, lugubrious, mortuary

16. soporific
(säp ə rif' ik)

(adj.) tending to cause sleep, relating to sleepiness or lethargy; (n.) something that induces sleep

He claimed that the musical, despite its energy, was _____soporific_____ and that he had slept through the entire second act.

Shakespeare's Juliet drinks a _____soporific_____ so as to appear to be dead—a trick she is soon to regret.

SYNONYMS: (n.) narcotic, anesthetic
ANTONYMS: (adj.) stimulating; (n.) stimulant, stimulus

17. straitlaced
(strāt' lāst)

(adj.) extremely strict in regard to moral standards and conduct; prudish, puritanical

Travelers may find people overseas _____straitlaced_____ in some ways but surprisingly free in others.

SYNONYMS: highly conventional, overly strict, stuffy
ANTONYMS: lax, loose, indulgent, permissive, dissolute

18. transient
(tran' shənt)

(adj.) lasting only a short time, fleeting; (n.) one who stays only a short time

His bad mood was _____transient_____, and by the time he'd finished his breakfast, he was smiling.

Many farm hands lived the lives of _____transients_____ during the Great Depression.

SYNONYMS: (adj.) impermanent, ephemeral, evanescent
ANTONYMS: (adj.) permanent, imperishable, immortal

19. unwieldy
(ən wēl' dē)

(adj.) not easily carried, handled, or managed because of size or complexity

We loaded the truck with the chairs and the coffee table, but the grand piano was too _____unwieldy_____.

SYNONYMS: cumbersome, bulky, clumsy, impractical
ANTONYMS: manageable, easy to handle

20. vapid
(vap' id)

(adj.) dull, uninteresting, tiresome; lacking in sharpness, flavor, liveliness, or force

While critics called the movie _____vapid_____, I thought the performers were very compelling.

SYNONYMS: insipid, lifeless, colorless
ANTONYMS: zesty, spicy, savory, colorful, lively

Completing the Sentence

From the words for this unit, choose the one that best completes each of the following sentences. Write the word in the space provided.

1. Her approach to the problem seems to have been guided by the time-honored _____**precept**_____ that "Force is the remedy for nothing."

2. Since the close of World War II, almost 100 former colonies have gained full _____**autonomy**_____ and joined the family of nations.

3. She has made so many contradictory promises to so many people that I don't see how she can _____**extricate**_____ herself from the situation.

4. Shivers went up and down our spines as, in a(n) _____**sepulchral**_____ voice, the teacher spoke to us of ghosts, vampires, and the "living dead."

5. It is _____**axiomatic**_____ that democracy, more than any other form of government, calls for the active participation of all the people in public affairs.

6. The decision was a disappointment to me, but after thinking it over, I had to agree that it was _____**equitable**_____.

7. The new government, seeking to restore normal conditions, declared a(n) _____**amnesty**_____ for all political prisoners.

8. It was Lincoln who said: "Fondly do we hope, fervently do we pray, that this mighty _____**scourge**_____ of war may speedily pass away."

9. The standards of behavior generally accepted in Victorian times would probably be rejected today as excessively _____**straitlaced**_____.

10. I tried to warn them of the dangers involved in such an undertaking, but all my _____**caveats**_____ and admonitions fell on deaf ears.

11. The carton was not heavy, but it was so _____**unwieldy**_____ that it took four of us to carry it to the shed.

12. Even the most talented actors could not breathe life and credibility into the _____**vapid**_____ lines of that silly play.

13. Who would have thought that the new treasurer could sink so low as to _____**filch**_____ money from the club's petty cash fund?

14. My teacher's criticism of my term paper was so _____**scathing**_____ that after reading it I felt thoroughly crushed.

15. It became clear that the squad of policemen would be unable to control the small but _____**fractious**_____ crowd of angry protesters.

16. His fame as a football star proved to be _____**transient**_____, and he found himself just another young man looking for a job.

17. Failures are always unpleasant, but if you learn from them, they may have a(n) _____**salutary**_____ effect on your future career.

Unit 5 ■ 61

18. Any unit of government—national or local—that _____**flouts**_____ sound economic principles is headed for disaster.
19. The fighter planes of World War II sometimes had the pictures of famous movie stars, like Betty Grable, _____**blazoned**_____ on the fuselage.
20. The _____**soporific**_____ effect of his droning lectures surpasses that of any sleeping pill now in use.

Synonyms

Choose the word from this unit that is **the same** or **most nearly the same** in meaning as the **boldface** word or expression in the given phrase. Write the word on the line provided.

1. guided by stern **principles** — precepts
2. a **doleful** atmosphere during the service — sepulchral
3. eager to **scoff at** the unknown — flout
4. a **warning** regarding possible difficulties — caveat
5. too **cumbersome** to carry home — unwieldy
6. **pardon** for the former rebels — amnesty
7. working toward a **reasonable** treaty — equitable
8. **disengage** the cat from the tree — extricate
9. to **purloin** some coins from petty cash — filch
10. an argumentative, **refractory** congress — fractious
11. **ephemeral** as a rainbow — transient
12. **flog** the oxen unmercifully — scourge
13. an **insipid** little five-note tune — vapid
14. unruffled by his **savage** tone — scathing

Antonyms

Choose the word from this unit that is **most nearly opposite** in meaning to the **boldface** word or expression in the given phrase. Write the word on the line provided.

15. a **dubious** motto to live by — axiomatic
16. the **detrimental** effects of sunshine — salutary
17. **subjection** of the small nation — autonomy
18. the **indulgent** grandmother — straitlaced
19. medicine that acted as a **stimulant** — soporific
20. to **conceal** the famous trademark — blazon

Choosing the Right Word

Circle the **boldface** word that more satisfactorily completes each of the following sentences.

1. I didn't expect the play to be particularly stimulating, but I certainly never anticipated its overwhelmingly (**equitable, soporific**) power.
2. How easy it is for a nation to become trapped in an inflationary price rise; how difficult to (**blazon, extricate**) itself from the upward spiral!
3. Instead of brooding about past wrongs, I suggest that you declare a personal (**amnesty, caveat**) and start thinking about the future.
4. I intend to be guided by the simple (**scourges, precepts**) that have proven their value over long periods of human experience.
5. Unabridged dictionaries often alert the reader to common mistakes in the use of a word by including brief (**caveats, scourges**).
6. The ghost of Hamlet's father whispered in (**sepulchral, salutary**) tones the story of his tragic death.
7. Appointed by the Governor to be Commissioner of Investigations, she soon became the (**scourge, autonomy**) of dishonest and incompetent officials.
8. You may regard her ideas as (**salutary, straitlaced**), but I think that they reflect good thinking and sound values.
9. Today our intricate network of mass communications can (**blazon, flout**) news of national importance across the country in a matter of minutes.
10. We had many talented players, but the (**fractious, scathing**) behavior of a few individuals impaired our team spirit and led to a losing season.
11. The rules of the club proved so (**equitable, unwieldy**) that it was all but impossible to carry on business.
12. I now know that *Gulliver's Travels*, far from being a "children's book," is a work of mature and (**scathing, vapid**) satire.
13. Some sadly misguided individuals seem to go through life trying to (**filch, blazon**) petty advantages from everyone they encounter.
14. Arriving at (**equitable, fractious**) arrangements in human affairs often requires sound judgment, as well as good intentions.
15. The Judeo-Christian tradition teaches that material things are (**transient, fractious**), while spiritual values are eternal.
16. Young people who consider themselves nonconformists often go to extremes in their determination to (**blazon, flout**) the conventions.
17. Isn't it strange that the basic ideas that some economists regard as (**sepulchral, axiomatic**) are rejected by others as absolutely false!
18. Young people, tired of being controlled by parents, teachers, and others, often have a strong impulse to gain (**amnesty, autonomy**).
19. In spite of the tremendous sales of that novel, I found it to be mediocre and (**vapid, salutary**) in every respect.
20. Few things are more (**salutary, unwieldy**) for a young person than an occasional painful reminder that life is not a bowl of cherries.

Vocabulary in Context

*Read the following passage, in which some of the words you have studied in this unit appear in **boldface** type. Then complete each statement given below the passage by circling the letter of the item that is **the same** or **almost the same** in meaning as the highlighted word.*

A Very Heavy Hitter

(Line)

Though he grew to be only 5′ 7″, the first baseball commissioner of the United States was named after a mountain. Kenesaw Mountain Landis (1866–1949) was named after the Georgia peak where his father was wounded in the Civil War. From boyhood, Kenesaw was said to have lived as if watching humanity from on high and laying down the law. Not surprisingly, he became a Chicago judge in (5) 1905 before he was forty years old.

He ruled his courtroom with a king's **autonomy**, and when John D. Rockefeller, head of Standard Oil and the richest man in America, declined to testify in a case against his own company, Landis forced him to appear. The clashing of wills between (10) these powerful men was **blazoned** across headlines nationwide.

Landis always loved power, but he may have loved baseball more. A devoted fan at Chicago games, he (15) called baseball "remarkable for the hold it has on the people, and equally remarkable for its cleanness." But by 1919 gamblers' schemes and warring team owners had so **flouted** that (20) cleanness that Chicago White Sox players deliberately lost the World Series in return for bribes. Officials

Bat meets ball

appointed Landis as baseball commissioner, with the job of saving the honor of the game. The owners expected to be treated gently, but Landis was **equitable** in his (25) reforms, and a **scourge** to all sides.

Players suspected of taking bribes were barred for life with no hope of an **amnesty**. Trades were canceled, star players suspended. Owners had to give up investments in race tracks, and fought Landis for years before they could schedule games at night. For two decades, Landis ruled. When he died in 1944 he was (30) known to all in baseball as "the judge."

---

1. The meaning of **autonomy** (line 7) is
   a. snobbery
   b. meanness
   c. home rule
   d. whim

2. **Blazoned** (line 11) most nearly means
   a. set fire to
   b. denounced
   c. praised
   d. trumpeted

3. **Flouted** (line 20) is best defined as
   a. mocked
   b. observed
   c. showed off
   d. misunderstood

4. The meaning of **equitable** (line 25) is
   a. surprising
   b. quick
   c. slow
   d. reasonable

5. **Scourge** (line 26) most nearly means
   a. bane
   b. comfort
   c. favorite
   d. instructor

6. **Amnesty** (line 28) is best defined as
   a. transfer
   b. general absolution
   c. apology
   d. explanation

UNIT 6

🎧 See page T21 for information.

Definitions

Note carefully the spelling, pronunciation, part(s) of speech, and definition(s) of each of the following words. Then write the word in the blank space(s) in the illustrative sentence(s) following. Finally, study the lists of synonyms and antonyms given at the end of each entry.

1. anomalous
(ə näm′ ə ləs)

(*adj.*) abnormal, irregular, departing from the usual
Feeling protective of my friend but knowing of his difficulties placed me in an ___**anomalous**___ position.
SYNONYMS: exceptional, atypical, unusual, aberrant
ANTONYMS: normal, regular, customary, typical, ordinary

2. aspersion
(ə spər′ zhən)

(*n.*) a damaging or derogatory statement; the act of slandering or defaming
Think twice before casting ___**aspersions**___ on his honesty, for he might be telling the truth.
SYNONYMS: innuendo, calumny, denigration
ANTONYMS: endorsement, testimonial, praise

3. bizarre
(bi zär′)

(*adj.*) extremely strange, unusual, atypical
Years from now I will look at this picture and wonder what sort of ___**bizarre**___ costume I was wearing.
SYNONYMS: grotesque, fantastic, outlandish
ANTONYMS: normal, typical, ordinary, expected

4. brusque
(brəsk)

(*adj.*) abrupt, blunt, with no formalities
His request for a large loan for an indefinite length of time was met with a ___**brusque**___ refusal.
SYNONYMS: curt, tactless, ungracious, gruff, rough
ANTONYMS: gracious, tactful, courteous, diplomatic

5. cajole
(kə jōl′)

(*v.*) to coax, persuade through flattery or artifice; to deceive with soothing thoughts or false promises
With a smile, a joke, and a second helping of pie, she would ___**cajole**___ him into doing what she wanted.
SYNONYMS: wheedle, inveigle, soft-soap, sweet-talk
ANTONYMS: coerce, force, strong-arm

6. castigate
(kas′ tə gāt)

(*v.*) to punish severely; to criticize severely
After he ___**castigated**___ the unruly children, they settled down to study quietly.
SYNONYMS: chastise, rebuke, censure, upbraid
ANTONYMS: reward, honor, praise, laud

7. contrive
(kən trīv′)

(v.) to plan with ingenuity, invent; to bring about as the result of a scheme or plan

She can __contrive__ wonderful excuses; but when she tries to offer them, her uneasiness gives her away.

SYNONYMS: think up, devise, concoct, fabricate

8. demagogue
(dem′ ə gäg)

(n.) a leader who exploits popular prejudices and false claims and promises in order to gain power

Often a show of angry concern conceals the self-serving tactics of a __demagogue__.

SYNONYMS: rabble-rouser, firebrand

9. disabuse
(dis ə byüz′)

(v.) to free from deception or error, set right in ideas or thinking

He thinks that all women adore him, but my sister will probably __disabuse__ him of that idea.

SYNONYMS: undeceive, enlighten, set straight
ANTONYMS: deceive, delude, pull wool over one's eyes

10. ennui
(än wē′)

(n.) weariness and dissatisfaction from lack of occupation or interest, boredom

Some people seem to confuse sophistication with __ennui__.

SYNONYMS: languor, world-weariness, listlessness
ANTONYMS: enthusiasm, liveliness, excitement, intensity

11. fetter
(fet′ ər)

(n.) a chain or shackle placed on the feet (often used in plural); anything that confines or restrains; (v.) to chain or shackle; to render helpless or impotent

The old phrase "chain gang" refers to prisoners made to work, each joined to the next by linked __fetters__.

It is said that good inventors do not __fetter__ themselves with conventional thinking.

SYNONYMS: (n.) bond, restraint; (v.) bind, hamper
ANTONYMS: (v.) free, liberate, emancipate

12. heinous
(hā′ nəs)

(adj.) very wicked, offensive, hateful

A town so peaceful, quiet, and law-abiding was bound to be horrified by so __heinous__ a crime.

SYNONYMS: evil, odious, abominable, outrageous
ANTONYMS: excellent, wonderful, splendid

13. immutable
(i myü′ tə bəl)

(adj.) not subject to change, constant

Scientists labored to discover a set of __immutable__ laws of the universe.

SYNONYMS: unchangeable, unalterable, fixed, invariable
ANTONYMS: changeable, inconstant, variable, fickle

14. insurgent
(in sər′ jənt)

(*n.*) one who rebels or rises against authority; (*adj.*) rising in revolt, refusing to accept authority; surging or rushing in or on

George Washington and his contemporaries were _____**insurgents**_____ against Britain.

The army was confident that they could crush the _____**insurgent**_____ forces.

SYNONYMS: (*adj.*) revolutionary, rebellious, mutinous
ANTONYMS: (*adj.*) loyalist, loyal, faithful

15. megalomania
(meg ə lō mā′ nē ə)

(*n.*) a delusion marked by a feeling of power, wealth, talent, etc., far in excess of reality

Sudden fame and admiration can make people feel unworthy—or it can bring on feelings of _____**megalomania**_____.

SYNONYM: delusions of grandeur
ANTONYMS: humility, modesty, self-abasement

16. sinecure
(si′ nə kyür)

(*n.*) a position requiring little or no work; an easy job

The office of Vice President of the United States was once considered little more than a _____**sinecure**_____.

SYNONYMS: "no-show" job, cushy job, "plum"

17. surreptitious
(sər əp tish′ əs)

(*adj.*) stealthy, secret, intended to escape observation; made or accomplished by fraud

The movie heroine blushed when she noticed the _____**surreptitious**_____ glances of her admirer.

SYNONYMS: furtive, covert, clandestine, concealed
ANTONYMS: open, frank, aboveboard, overt

18. transgress
(tranz gres′)

(*v.*) to go beyond a limit or boundary; to sin, violate a law

The penitent citizens promised to never again _____**transgress**_____ the laws of the land.

SYNONYMS: overstep, exceed, trespass, err
ANTONYMS: obey, toe the line

19. transmute
(tranz myüt′)

(*v.*) to change from one nature, substance, or form to another

To ___**transmute**___ distrust into friendship along that war-torn border will take more than wise politicians and just laws.

SYNONYMS: transform, convert, translate, metamorphose
ANTONYMS: maintain unchanged, preserve

20. vicarious
(vī kâr′ ē əs)

(*adj.*) performed, suffered, or otherwise experienced by one person in place of another

In search of _____**vicarious**_____ excitement, we watched movies of action and adventure.

SYNONYMS: surrogate, substitute, imagined, secondhand
ANTONYMS: real, actual, firsthand

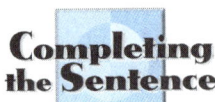

Completing the Sentence

From the words for this unit, choose the one that best completes each of the following sentences. Write the word in the space provided.

1. The __surreptitious__ way in which they planned the undertaking shows that they were aware of its illegal character.
2. Is there any other crime in history as __heinous__ as the attempt of the Nazis to annihilate so-called "inferior" racial groups?
3. Although the __insurgents__ were defeated by the government's forces, a small group escaped into the mountains, where they kept the spirit of rebellion alive.
4. Although most of us lead a quiet, humdrum sort of life, we can all get a(n) __vicarious__ thrill from the achievements of our astronauts.
5. The Emancipation Proclamation issued by Abraham Lincoln once and for all broke the __fetters__ that bound Southern blacks to a life of servitude and humiliation.
6. I find it hard to understand how they were able to __contrive__ such an elaborately underhanded scheme in so short a time.
7. His endless talk about himself and his interests is truly unexcelled for producing __ennui__ in others.
8. Wearing __bizarre__ masks at Halloween is a tradition that goes back many centuries.
9. Resorting to rather farfetched promises, I finally __cajoled__ Tina into going to the prom with me.
10. At the very outset of the term, I urged you to __disabuse__ yourself of the idea that you can pass this course without hard, regular work.
11. The one fact about nature that seems completely __immutable__ is that everything is subject to change.
12. His conceit is so great and so immune to the lessons of experience that this must be considered a kind of __megalomania__.
13. Anyone who refers to my job as a(n) __sinecure__ should spend just one day in my place!
14. The alchemists of the Middle Ages, who were both skilled magicians and primitive chemists, hoped to __transmute__ base metals into gold.
15. The speaker's blatant appeal to the emotions of the crowd smacked more of the __demagogue__ than the true leader of the people.
16. Since he had always been quiet and retiring, we were amazed when he stood up at the meeting and __castigated__ the chairperson for failing to give everyone a chance to speak.
17. Can you imagine anything as __anomalous__ as a successful drama coach who has never acted on the stage!

18. In his determination to be blunt and honest, he has ____**transgressed**____ the limits of good taste.
19. Rude questions call for ____**brusque**____ answers, and mine is "No!"
20. I welcome honest criticism, but I deeply resented their ____**aspersions**____ on my sincerity and good faith.

Synonyms

*Choose the word from this unit that is **the same** or **most nearly the same** in meaning as the **boldface** word or expression in the given phrase. Write the word on the line provided.*

1. **abominable** treatment of prisoners of war — heinous
2. an unwarranted **denigration** against my friend — aspersion
3. trying to **restrain** our imaginations — fetter
4. the fear-mongering of a **rabble-rouser** — demagogue
5. **undeceive** him of that belief — disabuse
6. wish to **rebuke** the vandals — castigate
7. the disposition of a **revolutionary** — insurgent
8. the cleverest plan we could **devise** — contrive
9. an **atypical** position — anomalous
10. **inveigle** a pay raise — cajole
11. a truly **outlandish** set of circumstances — bizarre
12. a woman of **unalterable** habits — immutable
13. a scandal involving **"no-show" jobs** — sinecures
14. **convert** ambition into action — transmute
15. sensed **furtive** movements in the darkness — surreptitious

Antonyms

*Choose the word from this unit that is **most nearly opposite** in meaning to the **boldface** word or expression in the given phrase. Write the word on the line provided.*

16. his usual **gracious** reply — brusque
17. the **excitement** of the ninth inning — ennui
18. the **modesty** of the real genius — megalomania
19. **obey** the week-night curfew — transgress
20. experienced **actual** thrills at the race — vicarious

Choosing the Right Word

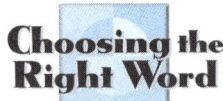

Circle the **boldface** word that more satisfactorily completes each of the following sentences.

1. A favorite ploy of the (**anomalous, demogogue**) is to appoint a convenient scapegoat upon whom a misguided populace can vent its anger.
2. By casting (**sinecures, aspersions**) on the ability and character of others, you reveal the misgivings you have about yourself.
3. The task of education, said the speaker, is to (**transgress, transmute**) the primitive selfishness of the child into socially useful modes of behavior.
4. His conduct after his mother's death was so (**anomalous, brusque**) that I must conclude he was not in full possession of his faculties.
5. With the innumerable activities open to a young person like you, I can't understand why you should suffer from (**ennui, megalomania**).
6. I cannot understand how she was able to (**disabuse, contrive**) a meeting between two people who had refused to have anything to do with each other.
7. If, as they now claim, they were not aware of the illegal character of their undertaking, why did they plan it so (**cajolingly, surreptitiously**)?
8. The President complained that government bureaucracy was hobbling his programs with (**fetters, aspersions**) of red tape.
9. He's so tight with his money that it's just about impossible to (**cajole, transmute**) a nickel out of him, no matter how worthy the cause.
10. Her description of the Western frontier was so vivid that I seemed to be (**vicariously, surreptitiously**) experiencing the realities of pioneer life.
11. In *Gulliver's Travels* and other writings, Jonathan Swift (**cajoled, castigated**) the human race for its follies and wickedness.
12. Her opinion of her own importance is so grotesquely exaggerated that we have come to regard her as a (**megalomaniac, demagogue**).
13. He may have kept within the letter of the law, but there is no doubt that he has (**cajoled, transgressed**) the accepted moral code.
14. For ancient Romans, fleeing from the battlefield was the most (**heinous, immutable**) act of cowardice a soldier could commit.
15. The institutions of our society, far from being (**immutable, anomalous**), are in the process of change at this very moment.
16. A(n) (**insurgent, heinous**) group at the convention refused to accept the choices of the regular party leaders.
17. Have you ever heard of anything as (**bizarre, brusque**) as an experimental technique to test the intelligence of cows!
18. What hurt my feelings was not so much his refusal to give me a job as the (**brusque, vicarious**) way in which he told me that he had nothing for me.
19. Although her new position bore a high-sounding title, it was really little more than a(n) (**insurgent, sinecure**).
20. Although she is well into middle age, my aunt Sally seems unable to (**cajole, disabuse**) herself of the idea that she is still a teenager.

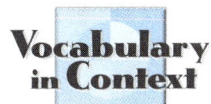

Vocabulary in Context

*Read the following passage, in which some of the words you have studied in this unit appear in **boldface** type. Then complete each statement given below the passage by circling the letter of the item that is **the same** or **almost the same** in meaning as the highlighted word.*

Kudzu

(Line)
Some readers may recognize kudzu as the name of a comic strip, but Southerners know it as a fact of nature too **bizarre** to be funny. This galloping vine, nearly impossible to kill, grows from a finger-like shoot that winds around any stump, car, shed, tree, house, or barn that stands in its way. In one day's time, kudzu
(5) (pronounced "kəd-zü") can grow up to twelve inches. All too soon, its trunk is the width of a one-quart milk bottle, and its leaves are as large as this book. Its flowers bloom purple and fragrant; its root can weigh
(10) well over two hundred pounds.

This **insurgent** weed, long common in Asia, was welcomed here in the late nineteenth century as a pretty porch decoration.
(15) Then the U.S. Government spread kudzu in the South to prevent soil erosion and to make cheap grazing for livestock. But the vine soon eluded the **fetters** of farm
(20) work, and in that damp, warm climate made its **surreptitious** way across seven million acres,

Kudzu covering a house in rural Georgia

mainly in North and South Carolina, Mississippi, Georgia, and Alabama. Now, neither farmers nor state governments can afford the labor needed to chop off the trunks
(25) and dig up the roots. Scientists put their hope in certain kinds of plant-eating beetles but must first make certain that the hungry little creatures will not **transgress** the bounds of their assignment and start new troubles of their own.

Whatever solution is **contrived** for the kudzu problem, it cannot be applied too soon. The vine has hitchhiked, flown, or wiggled through the mail to Massachusetts,
(30) New York, New Jersey, and Connecticut. Should it manage to acclimate itself to the cold Northern winter, it will stretch out and make itself at home there, too.

---

1. The meaning of **bizarre** (line 2) is
a. common   c. widespread
b. commercial   **d. strange** ✓

2. Insurgent (line 11) most nearly means
a. huge   **c. mutinous** ✓
b. widespread   d. sweet-smelling

3. Fetters (line 19) is best defined as
a. assignments   **c. restraints** ✓
b. weariness   d. complications

4. The meaning of **surreptitious** (line 21) is
a. furtive ✓   c. speedy
b. awkward   d. deliberate

5. Transgress (line 26) most nearly means
a. misunderstand   c. trample
b. overstep ✓   d. consume

6. Contrived (line 28) is best defined as
a. devised ✓   c. attempted
b. forbidden   d. praised

Review Units 4–6

Visit us at www.sadlier-oxford.com for interactive puzzles and games.

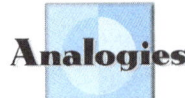

Analogies

In each of the following, circle the item that best completes the comparison.

See pages T38–T48 for explanations of answers.

1. **unwieldy** is to **handle** as
   a. immutable is to quiet
   b. salutary is to heal
   c. fractious is to control
   d. axiomatic is to purpose

2. **ennui** is to **bored** as
   a. ardor is to excited
   b. perplexity is to tired
   c. annoyance is to satisfied
   d. fatigue is to gleeful

3. **scurrilous** is to **unfavorable** as
   a. bizarre is to favorable
   b. sedulous is to unfavorable
   c. salutary is to favorable
   d. gossamer is to unfavorable

4. **alcohol** is to **soporific** as
   a. water is to enzyme
   b. milk is to pollutant
   c. tea is to intoxicant
   d. coffee is to stimulant

5. **erudite** is to **knowledge** as
   a. vapid is to intelligence
   b. insular is to sophistication
   c. cordial is to talent
   d. dexterous is to skill

6. **caveat** is to **warn** as
   a. amnesty is to chide
   b. precept is to teach
   c. aura is to compliment
   d. castigate is to advise

7. **merriment** is to **festive** as
   a. worry is to resilient
   b. gloom is to sepulchral
   c. despair is to equitable
   d. fear is to vapid

8. **produce** is to **farming** as
   a. sinecure is to manufacturing
   b. contraband is to smuggling
   c. gossamer is to mining
   d. propensity is to importing

9. **pickpocket** is to **filch** as
   a. cutthroat is to castigate
   b. scofflaw is to flout
   c. daredevil is to infer
   d. spoilsport is to cajole

10. **resilient** is to **recoil** as
    a. brittle is to bounce
    b. pliable is to soar
    c. buoyant is to float
    d. rigid is to bend

11. **affable** is to **aloof** as
    a. fractious is to incorrigible
    b. arrogant is to querulous
    c. sedulous is to nomadic
    d. courteous is to brusque

12. **straitlaced** is to **conventionality** as
    a. bizarre is to unconventionality
    b. soporific is to conventionality
    c. erudite is to unconventionality
    d. transient is to conventionality

13. **immutable** is to **change** as
    a. insurgent is to raise
    b. inscrutable is to erase
    c. insular is to tame
    d. irrevocable is to recall

14. **sleazy** is to **quality** as
    a. shoddy is to workmanship
    b. heinous is to durability
    c. scurrilous is to price
    d. scathing is to stylishness

15. **asymmetrical** is to **balance** as
    a. autonomous is to significance
    b. anomalous is to function
    c. amorphous is to shape
    d. axiomatic is to purpose

16. **gossamer** is to **heavy** as
    a. affable is to pleasant
    b. anomalous is to ordinary
    c. irrevocable is to decisive
    d. immutable is to noisy

17. **extricate** is to **embroil** as
    a. remonstrate is to expostulate
    b. reverberate is to echo
    c. repudiate is to avow
    d. remonstrate is to economize

18. **sneak thief** is to **surreptitious** as
    a. schnook is to fractious
    b. maven is to scurrilous
    c. kvetch is to querulous
    d. klutz is to vapid

72 ■ Review Units 4–6

REVIEW UNITS 4–6

Word Associations

In each of the following groups, circle the word that is best defined or suggested by the given phrase.

1. living through another
   a. affable b. salutary **c. vicarious** d. sleazy
2. a buoyant spirit
   a. resilient b. vapid c. transgressive d. insurgent
3. political prisoners set free
   a. ennui b. sinecure c. scourge **d. amnesty**
4. a curt reply
   a. resilient b. vapid **c. brusque** d. straitlaced
5. a leader who exploits
   a. demagogue b. scourge c. soporific d. caveat
6. rebuke the students
   a. flout **b. castigate** c. repudiate d. flatten
7. "We hold these truths to be self-evident"
   a. affable b. bizarre c. contraband **d. axiomatic**
8. transform his experiences into fiction
   a. transgress b. reverberate **c. transmute** d. remonstrate
9. a fair distribution of wealth
   a. salutary b. scathing **c. equitable** d. inscrutable
10. belligerent rebel forces
    a. insurgent b. contraband c. erudite d. surreptitious
11. the victim of an inflated ego
    a. vapid b. aura **c. megalomania** d. demagogue
12. plot a deception
    a. contrive b. scourge c. extricate d. transmute
13. bypass outdated conventions
    a. transgress b. infer c. disabuse d. extricate
14. a tendency to boast
    a. anathema **b. propensity** c. precept d. caveat
15. disregard advice
    a. infer **b. flout** c. blazon d. reverberate
16. shatter an illusion
    a. transmute b. repudiate c. fetter **d. disabuse**
17. healthy atmosphere of the park
    a. aura b. demagogue c. ennui d. aspersion
18. an abnormal set of circumstances
    a. gossamer **b. anomalous** c. inscrutable d. amorphous
19. formless creatures
    a. bizarre **b. amorphous** c. affable d. erudite
20. display conspicuously
    a. cajole **b. blazon** c. filch d. repudiate

Vocabulary in Context

*Read the following passage, in which some of the words you have studied in Units 4–6 appear in **boldface** type. Then complete each statement given below the passage by circling the item that is **the same** or **almost the same** in meaning as the highlighted word.*

Birth of Basketball

(Line)

Strange as it may seem, basketball was invented in the 1890s as an alternative to calisthenics and indoor marching at a YMCA school in
(5) Massachusetts. James Naismith, the physical education instructor at the school, noticed that his students, who played baseball in the spring and football in the fall, were not
(10) adequately challenged by indoor marching during New England's long, cold winters. Students' wintertime confinement, coupled by a lack of physical exertion, had a **soporific**
(15) effect. Naismith resolved to invent a new and **salutary** alternative.

To Naismith, it was **axiomatic** that the ideal team sport make use of a ball and some sort of goal. But the new
(20) game, which would be played on a hard gym floor, had to be gentler than football. He chose a basket as a goal because the ball had to be dropped into it rather than hurled straight at it. To
(25) prevent **fractious** scuffles and to keep the defense from ganging up on the offense, Naismith placed the goals up beyond an average person's grasp.

In 1892 Naismith's first game was
(30) played by his entire, eighteen-member gym class. But this proved too **unwieldy**, and the number of players on each side was later reduced and standardized to five. The sport was
(35) fortuitous for Naismith, and during the first women's basketball game, he met a teacher named Maude Sherman, whom he later married.

Colleges, including Vassar,
(40) Vanderbilt, and Yale, swiftly adopted the sport, and the YMCA formed several leagues of its own. Despite the benefits it offered, some **castigated** the game for being too
(45) rough, and a few YMCAs stuck to a schedule of good old-fashioned push-ups and marching instead. Basketball enthusiasts who still wanted to play the game simply rented dance halls or
(50) armories to compete in, and charged admission in order to pay rent. Professional basketball was born as a result of these admission fees and in 1896, players in Trenton, New Jersey
(55) were paid for the first time, $15 apiece, to compete in a game.

1. The meaning of **soporific** (line 14) is
   a. stimulating   c. wet
   b. exceptional   **d. sleep inducing**

2. **Salutary** (line 16) is best defined as
   a. deleterious   **c. healthful**
   b. unsanitary   d. probable

3. **Axiomatic** (line 17) most nearly means
   a. ridiculous   **c. obvious**
   b. inconvenient d. meaningless

4. The meaning of **fractious** (line 25) is
   a. refractory   c. slow
   b. confused   d. old-fashioned

5. **Unwieldy** (line 32) most nearly means
   a. rowdy   c. unskillful
   b. cumbersome d. expert

6. **Castigate** (line 44) is best defined as
   a. praise   c. attend
   b. rebuke   d. close down

REVIEW UNITS 4–6

Choosing the Right Meaning

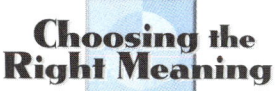

Read each sentence carefully. Then circle the item that best completes the statement below the sentence.

See pages T38–T48 for explanations of answers.

No one who has seen *Cool Hand Luke* will ever forget the shocking scenes of Paul Newman and the other convicts on that Georgia chain gang, fettered together more like animals than human beings. (2)

1. In line 2 the word **fettered** can best be defined as
- **(a. shackled)**
- b. roped
- c. tied
- d. linked

In small-town America one hundred years ago, the boardinghouse catered to long-term visitors, while the hotel met the needs of mere transients. (2)

2. The best definition of the word **transients** in line 2 is
- a. traveling salespeople
- b. tourists on holiday
- **(c. people just passing through)**
- d. displaced persons

The practice of scourging ordinary seamen severely for even petty offenses lasted well into the 19th century in both the British and the American navies. (2)

3. The word **scourging** in line 1 can best be defined as
- **(a. flogging)**
- b. reprimanding
- c. punishing
- d. fining

Smaller and smaller images of the chandeliers and candelabras forever reverberated in the mirrors that encrusted the wall of the great central reception hall. (2)

4. The best meaning for the word **reverberated** in line 1 is
- a. thundered
- **(b. were reflected)**
- c. resounded
- d. were enlarged

The fog that morning was so inscrutable that traffic officials were warning drivers not to proceed until it lifted. (2)

5. In line 1 the word **inscrutable** most nearly means
- a. incapable of being understood
- b. unlikely to cause harm
- c. unable to distinguish
- **(d. impossible to see through)**

Antonyms

In each of the following groups, circle the word or expression that is most nearly the **opposite** of the word in **boldface** type.

1. erudite
- **(a. uninformed)**
- b. wordy
- c. brief
- d. relevant

2. soporific
- a. adequate
- b. long-winded
- c. disorganized
- **(d. stimulating)**

3. aspersions
- **(a. praise)**
- b. advice
- c. slander
- d. rumors

4. insular
- **(a. cosmopolitan)**
- b. bigoted
- c. old-fashioned
- d. provincial

5. ennui
- a. adiposity
- b. depression
- **(c. excitement)**
- d. uncertainty

6. repudiate
- a. reject
- **(b. accept)**
- c. publish
- d. amend

7. vapid
- a. foreign
- b. dull
- c. prize-winning
- **(d. meaningful)**

8. autonomy
- **(a. dependence)**
- b. freedom
- c. stability
- d. financial ruin

9. affable
a. talkative
b. unfriendly ✓
c. long-standing
d. faithful

10. transient
a. selfish
b. permanent ✓
c. passing
d. innocent

11. surreptitious
a. hasty
b. brief
c. open ✓
d. unexpected

12. heinous
a. noble ✓
b. cruel
c. inadvertent
d. wicked

13. sleazy
a. colorful
b. well made ✓
c. inexpensive
d. dingy

14. irrevocable
a. considered
b. hasty
c. minor
d. reversible ✓

15. querulous
a. agreeable ✓
b. loud
c. hostile
d. complaining

16. scathing
a. complimentary ✓
b. bitter
c. ungrammatical
d. unjustified

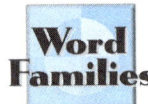

Word Families

A. On the line provided, write the word you have learned in Units 4–6 that is related to each of the following nouns.

EXAMPLE: reverberation—**reverberate**

1. affability — *affable*
2. erudition, eruditeness — *erudite*
3. inscrutability, inscrutableness — *inscrutable*
4. querulousness — *querulous*
5. remonstration, remonstrance, remonstrator — *remonstrate*
6. resilience, resiliency — *resilient*
7. scurrilousness, scurrility — *scurrilous*
8. inference, inferrer — *infer*
9. insularity, insularism, insulation, insulator — *insular*
10. cajolery, cajolement, cajoler — *cajole*
11. autonomist — *autonomy*
12. transiency, transience — *transient*
13. castigation — *castigate*
14. transmutation — *transmute*
15. anomaly, anomalousness — *anomalous*
16. cajolery — *cajole*

B. On the line provided, write the word you have learned in Units 4–6 that is related to each of the following verbs.

EXAMPLE: contrive—**contrivance**

17. insulate — *insular*
18. extract — *extricate*
19. scathe — *scathing*
20. asperse — *aspersion*

76 ■ Review Units 4–6

REVIEW UNITS 4–6

Two-Word Completions

Circle the pair of words that best complete the meaning of each of the following passages.

See pages T38–T48 for explanations of answers.

1. Rubber's remarkable _____ to resume its original shape makes it one of the world's most _____ materials.
   a. aura . . . fractious
   b. propensity . . . resilient
   c. autonomy . . . erudite
   d. ennui . . . gossamer

2. Only the sound of my footsteps _____ through the empty hallway disturbed the _____ silence in which the deserted office building was enveloped. "It's as quiet as a tomb in here at night," I thought as I made my way to the exit.
   a. transgressing . . . gossamer
   b. exacting . . . anomalous
   c. reverberating . . . sepulchral
   d. transmuting . . . bizarre

3. When I returned from lunch earlier than I had planned, I surprised a little sneak thief _____ attempting to _____ a few dollars from the petty cash drawer.
   a. brusquely . . . admonish
   b. irrevocably . . . wheedle
   c. rapidly . . . cajole
   d. surreptitiously . . . filch

4. "The American legal system is not _____, nor are our laws _____," the Chief Justice observed. "Like everything else in this fluid world of ours, they change and develop over time."
   a. anomalous . . . autonomous
   b. transient . . . resilient
   c. immutable . . . irrevocable
   d. axiomatic . . . inscrutable

5. He is usually so courteous and _____ that I was completely taken aback by his unaccountably _____ and surly reply to my question.
   a. affable . . . brusque
   b. fractious . . . scurrilous
   c. equitable . . . erudite
   d. straitlaced . . . querulous

6. "It took months of _____ effort and astute planning on my part to _____ this company from the mess in which I found it," the new owner smugly boasted. "If I hadn't worked like a dog, the firm would still be in financial hot water."
   a. amorphous . . . cajole
   b. sedulous . . . extricate
   c. immutable . . . contrive
   d. irrevocable . . . disabuse

Building with Classical Roots

grad, gress—to step, walk

This root appears in **transgress** (page 67), literally, "to step beyond." The word now means "to go beyond a limit or bound" or "to violate a command or law." Other words based on the same root are listed below.

| aggressive | digress | gradient | regress |
| congress | egress | gradualism | retrograde |

From the list of words above, choose the one that corresponds to each of the brief definitions below. Write the word in the blank space in the illustrative sentence below the definition.

1. a policy of approaching a desired end by slight degrees
   The moderates advocate a policy of __**gradualism**__.

2. attacking, taking the first step in an attack or quarrel; energetic, forceful (*"walking toward"*)
   Most wild animals are not __**aggressive**__ toward humans.

3. moving backward, contrary to the usual or normal order; tending toward a worse state
   They resisted the __**retrograde**__ tendencies of the small but vocal faction.

4. to move backward; to decline, grow worse
   Their reading skills will __**regress**__ if they do not work over the summer.

5. an exit; a going out (*"walking out"*)
   Be careful not to block the __**egress**__.

6. a part (as of a road or path) that slopes upward or downward
   The climbers struggled up the dangerously steep __**gradient**__.

7. a meeting (especially of persons or minds)
   We were invited to attend a(n) __**congress**__ of medical workers.

8. to turn aside, get off the main topic (*"to step away"*)
   She tried not to __**digress**__ from her speech.

From the list of words above, choose the one that best completes each of the following sentences. Write the word in the space provided.

1. Since their property does not border the road, their neighbor's private driveway is their only means of __**egress**__.

2. In her view, social problems in the community are too pressing to be dealt with through a policy of __**gradualism**__.

REVIEW UNITS 4–6

3. Since time was so limited, the moderator refused to allow the panel discussion to **digress**, even for a moment, from the topic.
4. A business concern either progresses or **regresses**; it never stands still.
5. The road spiraled around the mountain with a moderate **gradient**, making it passable even during stormy weather.
6. We had hoped that the UN could prevent **aggressive** nations from trampling on the rights of their neighbors.
7. After the first month of the term, I was considered an excellent math student, but then I began a(n) **retrograde** movement that carried me to the bottom of the class.
8. A special **congress** of religious leaders from all over the world will be held in London next month.

Circle the **boldface** word that more satisfactorily completes each of the following sentences.

1. Sometimes an older child will (**digress, (regress)**) in behavior when a new baby brother or sister seems to be getting all the parents' attention.
2. The radicals attacked the (**(gradualism,) congress**) of their opponents and accused them of caving in to established interests.
3. The purpose of a fire drill is to ensure the orderly (**regress, (egress)**) of the occupants from a building in case of fire.
4. The newspaper editorial condemned the (**(retrograde,) aggressive**) thinking of those who wished to halt all spending on space exploration.
5. Her competitive nature made her a(n) (**(aggressive,) retrograde**) opponent on the basketball court.
6. All the attendees at a recent (**gradient, (congress)**) of writers agreed to protest against attempts to ban books or limit freedom of speech.
7. While on vacation, we often like to (**regress, (digress)**) from the interstate highways and take some of the more picturesque back roads.
8. The (**(gradient,) gradualism**) of the road going up the mountain makes it a dangerous drive in icy conditions.

Read the following sentences, paying special attention to the words and phrases underlined. From the words in the box below, find better choices for these underlined words and phrases. Then use these choices to rewrite the sentences.

WORD BANK

aggrandize	blazon	erudite	infer	scourge
autonomy	caveat	fetter	inscrutable	scurrilous
axiomatic	disabuse	fractious	irrevocable	sedulous
bizarre	ennui	heinous	querulous	transmute

Mozart vs. Salieri?

1. The 1984 film *Amadeus* explores the <u>difficult to govern</u> relationship between musical genius Wolfgang Amadeus Mozart and the more conventional court composer, Antonio Salieri.
fractious

2. The film attempts to explain some of Mozart's <u>far-fetched</u> behavior by portraying him as an eccentric genius whose love of music renders all other aspects of his life immaterial.
bizarre

3. The makers of the film assert that it is <u>a universally accepted rule</u> that Mozart's musical brilliance drove Salieri into a jealous frenzy that ended in murder.
axiomatic

4. Since the film's debut, many historians have tried to <u>redress the conceptions of</u> the public of the widely held belief that Salieri poisoned his younger and more talented contemporary.
disabuse

5. In fact, Salieri worked hard to <u>increase the scope and strength of</u> his own popularity, and enjoyed both financial and critical success, teaching such illustrious musicians as Beethoven, Schubert, and Liszt.
aggrandize

6. But viewers will readily <u>gather</u> from the screenplay that Salieri was distracted by Mozart and wildly jealous of him.
infer

7. While true history is often <u>impossible to interpret</u>, most agree that the relationship between Mozart and Salieri, while complicated, did not include murder.
inscrutable

80 ■ Review Units 4–6

CUMULATIVE REVIEW I

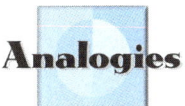

Analogies

In each of the following, circle the item that best completes the comparison.

See pages T38–T48 for explanations of answers.

1. **aggrandize** is to **bigger** as
   a. ascribe is to larger
   b. contrive is to smaller
   (c. ameliorate is to better)
   d. flout is to shorter

2. **meritorious** is to **heinous** as
   a. amorphous is to shapeless
   b. puzzling is to inscrutable
   c. immutable is to permanent
   (d. bland is to scathing)

3. **intermediary** is to **intercede** as
   (a. interloper is to intrude)
   b. proponent is to repudiate
   c. demagogue is to conciliate
   d. stalwart is to adjudicate

4. **propensity** is to **proclivity** as
   a. hiatus is to continuity
   (b. aura is to atmosphere)
   c. aspersion is to remark
   d. approbation is to disapproval

5. **remonstrate** is to **expostulate** as
   a. abominate is to intercede
   b. castigate is to precipitate
   (c. wheedle is to cajole)
   d. ingratiate is to commiserate

6. **lassitude** is to **tired** as
   a. sangfroid is to excited
   b. resilience is to annoyed
   (c. ennui is to wearied)
   d. aplomb is to mortified

7. **tenuous** is to **strength** as
   a. vitriolic is to rancor
   (b. transient is to permanence)
   c. equitable is to fairness
   d. stringent is to durability

8. **provincial** is to **insular** as
   (a. occult is to esoteric)
   b. inadvertent is to deliberate
   c. salutary is to baneful
   d. fractious is to docile

9. **querulous** is to **fret** as
   a. affable is to bellyache
   (b. petulant is to fuss)
   c. bizarre is to gripe
   d. noncommittal is to complain

10. **vapid** is to **flavor** as
    a. sedulous is to industry
    b. intrinsic is to value
    (c. hackneyed is to novelty)
    d. brusque is to brevity

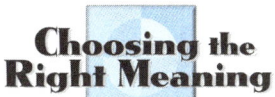

Choosing the Right Meaning

Read each sentence carefully. Then circle the item that best completes the statement below the sentence.

See pages T38–T48 for explanations of answers.

On the retreat from Moscow, Napoleon's once invincible Grand Armée degenerated into an amorphous mass of frightened fugitives, thanks to the Cossacks and the Russian winter. (2)

1. The word **amorphous**, as used in line 2, most nearly means
   a. lacking substance
   b. lacking character
   (c. lacking cohesion)
   d. lacking limits

For certain types of wheel-thrown ceramics, a fine, unctuous clay is best; for others, a less malleable medium is preferable. (2)

2. The word **unctuous** in line 1 may best be defined as
   a. servile   b. dry   c. smug   (d. plastic)

ICBMs and other types of guided missiles are unfortunately much too fractious to allow for testing anywhere near populated areas, however thinly inhabited. (2)

3. The best definition for the word **fractious** in line 1 is
   - (a. unpredictable)
   - b. explosive
   - c. quarrelsome
   - d. expensive

"That particular artist is so eclectic," the critic admitted, "that it is impossible to track down absolutely all the tenuous influences on his work." (2)

4. The best meaning for the word **tenuous** in line 2 is
   - a. unusual
   - (b. vague)
   - c. flimsy
   - d. various

"Or like stout Cortez when with eagle eyes
He star'd at the Pacific—and all his men (2)
Looked at each other with a wild surmise—
Silent, upon a peak in Darien." (4)
(Keats, "On First Looking into Chapman's Homer," 11–14)

5. The word surmise in line 3 most nearly means
   - a. smile of recognition
   - (b. flash of intuition)
   - c. peal of laughter
   - d. yawn of boredom

Two-Word Completions

Circle the pair of words that best complete the meaning of each of the following sentences.

See pages T38–T48 for explanations of answers.

1. The flames from the tire factory bathed the whole neighborhood in a(n) _____ glow and the stench of burning rubber _____ the air.
   - a. vapid . . . transmuted
   - (b. lurid . . . permeated)
   - c. sleazy . . . transcended
   - d. amorphous . . . simulated

2. The sonorous notes of the mighty organ _____ through the _____ vaults and cavernous expanses of the cathedral like the distant roar of thunder.
   - (a. reverberated . . . sepulchral)
   - b. blazoned . . . unctuous
   - c. expostulated . . . surreptitious
   - d. debased . . . circuitous

3. Though _____ have passed since the day Moses brought them down from the top of Mt. Sinai, the _____ contained in the Ten Commandments are still revered by many throughout the world.
   - a. epitomes . . . caveats
   - (b. millennia . . . precepts)
   - c. addenda . . . coalitions
   - d. umbrages . . . archetypes

4. In many ancient religions, the _____ of an entire community would periodically be placed on the head of a single sacrificial animal, so that the death of one might _____ the sins of all.
   - a. innuendoes . . . fetter
   - b. surmises . . . enjoin
   - c. aspersions . . . expedite
   - (d. transgressions . . . expiate)

5. If the job you have is nothing more than a(n) _____, you don't have to be a particularly _____ or talented worker to handle it.
   - a. hiatus . . . erudite
   - b. prerogative . . . noncommittal
   - (c. sinecure . . . sedulous)
   - d. anathema . . . soporific

CUMULATIVE REVIEW I

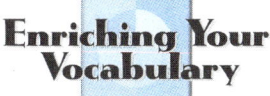

Enriching Your Vocabulary

Read the passage below. Then complete the exercise at the bottom of the page.

Living Latin

While some might consider Latin a "dead language" because it is no longer spoken in the modern world, most scholars can attest to the fact that Latin has contributed many roots, conjugations, and phrases to the English language. We can determine the meanings of some Latin expressions based on the familiar word roots that appear in other Anglicized words. For example, the phrase *e pluribus unum* appears on American money. Recognizing the *e* prefix as in *e*ject as meaning *out* or *from*, the *plur* root as in *plur*al as meaning *many*, and the *un* root as in *un*ited as meaning *one*, we can figure out the meaning of this phrase representing American democracy: out of many, one.

The forms of other Latin phrases may not be as easily recognizable, yet these words play a significant role in our lexicon. For example, *ex officio* (Unit Two) means "by virtue of holding a certain office"; a play's producer may distribute parts *ex officio* as the head of the production. *Ex post facto* means "after the fact." *Habeas corpus* refers to the need for absolute proof. And of course, where would our lists be without the popular abbreviation *etc.*, short for *et cetera*, meaning, "and other things"?

Alumni and *alumnae* come from the Latin for "stepchild."

With or without a dictionary, select the item in the box below that completes each sentence.

| alma mater | modus operandi | pro tempore |
| de facto | persona non grata | status quo |

1. The football player donated a large sum to his _____**alma mater**_____.
2. The burglar's _____**modus operandi**_____ included climbing in a second story window.
3. After I decided not to sign the petition to plant more trees on our block, I became _____**persona non grata**_____ in our neighborhood.
4. The governor decided to maintain the _____**status quo**_____ and not raise taxes.
5. Until we hire a new principal, the assistant principal will be the principal **pro tempore**.
6. While the monarchy of England plays a ceremonial role, the _____**de facto**_____ head of government is the prime minister.

Unit 7

 See page T21 for information.

 Note carefully the spelling, pronunciation, part(s) of speech, and definition(s) of each of the following words. Then write the word in the blank space(s) in the illustrative sentence(s) following. Finally, study the lists of synonyms and antonyms given at the end of each entry.

1. austere
(ô stēr′)

(*adj.*) severe or stern in manner; without adornment or luxury, simple, plain; harsh or sour in flavor

The _____**austere**_____ clothing and conduct of the Puritans expressed their religious humility.

SYNONYMS: forbidding, rigorous, puritanical, ascetic, unadorned, subdued
ANTONYMS: mild, indulgent, luxurious, flamboyant

2. beneficent
(bə nef′ ə sənt)

(*adj.*) performing acts of kindness or charity; conferring benefits, doing good

From them I learned that purely _____**beneficent**_____ acts can require as much hard work as a nine-to-five job.

SYNONYMS: humanitarian, magnanimous, charitable
ANTONYMS: selfish, cruel, harmful, deleterious

3. cadaverous
(kə dav′ ər əs)

(*adj.*) pale, gaunt, resembling a corpse

Weak from hunger and _____**cadaverous**_____ in appearance, the rescued captives were carried from the plane.

SYNONYMS: corpselike, wasted, haggard, emaciated, ghastly
ANTONYMS: robust, portly, rosy, the picture of health

4. concoct
(kän käkt′)

(*v.*) to prepare by combining ingredients, make up (as a dish); to devise, invent, fabricate

He _____**concocts**_____ a savory stew with fresh herbs and vegetables from the garden.

SYNONYMS: create, fashion, rustle up

5. crass
(kras)

(*adj.*) coarse, unfeeling; stupid

We feel that the positions of our representative show a _____**crass**_____ indifference to our problems.

SYNONYMS: crude, vulgar, tasteless, oafish, obtuse
ANTONYMS: refined, elegant, tasteful, polished, brilliant

6. debase
(di bās′)

(*v.*) to lower in character, quality, or value; to degrade, adulterate; to cause to deteriorate

Every time a new rule is introduced in a popular sport, there are fans who say it will _____**debase**_____ the game.

SYNONYMS: cheapen, corrupt, demean, depreciate
ANTONYMS: elevate, uplift, improve, enhance

7. **desecrate**
(des' ə krāt)

(v.) to commit sacrilege upon, treat irreverently; to contaminate, pollute

The search continues for the vandals who __desecrated__ the cemetery.

SYNONYMS: profane, defile, violate
ANTONYMS: revere, honor, venerate, consecrate

8. **disconcert**
(dis kən sərt')

(v.) to confuse; to disturb the composure of

They had hoped to __disconcert__ him with an unexpected question, but he was well prepared.

SYNONYMS: upset, rattle, ruffle, faze, perturb
ANTONYMS: relax, calm, put at ease

9. **grandiose**
(gran' dē ōs)

(adj.) grand in an impressive or stately way; marked by pompous affectation or grandeur, absurdly exaggerated

In how many stories, I wonder, does an ambitious villain become the victim of __grandiose__ plans?

SYNONYMS: majestic, bombastic, highfalutin
ANTONYMS: simple, modest, unaffected, humble

10. **inconsequential**
(in kän sə kwen' shəl)

(adj.) trifling, unimportant

Feel free to ignore the __inconsequential__ details, provided that you know exactly which ones they are.

SYNONYMS: trivial, negligible, petty, paltry
ANTONYMS: important, essential, crucial, vital

11. **infraction**
(in frak' shən)

(n.) a breaking of a law or obligation

His uncle paid a fine for his __infraction__ of the local recycling regulations.

SYNONYMS: violation, transgression, breach, offense

12. **mitigate**
(mit' ə gāt)

(v.) to make milder or softer, to moderate in force or intensity

I had hoped to __mitigate__ her anger by offering an apology.

SYNONYMS: lessen, relieve, alleviate, diminish
ANTONYMS: aggravate, intensify, irritate, exacerbate

13. **pillage**
(pil' ij)

(v.) to rob of goods by open force (as in war), plunder; (n.) the act of looting; booty

The commanding officer warned his troops not to __pillage__ the conquered city.

__Pillage__ and murder became a fact of life in Europe during the Dark Ages.

SYNONYMS: (v.) ravage, sack, loot; (n.) booty

14. **prate**
    (prāt)

    (*v.*) to talk a great deal in a foolish or aimless fashion
       He would _____**prate**_____ endlessly about the past but say nothing useful about our present dilemma.
    SYNONYMS: chatter, prattle, blab, blabber, palaver
    ANTONYMS: come to the point, not waste words

15. **punctilious**
    (pəŋk til′ ē əs)

    (*adj.*) very careful and exact, attentive to fine points of etiquette or propriety
       The clerk was so _____**punctilious**_____ in obeying court rules that I had to remind him why I was there.
    SYNONYMS: precise, scrupulous, exacting, fussy, finicky
    ANTONYMS: careless, negligent, lax, perfunctory

16. **redoubtable**
    (ri daủ′ tə bəl)

    (*adj.*) inspiring fear or awe; illustrious, eminent
       As a ruler he was _____**redoubtable**_____ but, like all such rulers, not much loved.
    SYNONYMS: formidable, fearsome, awesome, august
    ANTONYMS: laughable, risible, contemptible

17. **reprove**
    (ri prüv′)

    (*v.*) to find fault with, scold, rebuke
       She _____**reproved**_____ her staff for having followed orders blindly.
    SYNONYMS: chide, chastise, upbraid, reproach
    ANTONYMS: praise, commend, laud, pat on the back

18. **restitution**
    (res tə tü′ shən)

    (*n.*) the act of restoring someone or something to the rightful owner or to a former state or position; making good on a loss or damage
       They made _____**restitution**_____ for the damage to the car but never fully regained the friendship of its owner.
    SYNONYMS: compensation, reimbursement, redress, restoration

19. **stalwart**
    (stôl′ wərt)

    (*adj.*) strong and sturdy; brave; resolute; (*n.*) a brave, strong person; a strong supporter; one who takes an uncompromising position
       She became as _____**stalwart**_____ on the basketball court as she was quick at mathematical puzzles.
       The enemy had broken through our first line but was repulsed by the _____**stalwarts**_____ defending the gates.
    SYNONYMS: (*adj.*) sturdy, stout, intrepid, valiant; (*n.*) mainstay
    ANTONYMS: (*adj.*) weak, infirm, irresolute, vacillating

20. **vulnerable**
    (vəl′ nər ə bəl)

    (*adj.*) open to attack; capable of being wounded or damaged; unprotected
       Those brave enough to have opposed the dictator's rise now found themselves in a _____**vulnerable**_____ position.
    SYNONYMS: defenseless, exposed, unguarded
    ANTONYMS: invincible, protected, safe, secure

Completing the Sentence

From the words for this unit, choose the one that best completes each of the following sentences. Write the word in the space provided.

1. Though most of our players were the equals of theirs, the awesome size of their __redoubtable__ center filled us with apprehension.

2. I became desperately tired of listening to him __prate__ about how important he was, how much money he had, and so forth.

3. Who can ever forget those pictures showing the __cadaverous__ faces of the people who had been in concentration camps!

4. Whenever she serves as chairperson, she is so __punctilious__ that she insists on observing every fine point of parliamentary procedure.

5. I found that beneath his rather __austere__ manner and appearance there was a warm, sympathetic person.

6. An official who is responsible for shaping vital national policies should not waste time and energy on such __inconsequential__ matters.

7. Even a so-called minor __infraction__ of the traffic laws may lead to a serious accident.

8. At a time when we need a modest, low-cost housing program, how can we be expected to accept such a(n) __grandiose__ scheme?

9. His work on behalf of the homeless was merely the latest in a long line of __beneficent__ undertakings.

10. Is there any way that we can make __restitution__ for the terrible wrong we have done them?

11. Fond remembrances of happy days of family life intensified rather than __mitigated__ her grief.

12. They __desecrated__ the funeral service by talking loudly during the ceremonies, laughing, and generally showing a complete lack of respect.

13. Before they arrived home from the party, they __concocted__ an elaborate story that they hoped would excuse their being two hours late.

14. It is hard to forgive the __crass__ selfishness with which they took most of the food supplies for their own use.

15. Our democracy, I believe, is more __vulnerable__ to decay from within than it is to attack from the outside.

16. Though she looked rather frail, her __stalwart__ spirit made her a tireless crusader for women's rights.

17. We are, I trust, long past the time when it was considered quite "natural" for newly elected officials to __pillage__ the city treasury.

Unit 7 ■ 87

18. She has ____debased____ her considerable talents by writing books that are designed to appeal to the lowest tastes.
19. I'm telling you this not to ____reprove____ you for having made a mistake but to prevent the mistake from being repeated.
20. He went right on with his speech, refusing to be ____disconcerted____ by the heckling of a few loudmouths.

Synonyms

Choose the word from this unit that is **the same** or **most nearly the same** in meaning as the **boldface** word or expression in the given phrase. Write the word on the line provided.

1. not **perturbed** by the noise — disconcerted
2. **vulgar** appeal for money — crass
3. to **chatter** boringly about the weather — prate
4. **compensation** for his misdeeds — restitution
5. **diminish** the horror of the crime — mitigate
6. **fabricate** an excuse — concoct
7. exaggerating **trivial** flaws — inconsequential
8. a **breach** of our agreement — infraction
9. **exposed** to wind and high water — vulnerable
10. **loot** the museum of valuables — pillage
11. to **demean** our group's reputation — debase
12. an **intrepid** and faithful sidekick — stalwart
13. an **ascetic** life of plain food and little sleep — austere
14. was **reproached** for his mistakes — reproved
15. happy results from **magnanimous** choices — beneficent

Antonyms

Choose the word from this unit that is **most nearly opposite** in meaning to the **boldface** word or expression in the given phrase. Write the word on the line provided.

16. a **robust** specimen — cadaverous
17. her **unaffected** delivery of Shakespeare's lines — grandiose
18. **honor** this ritual of the tribe — desecrate
19. **laughable** as a challenger — redoubtable
20. **negligent** in filling out the form — punctilious

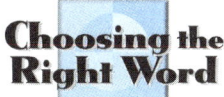

Choosing the Right Word

Circle the **boldface** word that more satisfactorily completes each of the following sentences.

1. That sum may seem (**inconsequential**, **vulnerable**) to you, but to me it is a great deal of money.
2. By concentrating on personal gain, he has (**debased**, **disconcerted**) both himself and the high office to which he was elected.
3. The starving children shown in the TV special looked more like (**cadavers**, **stalwarts**) than living creatures.
4. Whenever I go to a concert, I seem to spend half my time shushing the (**crass**, **austere**) boors who chitchat while the orchestra is playing.
5. As (**restitution**, **infraction**) for the damage he had caused to the family car, Phil promised to clean and polish it regularly for a full year.
6. Since my next paycheck was not to be had until the first of the month, I reconciled myself to living (**austerely**, **inconsequentially**) until then.
7. The woman is known and loved throughout the community for her many (**redoubtable**, **beneficent**) acts on behalf of all types of unfortunates.
8. The principal (**disconcerted**, **reproved**) the entire student body for their discourteous behavior toward the guest speaker at the school assembly.
9. His (**grandiose**, **beneficent**) schemes for world conquest collapsed in a nightmare of military defeat and internal revolt.
10. In her clumsy efforts to be recognized as an "intellectual," she (**prates**, **desecrates**) endlessly about matters she does not really understand.
11. All the power of Great Britain could not shake the American colonists in their (**stalwart**, **beneficent**) opposition to measures that they considered unfair and tyrannical.
12. She is such a (**redoubtable**, **crass**) foe of the trite phrase that her students tremble lest her wrath descend on them for using a cliché.
13. The sale of so many great works of art to foreign collectors is, in my eyes, little more than (**pillage**, **mitigation**) of our cultural heritage.
14. The master chef has (**debased**, **concocted**) a dessert that is so rich that it will be a menace to weight watchers throughout the country.
15. He is so (**punctilious**, **austere**) about every detail that it is said he irons his shoelaces before wearing them.
16. Her self-confidence is so unshakeable that she is simply not (**grandiose**, **vulnerable**) to "put-down" remarks that would annoy other people.
17. The fact that he did everything possible to help the poor child after the accident tends to (**mitigate**, **desecrate**) his responsibility for the tragedy.
18. It is a (**desecration**, **restitution**) of the memory of Lincoln to involve his name in defense of such a racist policy.
19. Although his conduct may not have violated any law, I consider it a gross (**cadaver**, **infraction**) of conventional ethical standards.
20. The conductor of the orchestra was so (**desecrated**, **disconcerted**) by the noisy audience that he stopped the performance and asked for quiet.

Vocabulary in Context

Read the following passage, in which some of the words you have studied in this unit appear in **boldface** type. Then complete each statement given below the passage by circling the letter of the item that is **the same** or **almost the same** in meaning as the highlighted word.

Walker Evans: Life As It Is

(Line)

In the 1920s still cameras were considered mere gadgets. They took only black-and-white pictures and one used them to record weddings or to let friends see how fast the children were growing. Almost no one encouraged Walker Evans, a shy young Midwesterner, in his belief that photography could be an art. (5)

The few older photographers who shared Evans' view chose foreign locations or poetical subjects in which billowing mists or sharply contrasted tones made the viewer marvel that a photo could so dramatically resemble a painting. But Evans thought (10) that imitating paintings **debased** photography. He wanted to show life as we ourselves commonly see it—but show it more clearly than we usually see. As with this photo of a cotton harvest worker in Alabama (left), Evans learned to find the wonderful within the ordinary. (15)

In 1936 Evans was hired to go South with the writer James Agee to produce a magazine article on tenant farmers, the largest group of abjectly poor workers in the nation. Other articles had presented these farmers as nobly heroic or pitifully **vulnerable**, (20) or as **cadaverous** scarecrows dramatic in their poverty, posed with lighting to match. Evans photographed them as he found them, **austere**, likeable people doing their best with the little they had. No contrived drama **mitigated** their terrible, (25) actual lives. His pictures were **disconcerting**

Hale County, Alabama, Summer 1936

because they were so clear and obviously true. But they also respected their subjects, and this aura of respect made them unforgettable.

Though Evans died in 1975, his honest and evocative photographs of American life serve as a testament to the art of the camera. (30)

---

1. The meaning of **debased** (line 11) is
   a. glorified   c. depreciated
   b. strained   d. broke

2. **Vulnerable** (line 20) most nearly means
   a. defenseless   c. funny
   b. hungry   d. poor

3. **Cadaverous** (line 21) is best defined as
   a. waving   c. comical
   b. emaciated   d. menacing

4. The meaning of **austere** (line 23) is
   a. unhappy   c. unadorned
   b. busy   d. relaxed

5. **Mitigated** (line 25) most nearly means
   a. diminished   c. broadcast
   b. hid   d. saved

6. **Disconcerting** (line 26) is best defined as
   a. puzzling   c. interesting
   b. enlightening   d. upsetting

See page T21 for information.

UNIT 8

Definitions

Note carefully the spelling, pronunciation, part(s) of speech, and definition(s) of each of the following words. Then write the word in the blank space(s) in the illustrative sentence(s) following. Finally, study the lists of synonyms and antonyms given at the end of each entry.

1. **acrimonious**
   (ak rə mō′ nē əs)

   (*adj.*) stinging, bitter in temper or tone

   She whirled to face me when I spoke, and her answer startled me by its _____acrimonious_____ bluntness.

   SYNONYMS: biting, caustic, rancorous, hostile, peevish
   ANTONYMS: gentle, warm, mild, friendly, cordial

2. **bovine**
   (bō′ vīn)

   (*adj.*) resembling a cow or ox; sluggish, unresponsive

   After I told him what had happened, he sat there with a _____bovine_____ expression and said nothing.

   SYNONYMS: stolid, dull, slow, stupid
   ANTONYMS: alert, sharp, bright, keen, quick

3. **consternation**
   (kän stər nā′ shən)

   (*n.*) dismay, confusion

   His father looked at the mess with _____consternation_____, hardly knowing what to say first.

   SYNONYMS: shock, amazement, bewilderment, dismay
   ANTONYMS: calm, composure, aplomb

4. **corpulent**
   (kôr′ pyə lənt)

   (*adj.*) fat; having a large, bulky body

   Though she had grown _____corpulent_____ with the years, the opera singer's voice and her way with a song were the same.

   SYNONYMS: overweight, heavy, obese, stout, portly
   ANTONYMS: slender, lean, spare, gaunt, emaciated

5. **disavow**
   (dis ə vaủ′)

   (*v.*) to deny responsibility for or connection with

   The suspect stubbornly continued to _____disavow_____ any part in the kidnapping plot.

   SYNONYMS: disown, disclaim, retract, abjure
   ANTONYMS: acknowledge, admit, grant, certify

6. **dispassionate**
   (dis pash′ ə nət)

   (*adj.*) impartial; calm, free from emotion

   Being a neighbor but not quite a family friend, he was called in to give a _____dispassionate_____ view of our plan.

   SYNONYMS: unbiased, disinterested, cool, detached
   ANTONYMS: committed, engaged, partial, biased

7. **dissension**
   (di sen' shən)

   (*n.*) disagreement, sharp difference of opinion
   The political party was torn by _____dissension_____ and finally split into two wings.
   SYNONYMS: strife, discord, contention
   ANTONYMS: agreement, accord, harmony

8. **dissipate**
   (dis' ə pāt)

   (*v.*) to cause to disappear; to scatter, dispel; to spend foolishly, squander; to be extravagant in pursuit of pleasure
   As chairman he is fair and open, but he _____dissipates_____ his energies on trivial things.
   SYNONYMS: disperse, strew, diffuse, waste
   ANTONYMS: gather, collect, conserve, husband

9. **expurgate**
   (ek' spər gāt)

   (*v.*) to remove objectionable passages or words from a written text; to cleanse, purify
   According to the unwritten law of journalism, the editor alone has the right to _____expurgate_____ the article.
   SYNONYMS: purge, censor, bowdlerize

10. **gauntlet**
    (gônt' lət)

    (*n.*) an armored or protective glove; a challenge; two lines of men armed with weapons with which to beat a person forced to run between them; an ordeal
    In the Middle Ages, a knight threw down his _____gauntlet_____ as a challenge, and another knight picked it up only if he accepted.
    SYNONYMS: dare, provocation, trial, punishment

11. **hypothetical**
    (hī pə thet' ə kəl)

    (*adj.*) based on an assumption or guess; used as a provisional or tentative idea to guide or direct investigation
    Science is not based on _____hypothetical_____ assumptions, but on proven facts.
    SYNONYMS: assumed, supposed, conjectural, conditional
    ANTONYMS: actual, real, tested, substantiated

12. **ignoble**
    (ig nō' bəl)

    (*adj.*) mean, low, base
    Most people will agree that a noble purpose does not justify _____ignoble_____ means.
    SYNONYMS: inferior, unworthy, dishonorable, sordid
    ANTONYMS: admirable, praiseworthy, lofty, noble

13. **impugn**
    (im pyün')

    (*v.*) to call into question; to attack as false
    You can _____impugn_____ the senator's facts, but you cannot accuse her of concealing her intentions.
    SYNONYMS: challenge, deny, dispute, query, question
    ANTONYMS: confirm, prove, verify, validate

14. intemperate
(in tem' pər ət)

(*adj.*) immoderate, lacking in self-control; inclement

Experience taught her to control her ____intemperate____ outbursts of anger.

SYNONYMS: excessive, extreme, unrestrained, inordinate
ANTONYMS: moderate, restrained, cool and collected

15. odium
(ō' dē əm)

(*n.*) hatred, contempt; disgrace or infamy resulting from hateful conduct

Those eager to heap ____odium____ on the fallen tyrant learned that he had escaped in the night.

SYNONYMS: abhorrence, opprobrium, shame, ignominy
ANTONYMS: esteem, admiration, approbation

16. perfidy
(pər' fə dē)

(*n.*) faithlessness, treachery

Rulers in Shakespeare's plays often find themselves armed against enemies but not against the ____perfidy____ of their friends.

SYNONYMS: betrayal, disloyalty, treason, duplicity
ANTONYMS: faithfulness, loyalty, steadfastness

17. relegate
(rel' ə gāt)

(*v.*) to place in a lower position; to assign, refer, turn over; to banish

Even if they ____relegate____ him to a mere clerical job, he is determined to make his presence felt.

SYNONYMS: transfer, consign, demote, exile
ANTONYMS: promote, elevate, advance, recall

18. squeamish
(skwē' mish)

(*adj.*) inclined to nausea; easily shocked or upset; excessively fastidious or refined

If I am called ____squeamish____ for disliking the horror movie, what do we call those who say that they liked it?

SYNONYMS: nauseated, queasy, delicate, oversensitive, priggish

19. subservient
(səb sər' vē ənt)

(*adj.*) subordinate in capacity or role; submissively obedient; serving to promote some end

The officers were taught to be respectful of but not blindly ____subservient____ to their superior's wishes.

SYNONYMS: secondary, servile, obsequious, useful
ANTONYMS: primary, principal, bossy, domineering

20. susceptible
(sə sep' tə bəl)

(*adj.*) open to; easily influenced; lacking in resistance

The trouble with being ____susceptible____ to flattery is that you can never be sure that the flatterer is sincere.

SYNONYMS: vulnerable, receptive, impressionable
ANTONYMS: resistant, immune

Completing the Sentence

From the words for this unit, choose the one that best completes each of the following sentences. Write the word in the space provided.

1. We have had enough of high-powered, excited oratory; what we need now is a(n) _____dispassionate_____ examination of the facts.

2. Although she seems rather plodding in her behavior and rarely becomes excited, I think it is unfair to call her "_____bovine_____."

3. She is a person of such fine moral standards that she seems incapable of a(n) _____ignoble_____ act.

4. Instead of using all their forces in one concerted attack on the enemy, they _____dissipated_____ their strength in minor engagements.

5. The job of cleaning up the field and the stands after the big game was _____relegated_____ to the freshmen.

6. Our discussion that day was a(n) _____hypothetical_____ one, based on the possibility—still far from definite—that I would take the job.

7. Far from presenting a unified front, the party is torn by all kinds of strife and _____dissension_____.

8. I am not trying to _____impugn_____ his truthfulness, but I still do not see how the facts support his claims.

9. Now that these ugly facts about his business dealings have come to light, I must _____disavow_____ my support of his candidacy.

10. Vigorous debate is fine, but is there any real need for such unrestrained and _____acrimonious_____ name-calling?

11. He is so _____susceptible_____ to flattery that with a few complimentary words I can get him to do almost anything I want.

12. Though her overall position seemed to be sensible, her language was so unrestrained and _____intemperate_____ that people wouldn't support her.

13. Anyone as _____squeamish_____ as that trainee will have trouble accustoming himself to the sights, sounds, and smells of hospital work.

14. Because Vidkun Quisling cooperated with the Nazis, his name has become a symbol of _____perfidy_____ in his home country of Norway.

15. The _____odium_____ for this tragic failure does not belong to any individual or small group but to the community as a whole.

16. To the _____consternation_____ of the people in the stands, the lion leaped out of the cage and bounded toward the exit.

17. Thomas Bowdler _____expurgated_____ certain words from Shakespeare's plays because he felt that they were unfit to "be read aloud in a family."

18. Under the American form of government, all branches of the military are clearly _____subservient_____ to the civilian authority.
19. The bold candidate threw down the _____gauntlet_____ and dared her opponent to face her in a televised debate.
20. People with a tendency toward being _____corpulent_____ must wage a lifelong struggle against rich foods.

Synonyms

Choose the word from this unit that is **the same** or **most nearly the same** in meaning as the **boldface** word or expression in the given phrase. Write the word on the line provided.

1. standing before us in **bewilderment** — consternation
2. to **disown** any credit for herself — disavow
3. deciding to **bowdlerize** the passage — expurgate
4. unwilling to **question** his honor — impugn
5. setting aside her **conjectural** motive — hypothetical
6. the brutal **challenge** he endured — gauntlet
7. a **dishonorable** end to a shadowy life — ignoble
8. feeling **queasy** at the very thought — squeamish
9. **consigned** to the highest bleachers — relegated
10. not a hint of **duplicity** in him — perfidy
11. a show of **unrestrained** scorn — intemperate
12. a **stolid**, faithful devotion — bovine
13. to deliberately **waste** her wealth — dissipate
14. give a **detached** account — dispassionate
15. his **caustic** way of speaking — acrimonious

Antonyms

Choose the word from this unit that is **most nearly opposite** in meaning to the **boldface** word or expression in the given phrase. Write the word on the line provided.

16. a slow, **gaunt** old man — corpulent
17. the **esteem** attached to that name — odium
18. a family vacation marked by **harmony** — dissension
19. quite **immune** to outside influences — susceptible
20. an intern's **domineering** manner — subservient

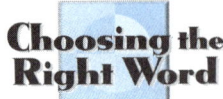

Choosing the Right Word

Circle the **boldface** word that more satisfactorily completes each of the following sentences.

1. A certain amount of disagreement is healthy in any organization, but in our club (**dissension**, **perfidy**) has almost become a way of life.
2. I noticed with some distaste how her usually overbearing manner became (**susceptible**, **subservient**) when our employer joined the group.
3. If we are going to be required to perform a(n) (**expurgated**, **relegated**) version of the play, then I think it is not worth doing.
4. Imagine our (**consternation**, **dissension**) when the brakes failed and we headed full speed toward the busy intersection!
5. Students who have been well trained in the social sciences should not be (**susceptible**, **ignoble**) to the cheap fallacies of racism.
6. The estate he had inherited from his father was (**dissipated**, **disavowed**) in a long series of impractical and/or mismanaged business enterprises.
7. Try your best to subdue your natural reluctance and make a (**squeamish**, **dispassionate**) decision that will be in your son's best interests.
8. My Spanish friend finds it hard to understand the (**odium**, **dissension**) attached to bullfighting in most non-Hispanic countries.
9. Their (**susceptible**, **bovine**) stares and obvious inability to understand the seriousness of the situation made me doubt their mental capacity.
10. Though I was annoyed by the child's behavior, the father's outburst of anger seemed to me deplorably (**intemperate**, **bovine**).
11. I am not ordinarily a (**corpulent**, **squeamish**) person, but the sight of that terrible automobile accident haunted me for weeks.
12. By reference to (**hypothetical**, **ignoble**) cases, you may be able to clarify the difference between "murder" and "manslaughter" for the law students.
13. It is not for me to (**expurgate**, **impugn**) his motives, but how could anyone except an overambitious scoundrel have misled his friends in that way?
14. Aren't you going a little far when you accuse me of (**consternation**, **perfidy**) because I didn't vote for you in the beauty contest?
15. The retiring coach said he no longer had the stomach to run the (**gauntlet**, **odium**) of critics who assailed him after every loss.
16. There is often a thin line between the kind of debate that is spirited and useful and that which is (**acrimonious**, **hypothetical**) and nonproductive.
17. Not too long ago in our society, a (**corpulent**, **bovine**) body was generally admired as a sign of prosperity and physical vigor.
18. When Mr. Kummer saw my pathetically inept efforts to prepare a banana split, I was (**impugned**, **relegated**) to the ranks of the unemployed.
19. The prisoner attempted to (**disavow**, **dissipate**) his confession on the grounds that he had not been informed of his legal rights.
20. Far from being (**ignoble**, **dispassionate**), her failure after making a valiant effort may serve as an inspiration to young people.

Vocabulary in Context

*Read the following passage, in which some of the words you have studied in this unit appear in **boldface** type. Then complete each statement given below the passage by circling the letter of the item that is **the same** or **almost the same** in meaning as the highlighted word.*

Monster in the Lake

(Line)

Mysteries become more popular the older they get, and the so-called mystery of the Loch Ness Monster is at least fifteen hundred years old. The creature, called everything from a fish to a dragon, was reportedly seen by a monk in 565 A.D., in a lake in Scotland (the "loch," to the Scots) that she has ever
(5) since been said to inhabit. For some reason, the **hypothetical** "Nessie" is always referred to as "she." Her size can only be guessed at, but the loch itself is 788 feet deep and twenty-three miles long.

For centuries, local people kept the mystery alive, but not until 1933 did newspapers cause
(10) **consternation** among the general public by publishing reports of "Nessie" sightings. Shortly thereafter, hunters, scientists, and tourists began arriving to see if she existed. One popular theory said that Nessie was a kind of
(15) dinosaur left over from another age. Such talk was like a **gauntlet** thrown down to scientists, who had repeatedly examined the stories of sightings and the photographs said to show Nessie's hump, flippers, and head (right). So
(20) far, most such pictures have been proven to be large logs or floating tree stumps, waves made by boats, rocks seen at a distance, or deer out swimming. Small submarines have searched the water, and thirty motorboats once lined up
(25) from shore to shore and scanned the length of the loch with equipment to detect objects under water. They discovered no monster. Those **susceptible** to the legend said Nessie was hiding in a cave.

Arguments over Nessie have at times been **acrimonious**. Nonbelievers **relegate** her to a folk tale. Still, all agree that the local tourist trade has never
(30) been better.

A "sighting" of the Loch Ness Monster?

---

1. The meaning of **hypothetical** (line 5) is
   a. secret   c. huge
   b. conjectural   d. ancient

2. Consternation (line 10) most nearly means
   a. mockery   c. shock
   b. boredom   d. happiness

3. Gauntlet (line 16) is best defined as
   a. provocation   c. clue
   b. joke   d. explanation

4. The meaning of **susceptible** (line 27) is
   a. suspicious   c. profiting
   b. amused   d. receptive

5. Acrimonious (line 28) most nearly means
   a. entertaining   c. long
   b. rancorous   d. illegal

6. Relegate (line 29) is best defined as
   a. consign   c. raise
   b. compare   d. describe

Unit 9

 See page T21 for information.

Note carefully the spelling, pronunciation, part(s) of speech, and definition(s) of each of the following words. Then write the word in the blank space(s) in the illustrative sentence(s) following. Finally, study the lists of synonyms and antonyms given at the end of each entry.

1. **abate**
   (ə bāt′)

   (*v.*) to make less in amount, degree, etc.; to subside, become less; to nullify; to deduct, omit

   We stood on the dock on that moonless night, waiting for the storm to _____**abate**_____.

   SYNONYMS: diminish, decrease, subside, let up
   ANTONYMS: intensify, increase, magnify, wax

2. **adulation**
   (aj ə lā′ shən)

   (*n.*) praise or flattery that is excessive

   Athletes have little choice but to enjoy the sometimes puzzling _____**adulation**_____ of their fans.

   SYNONYMS: adoration, idolization, hero-worship
   ANTONYMS: ridicule, derision, scorn, odium

3. **anathema**
   (ə nath′ ə mə)

   (*n.*) an object of intense dislike; a curse or strong denunciation (often used adjectivally without the article)

   The author's views on bringing up children are _____**anathema**_____ to my dad but a delight to my mother.

   SYNONYMS: malediction, imprecation, abomination
   ANTONYMS: benediction, blessing

4. **astute**
   (ə stüt′)

   (*adj.*) shrewd, crafty, showing practical wisdom

   The _____**astute**_____ management of money is a valuable skill but may not by itself make a good executive.

   SYNONYMS: shrewd, acute, sagacious, judicious, wily
   ANTONYMS: obtuse, doltish, empty-headed, dumb

5. **avarice**
   (av′ ər is)

   (*n.*) a greedy desire, particularly for wealth

   Her career exhibited both the miser's ever-growing _____**avarice**_____ and the miser's diminishing charm.

   SYNONYMS: cupidity, rapacity, acquisitiveness

6. **culpable**
   (kəl′ pə bəl)

   (*adj.*) deserving blame, worthy of condemnation

   It was the inspectors' _____**culpable**_____ neglect of duty that left such old buses in service.

   SYNONYMS: guilty, delinquent, peccant, blameworthy
   ANTONYMS: blameless, innocent, laudable, meritorious

7. dilatory
(dil′ ə tôr ē)

(*adj.*) tending to delay or procrastinate, not prompt; intended to delay or postpone

She hired an assistant because, on her own, she was always _____**dilatory**_____ in paying her bills.

SYNONYMS: stalling, slow, tardy, laggard
ANTONYMS: prompt, punctual, speedy, expeditious

8. egregious
(i grē′ jəs)

(*adj.*) conspicuous, standing out from the mass (used particularly in an unfavorable sense)

Whoever allowed that man on a stage is guilty of an _____**egregious**_____ blunder.

SYNONYMS: glaring, flagrant, blatant
ANTONYMS: unnoticeable, paltry, piddling

9. equivocate
(i kwiv′ ə kāt)

(*v.*) to speak or act in a way that allows for more than one interpretation; to be deliberately vague or ambiguous

I won't soon give my vote to a candidate who shows such a marked tendency to _____**equivocate**_____.

SYNONYMS: to talk out of both sides of one's mouth, palter, hedge
ANTONYM: to speak one's mind plainly

10. evanescent
(ev ə nes′ ənt)

(*adj.*) vanishing, soon passing away; light and airy

Looking back, I see that the magic of that summer was _____**evanescent**_____.

SYNONYMS: ephemeral, transient, transitory
ANTONYMS: everlasting, immortal, imperishable

11. irresolute
(ir ez′ ə lüt)

(*adj.*) unable to make up one's mind, hesitating

In *Hamlet*, the prince is _____**irresolute**_____ about whether to obey his father's ghost or to go on as if nothing has happened.

SYNONYMS: indecisive, vacillating, wavering
ANTONYMS: determined, decisive, unwavering

12. nebulous
(neb′ yə ləs)

(*adj.*) cloudlike, resembling a cloud; cloudy in color, not transparent; vague, confused, indistinct

By the time everyone present had expressed an opinion, the original idea had become somewhat _____**nebulous**_____.

SYNONYMS: hazy, fuzzy, cloudy, vague, murky, opaque, indeterminate
ANTONYMS: definite, distinct, clear, sharply focused

13. novice
(näv′ is)

(*n.*) one who is just a beginner at some activity requiring skill and experience (also used adjectivally)

You must be patient and realize that all his mistakes are typical of a _____**novice**_____ in this line of work.

SYNONYMS: neophyte, tyro, trainee, apprentice
ANTONYMS: veteran, past master, pro, expert

14. penury
(pen′ yə rē)

(*n.*) extreme poverty; barrenness, insufficiency

We never seem to tire of stories of people who go from _____**penury**_____ to sudden wealth.

SYNONYMS: destitution, want, indigence
ANTONYMS: affluence, abundance, luxury, opulence

15. pretentious
(prē ten′ shəs)

(*adj.*) done for show, striving to make a big impression; claiming merit or position unjustifiably; making demands on one's skill or abilities, ambitious

Talking about one's wealth is thought to be _____**pretentious**_____ and in poor taste.

SYNONYMS: inflated, ostentatious, affected
ANTONYMS: unassuming, unaffected, modest

16. recapitulate
(rē ka pich′ ə lāt)

(*v.*) to review a series of facts; to sum up

Don't bother to _____**recapitulate**_____ the plot of the book; instead, tell me if you liked it.

SYNONYMS: review, summarize, sum up, go over

17. resuscitate
(ri səs′ ə tāt)

(*v.*) to revive, bring back to consciousness or existence

We need someone who can _____**resuscitate**_____ our neighborhood council and thus perk up the community spirit.

SYNONYMS: revitalize, reanimate, restore, reactivate

18. slovenly
(sləv′ ən lē)

(*adj.*) untidy, dirty, careless

Her room was in a _____**slovenly**_____ state, and it took her an entire Saturday to clean it.

SYNONYMS: unkempt, slatternly, slipshod, lax
ANTONYMS: neat, tidy, careful, meticulous

19. supposition
(səp ə zish′ ən)

(*n.*) something that is assumed or taken for granted without conclusive evidence

Guided by a _____**supposition**_____ that turned out to be false, they made some disastrous decisions.

SYNONYMS: assumption, presumption, hypothesis

20. torpid
(tôr′ pid)

(*adj.*) inactive, sluggish, dull

We all felt _____**torpid**_____ after that long, dull lecture.

SYNONYMS: sluggish, lethargic, otiose, languid
ANTONYMS: energetic, dynamic, vigorous

Completing the Sentence

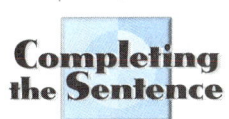

From the words for this unit, choose the one that best completes each of the following sentences. Write the word in the space provided.

1. I don't think I'd call such a(n) _____**egregious**_____ grammatical mistake a minor "slip of the pen."

2. It will mean more to him to gain the approval of the few people who can appreciate his work than to receive the _____**adulation**_____ of the crowd.

3. He holds forth in great detail on what is wrong with our city government, but the remedies he suggests are exceedingly _____**nebulous**_____.

4. Her mind, _____**torpid**_____ as a result of hours of exposure to the bitter cold, was not alert enough to sense the impending danger.

5. Since he was a(n) _____**novice**_____ at bridge, the three veteran players hoped to find someone more suitable to fill out their table.

6. Using the most up-to-date equipment, the firefighters worked tirelessly to _____**resuscitate**_____ the victim of smoke inhalation.

7. The study of history teaches us that a hunger for land, like other kinds of _____**avarice**_____, is the cause of a great many wars.

8. Your brilliant plan is based on one false _____**supposition**_____—that I am willing to work without pay.

9. The _____**penury**_____ she had experienced in her childhood and youth made her keenly aware of the value of money.

10. Sure, it's great to be a big-league ballplayer, but bear in mind that the years of stardom are brief and _____**evanescent**_____.

11. I told my friend that dress for the party was casual, but he showed up looking, in my opinion, just plain _____**slovenly**_____.

12. Does he use all those quotations as a means of clarifying his meaning, or simply as a(n) _____**pretentious**_____ display of his learning?

13. I was so _____**irresolute**_____ about whether to go out for basketball or for swimming that I ended up going out for neither.

14. As her anger slowly _____**abated**_____, she realized that such childish outbursts of emotion would do nothing to help solve her problems.

15. I was impressed by the _____**astute**_____ way our hostess guided the conversation away from topics that might be embarrassing to her guests.

16. Since I truly loathe people who think they are "above the common herd," any form of snobbery is absolutely _____**anathema**_____ to me.

17. Although she tried to _____**equivocate**_____, we insisted on a simple "yes" or "no" answer.

Unit 9 ■ 101

18. When you are **dilatory** in returning a book to the library, you are preventing someone else from using it.
19. After giving us extremely detailed instructions for more than an hour, she briefly **recapitulated** and then sent us out on our assignments.
20. How can you consider him **culpable** when the accident was caused by a landslide that no one could have foreseen or prevented?

Synonyms

Choose the word from this unit that is **the same** or **most nearly the same** in meaning as the **boldface** word or expression in the given phrase. Write the word on the line provided.

1. driven by a limitless **cupidity** — avarice
2. guilty of **flagrant** rudeness — egregious
3. a delicate and **transitory** beauty — evanescent
4. **sum up** your requirements — recapitulate
5. ashamed of a **slipshod** job — slovenly
6. struggle along in **destitution** — penury
7. **revive** the dull party — resuscitate
8. made **sluggish** by the heat — torpid
9. a maddeningly **murky** explanation — nebulous
10. demonstrated **shrewd** understanding — astute
11. a reasonable **presumption** — supposition
12. the clumsiness of a **neophyte** — novice
13. the hurricane's wind **subsided** — abated
14. **vacillating** over a choice — irresolute
15. a last, muttered **imprecation** — anathema

Antonyms

Choose the word from this unit that is **most nearly opposite** in meaning to the **boldface** word or expression in the given phrase. Write the word on the line provided.

16. a **laudable** decision to walk away — culpable
17. ready to meet the **scorn** of the crowd — adulation
18. a **prompt** reckoning of their losses — dilatory
19. **speak plainly** on important subjects — equivocate
20. an **unassuming** house near the city limits — pretentious

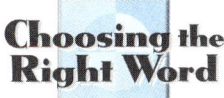

Choosing the Right Word

Circle the **boldface** word that more satisfactorily completes each of the following sentences.

1. What do you think of the concept that when a crime is committed, society is often as (**culpable**, **astute**) as the criminal?

2. The heat in the room, the quiet drone of the fly at the window, and the bright sunlight put me into a (**torpid**, **slovenly**) state.

3. As a result of (**irresolution**, **egregiousness**) when that novel was first submitted, the publishing house lost the biggest best-seller of the year.

4. What she calls her "philosophy of life" seems to me a hodgepodge of childish fallacies and (**nebulous**, **dilatory**) generalizations.

5. As the election drew nearer, the candidates went from reasonable discussion to quarrelsomeness to (**anathematizing**, **recapitulating**) each other.

6. The glory of this perfect spring day sems to be all the more precious because it is so (**torpid**, **evanescent**).

7. Biologists have a theory that every plant or animal in the course of its development (**abates**, **recapitulates**) all the stages of its evolution.

8. Only a (**penury**, **novice**) at golf would have tried to use a driver when hitting into such a strong wind.

9. In everyone's life, a situation may arise that calls for a basic moral choice to be made, without compromise or (**abatement**, **equivocation**).

10. Is it any wonder that a 17-year-old star athlete becomes smug when she receives such (**recapitulation**, **adulation**) from the entire school?

11. Since he is known to be a multimillionaire, it seems almost (**culpable**, **pretentious**) of him, in an inverted sense, to drive around in a small, battered, inexpensive car.

12. He is completely indifferent to wealth and luxurious living; his (**anathema**, **avarice**) is directed instead toward fame and prestige.

13. Sportswriters attribute the success of the pennant-winning team largely to the (**astute**, **evanescent**) managing of old Buck Coakley.

14. In the densely populated and underdeveloped countries we visited, we saw the depths to which people can be reduced by (**penury**, **anathema**).

15. The (**slovenly**, **pretentious**) physical appearance of the report was matched by its careless writing and disorganized content.

16. They say that school spirit at Central High is dead, but I am confident that it can be (**resuscitated**, **equivocated**) if the right methods are used.

17. When the results of her mistakes became public knowledge, she gained a well-deserved reputation for being an (**astute**, **egregious**) blunderer.

18. In playing chess, she deliberately uses (**dilatory**, **nebulous**) tactics to make her opponent impatient and tense.

19. You may be right in your belief that she won't let us use her car, but remember that this is still only a(n) (**anathema**, **supposition**).

20. As soon as the hurricane (**abated**, **equivocated**), rescue teams rushed out to help people in the devastated area.

Vocabulary in Context

*Read the following passage, in which some of the words you have studied in this unit appear in **boldface** type. Then complete each statement given below the passage by circling the letter of the item that is **the same** or **almost the same** in meaning as the highlighted word.*

A Writer Finds Her Way

(Line)

Edith Wharton (1862–1937) faced some interesting hurdles in becoming the important writer of fiction that she aspired to be. She was female at a time when the rich trained their daughters to be pretty hostesses on the lookout to marry wealthy men. Luckily, young Edith and her family lived in Europe for a time, and she was encouraged to read books. From both experiences, (5) she saw that life could be led in other ways.

Back in America, she published some stories and poems that received little attention. Soon she did indeed marry a rich banker. In redecorating their mansion, Wharton discovered that she had (10) **astute** judgment regarding furnishings and, with her designer, published a popular book on interior design. But she was learning that the pleasures of glittering society parties were **evanescent**. It was a prosperous time; Mark (15) Twain had called it "the Gilded Age." New York seemed full of **novice** millionaires. Wharton thought many **egregious** in their **avarice**, in their **pretentious** tastes, and, above all, in their lack of human kindness. (20)

She began to publish stories and novels, witty and powerful, in which she showed high society as it had never been shown before. Wharton used her friend and contemporary Henry James as her literary role model, but, though she shared (25)

Wharton in her early twenties

his thematic concerns, her style was all her own. In 1921 Wharton became the first woman to be awarded the Pulitzer Prize for a novel.

Quite a few of Wharton's stories and novels have been adapted as plays, films, and TV series. Three recent films are "The House of Mirth," "Ethan Frome," and "The Age of Innocence." (30)

1. **Astute** (line 11) most nearly means
   a. profitable
   c. sagacious ✓
   b. expensive
   d. forceful

2. **Evanescent** (line 15) most nearly means
   a. transitory ✓
   c. lasting
   b. deceiving
   d. childish

3. **Novice** (line 17) is best defined as
   a. modest
   c. neophyte ✓
   b. witty
   d. famous

4. The meaning of **egregious** (line 18) is
   a. secret
   c. amusing
   b. blatant ✓
   d. unsolvable

5. **Avarice** (line 18) most nearly means
   a. cupidity ✓
   c. rudeness
   b. curiosity
   d. competitiveness

6. **Pretentious** (line 19) is best defined as
   a. ostentatious ✓
   c. bad
   b. picky
   d. wonderful

REVIEW UNITS 7–9

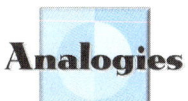

Visit us at www.sadlier-oxford.com for interactive puzzles and games.

Analogies

In each of the following, circle the item that best completes the comparison.

See pages T38–T48 for explanations of answers.

1. laggard is to **dilatory** as
a. (novice is to inexperienced)
b. cadaver is to lively
c. coward is to grandiose
d. bully is to torpid

2. nebulous is to **clarity** as
a. egregious is to significance
b. (torpid is to energy)
c. wit is to brevity
d. hypothetical is to relevance

3. starvation is to **cadaverous** as
a. dieting is to corpulent
b. (gluttony is to obese)
c. austerity is to plump
d. revelry is to squeamish

4. dapper is to **slovenly** as
a. shrewd is to astute
b. punctilious is to scrupulous
c. (modest is to pretentious)
d. beneficent is to urbane

5. redoubtable is to **awe** as
a. (piteous is to compassion)
b. evanescent is to adulation
c. squeamish is to misgiving
d. dispassionate is to enthusiasm

6. traitor is to **perfidy** as
a. dunce is to compassion
b. novice is to penury
c. judge is to restitution
d. (miser is to avarice)

7. consternation is to **disconcert** as
a. adulation is to disavow
b. aspersion is to impugn
c. (astonishment is to dumfound)
d. élan is to debase

8. bovine is to **sluggish** as
a. horsey is to squeamish
b. canine is to corpulent
c. feline is to crass
d. (swinish is to slovenly)

9. egregious is to **mountain** as
a. punctilious is to pigsty
b. grandiose is to foxhole
c. dispassionate is to toadstool
d. (inconsequential is to molehill)

10. aggravate is to **mitigate** as
a. repudiate is to disavow
b. pillage is to betray
c. (intensify is to abate)
d. reprove is to falsify

11. irresolute is to **determination** as
a. ignoble is to simplicity
b. inconsequential is to patience
c. dispassionate is to fairness
d. (intemperate is to moderation)

12. expurgate is to **censor** as
a. impugn is to lie
b. (pillage is to plunder)
c. desecrate is to cheat
d. dissipate is to steal

13. avarice is to **grasping** as
a. humility is to bare-knuckled
b. perfidy is to tight-fisted
c. acrimony is to light-fingered
d. (generosity is to open-handed)

14. idol is to **adulation** as
a. (anathema is to odium)
b. crony is to acrimony
c. novice is to supposition
d. scholar is to consternation

15. crass is to **refinement** as
a. squeamish is to conscience
b. punctilious is to etiquette
c. (ignoble is to honor)
d. stalwart is to decisiveness

16. gauntlet is to **hand** as
a. visor is to leg
b. (helmet is to head)
c. javelin is to arm
d. shield is to foot

17. susceptible is to **immunity** as
a. (vulnerable is to protection)
b. worthy is to exemption
c. culpable is to infraction
d. acrimonious is to dissension

18. palace is to **grandiose** as
a. mansion is to austere
b. shack is to pretentious
c. (hovel is to penurious)
d. cottage is to slovenly

Review Units 7–9 ■ 105

Word Associations

In each of the following groups, circle the word that is best defined or suggested by the given phrase.

1. behavior that is dishonest, selfish, and cowardly
   a. inconsequential   b. vulnerable   **c. ignoble**   d. pretentious
2. regained her citizenship by act of Congress
   a. dissension   **b. restitution**   c. perfidy   d. supposition
3. a tennis player who we know is too good for any of us
   a. austere   b. punctilious   c. grandiose   **d. redoubtable**
4. living in acute want
   a. penury   b. pillage   c. odium   d. adulation
5. provide some comfort for our deep sorrow
   a. debase   b. intemperate   **c. mitigate**   d. equivocate
6. pander to both sides of the issue
   a. prate   **b. equivocate**   c. concoct   d. mitigate
7. testimony that is unemotional and unprejudiced
   a. crass   **b. dispassionate**   c. evanescent   d. culpable
8. "I do not believe that his motives are as unselfish as he pretends."
   a. concoct   b. torpid   c. hypothetical   **d. impugn**
9. a lengthy speech that made few insightful points
   a. resuscitate   b. debase   c. mitigate   **d. prate**
10. demoted me to the second team
    a. disavow   **b. relegate**   c. desecrate   d. abate
11. an event planned out down to the last detail
    a. punctilious   b. squeamish   c. torpid   d. susceptible
12. revive a plan that had been abandoned
    a. resuscitate   b. prate   c. disconcert   d. disavow
13. scold the disruptive audience
    a. pillage   b. concoct   **c. reprove**   d. expurgate
14. someone who has just learned to play bridge
    a. novice   b. consternation   c. corpulent   d. hypothetical
15. a keen perception of that nation's motives
    a. astute   b. corpulent   c. ignoble   d. nebulous
16. "I can't stand the sight of blood!"
    a. dilatory   b. evanescent   **c. squeamish**   d. bovine
17. a conspicuous error
    a. egregious   b. dissipate   c. irresolute   d. slovenly
18. "Now, let's review the main points, one by one."
    a. recapitulate   b. nebulous   c. reprove   d. concoct
19. deserving of blame
    a. intemperate   **b. culpable**   c. dispassionate   d. pretentious
20. a kind act
    a. stalwart   **b. beneficent**   c. odium   d. adulation

REVIEW UNITS 7–9

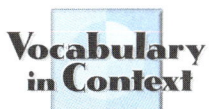

Vocabulary in Context

Read the following passage, in which some of the words you have studied in Units 7–9 appear in **boldface** type. Then complete each statement given below the passage by circling the item that is **the same** or **almost the same** in meaning as the highlighted word.

Between Elephants

(Line)

At first look, the counting of elephants would seem no harder than the counting of slow-moving trucks. But garnering information about the
(5) population density of elephants has proven to be no easy task for scientists from Cornell University. It is believed that half of the close-knit elephant families in Southern Africa live in
(10) dense and tangled forests, and counting these **corpulent** creatures raises several interesting questions.

A full-grown elephant must eat 500 pounds of leaves a day. This means
(15) that family members, though deeply devoted, spend much time apart— far apart, so as not to **pillage** one another's lunch. How do they keep in touch? And how many humans would
(20) it take to hack through a jungle trying to count an unknown number of widely separated subjects?

Fortunately, these royal families of the southern forest do keep in touch,
(25) and not only by the high pitched, trumpet-like blasts we've heard in the movies. Some years ago, scientists discovered that elephants also make sounds too deep for human ears to
(30) detect. These **nebulous** rumblings are not **inconsequential** in meaning. They seem to keep widely scattered family members moving in the same direction and headed toward the same
(35) destination. They also seem to signal comfort to a strayed elephant calf whose elders are coming to retrieve it. While the high pitched call is absorbed by trees or **dissipated** into the air, the
(40) deep call is able to travel much greater distances. Are these low rumblings a sophisticated form of communication, or even language? The Cornell team hopes to find out.

(45) Meanwhile, scientists mount recording devices in many parts of the forest, converting the inaudible elephant sounds to visual signs on computer disks. The team determines
(50) how long each call took to reach each recorder and eventually charts both the number of elephants in an area and the course of their movements.

As for decoding the calls, this
(55) process may be greatly helped when cameras join the recording devices in the forest. Researchers hope that when they **recapitulate** both the "soundless" calls and the visual
(60) records of the elephants' actions, clues will emerge as to what these sociable creatures are saying.

1. The meaning of **corpulent** (line 11) is
a. shy
b. invisible
c. affectionate
(d. portly)

2. Pillage (line 17) most nearly means
(a. loot)
b. step on
c. conceal
d. share

3. The meaning of **nebulous** (line 30) is
(a. vague)
b. strange
c. surprising
d. dangerous

4. Inconsequential (line 31) is best defined as
a. unfriendly
b. pleasant
(c. trivial)
d. frequent

5. Dissipated (line 39) most nearly means
(a. diffused)
b. mixed up
c. enhanced
d. blocked

6. Recapitulate (line 58) is best defined as
(a. repeat)
b. record
c. reorganize
d. redress

Choosing the Right Meaning

Read each sentence carefully. Then circle the item that best completes the statement below the sentence.

See pages T38–T48 for explanations of answers.

A teaspoonful of "Roach-Rout" powder, mixed with a quart of water, produces a nebulous, strong-smelling liquid that is highly toxic to cockroaches. (2)

1. The best meaning for the word **nebulous** in line 2 is
   a. fuzzy   (b. cloudy)   c. vague   d. confused

The grapes from that region produce a full-bodied wine with a decidedly austere flavor—quite the opposite of the smooth, fruity, but somewhat watery vintages characteristic of other parts of the country. (2)

2. The word **austere** in line 1 is used to mean
   a. solemn   b. plain   c. subdued   (d. harsh)

Not surprisingly, the tyrant's much-touted troop of stalwarts, once on the battlefield, proved utter cravens, turning and fleeing at the mere sound of gunfire. (2)

3. In line 1 the word **stalwarts** most nearly means
   (a. valiants)   b. supporters   c. loyalists   d. bullies

Among their many gods the ancient Egyptians were particularly attached to the bovine Hathor, the goddess of love and mirth and the personification of the sky. (2)

4. The best meaning for the word **bovine** in line 2 is
   (a. represented as a cow)   c. sluggish and unresponsive
   b. represented as a sheep   d. dim-witted

"Aurora's rosy fingers gently stroke the sky
And dissipate the inky vestiges of Night." (2)
   (A.E. Glug, "Prating in the Prater," 77–78)

5. The word **dissipate** in line 2 may best be defined as
   a. squander   b. carouse   (c. dispel)   d. waste

Antonyms

In each of the following groups, circle the word or expression that is most nearly the **opposite** of the word in **boldface** type.

1. **adulation**
   a. protection
   b. admiration
   (c. hostility)
   d. patronage

2. **pretentious**
   a. proud
   b. self-respecting
   (c. self-effacing)
   d. unpleasant

3. **inconsequential**
   a. foolish
   (b. significant)
   c. clever
   d. minor

4. **dissension**
   a. fighting
   b. discussion
   c. discipline
   (d. agreement)

5. **austere**
   a. obscure
   (b. self-indulgent)
   c. simple
   d. wholesome

6. **abates**
   a. passes
   (b. intensifies)
   c. rends
   d. occurs

7. **grandiose**
   (a. modest)
   b. intricate
   c. unselfish
   d. far-ranging

8. **debase**
   (a. elevate)
   b. examine
   c. criticize
   d. dress

REVIEW UNITS 7–9

9. beneficial
a. humanitarian
b. harmful ✓
c. well-planned
d. constructive

10. egregious
a. laughable
b. conspicuous
c. unnoticeable ✓
d. unpredictable

11. stalwart
a. uninformed
b. delicate ✓
c. armed
d. redoubtable

12. intemperate
a. restrained ✓
b. bitter
c. eloquent
d. irrational

13. slovenly
a. conspicuous
b. well-groomed ✓
c. unattractive
d. vulgar

14. disavow
a. accept ✓
b. reject
c. pay for
d. be ashamed of

15. culpable
a. meritorious ✓
b. criminal
c. bizarre
d. deliberate

16. disconcert
a. reassure ✓
b. ignore
c. mortify
d. announce

Word Families

A. On the line provided, write the word you have learned in Units 7–9 that is related to each of the following nouns.
EXAMPLE: grandiosity—**grandiose**

1. austerity, austereness — austere
2. recapitulation — recapitulate
3. irresolution, irresoluteness — irresolute
4. evanescence — evanescent
5. culpability — culpable
6. nebula — nebulous
7. astuteness — astute
8. abatement — abate
9. resuscitation, resuscitator — resuscitate
10. torpidity — torpid
11. relegation — relegate
12. dissent, dissenter — dissension
13. dissipation — dissipate
14. beneficence, beneficiary — beneficent

B. On the line provided, write the word you have learned in Units 7–9 that is related to each of the following verbs.
EXAMPLE: dissipate—**dissipation**

15. evanesce — evanescent
16. adulate — adulation
17. suppose — supposition
18. pretend — pretentious
19. hypothecate, hypothesize — hypothetical
20. anathematize — anathema

Two-Word Completions

Circle the pair of words that best complete the meaning of each of the following passages.

See pages T38–T48 for explanations of answers.

1. Though a few lucky "haves" are able to provide themselves with all the comforts of life on a truly _____ scale, the bulk of the people in many third-world countries seem to live like paupers in the most extreme state of _____ and neglect.
   a. egregious . . . avarice
   b. crass . . . dissension
   c. redoubtable . . . perfidy
   d. grandiose . . . penury

2. "Those who circumvent the law are often as _____ as those who actually break it," the lawyer remarked. "The seriousness of such an offense is rarely _____ by the fact that, technically, no crime has been committed."
   a. culpable . . . mitigated
   b. crass . . . abated
   c. vulnerable . . . impugned
   d. susceptible . . . disavowed

3. For a minor _____ of the rules of a hockey game, the offending player is _____ to the penalty box, or "sin bin," for two minutes. For a more serious violation, he is put there for five.
   a. anathema . . . recapitulated
   b. infraction . . . relegated
   c. supposition . . . disavowed
   d. dissension . . . debased

4. A person has to have a strong stomach to work in a funeral parlor or morgue. Handling _____ is definitely not a job for the _____.
   a. modicums . . . slovenly
   b. novices . . . redoubtable
   c. cadavers . . . squeamish
   d. concoctions . . . acrimonious

5. The _____ of history forever attaches itself to the name of Benedict Arnold for his villainous act of _____ during the American Revolution.
   a. acrimony . . . beneficence
   b. odium . . . perfidy
   c. consternation . . . equivocation
   d. anathema . . . restitution

6. In A.D. 267, a band of barbarous Heruli raided the ancient Greek religious center at Delphi. For several days they _____ the town and _____ its temples. Then they rode off, laden with booty.
   a. relegated . . . dissipated
   b. resuscitated . . . debased
   c. pillaged . . . desecrated
   d. disconcerted . . . expurgated

110 ■ Review Units 7–9

REVIEW UNITS 7-9

Building with Classical Roots

mor—form, shape; **the**—to put or place

The root **mor** appears in **amorphous** (page 51), "shapeless, without definite form." The root **the** appears in **anathema** (page 98), meaning "an object of intense dislike." Some other words based on these roots are listed below.

anthropomorphic	**metamorphosis**	**morphology**	**pseudomorph**
epithet	**parenthetical**	**theme**	**thesis**

From the list of words above, choose the one that corresponds to each of the brief definitions below. Write the word in the blank space in the illustrative sentence below the definition.

1. a marked change, a transformation
   The child was amazed by the __metamorphosis__ of the caterpillar.

2. contained in parenthesis; qualifying or explanatory
   She made a few __parenthetical__ remarks before starting her speech.

3. a false, deceptive, or irregular form
   Scientists are seldom fooled by a(n) __pseudomorph__.

4. a topic of discourse or discussion; an idea, point of view
   The __theme__ of the essay was the misuse of technology.

5. the study of form and structure
   Students of biological __morphology__ analyze animal forms.

6. a term used to characterize the nature of a person or thing
   "The King" is the __epithet__ used by Elvis fans for their hero.

7. characterized by the attribution of human qualities to nonhuman phenomena
   Giving pets human names is a common __anthropomorphic__ practice.

8. a proposition that is put forth for argument
   The professor offered evidence in support of her __thesis__.

From the list of words above, choose the one that best completes each of the following sentences. Write the word in the blank space provided.

1. The gods and goddesses of ancient Greece had many __anthropomorphic__ qualities that made them seem human as well as divine.

2. The use of a(n) __epithet__ to briefly describe a character is a common device in epic poems such as *Beowulf*.

3. After taking a course in ____morphology____ in the linguistics department, I had a much better understanding of the formation of words.

4. In order to earn a degree, doctoral candidates are expected to defend their ____theses____ before a committee of tenured faculty.

5. The new drug therapy brought about a medical ____metamorphosis____, restoring the patient to good health in two months.

6. The ____theme____ of last year's presidential campaign was extending economic opportunity to all segments of society.

7. The rock was a(n) ____pseudomorph____, having the crystalline composition of a mineral other than its own.

8. If the ____parenthetical____ information begins to overwhelm the main text in an essay or article, the reader is apt to get bored and confused.

---

*Circle the **boldface** word that more satisfactorily completes each of the following sentences.*

1. Poets dabble in a type of (**metamorphosis**, **anthropomorphism**) when they write of clouds weeping, oceans raging, and winds singing.

2. First, the lecturer outlined the (**parenthesis**, **thesis**) he wished to propose and then presented detailed arguments in support of his idea.

3. The student asked if a chameleon was an example of a (**pseudomorph**, **morphology**), since it changes its appearance but not its form.

4. The English teacher asked the students to hold a class discussion on the (**theme**, **epithet**) of Robert Frost's poem, "Mending Wall."

5. In Shakespeare's *A Midsummer Night's Dream,* the character Bottom undergoes an embarrassing (**metamorphosis**, **anthropomorphism**) when he turns into a donkey.

6. It was hard to follow the writer's train of thought because she did not put her explanatory ideas in (**parentheses**, **theses**).

7. In their (**morphology**, **pseudomorph**) classes, the medical students learned the complete structure of the human body and all its parts.

8. Those (**epithets**, **themes**) that attempt to characterize a person according to a stereotype can be hurtful and unfair.

REVIEW UNITS 7–9

Writer's Challenge

Read the following sentences, paying special attention to the words and phrases underlined. From the words in the box below, find better choices for these underlined words and phrases. Then use these choices to rewrite the sentences.

WORD BANK

acrimonious	(concocted)	(dissension)	novice	slovenly
astute	crass	(grandiose)	perfidy	(stalwart)
(austere)	(culpable)	ignoble	redoubtable	subservient
beneficent	dispassionate	mitigate	resuscitate	(susceptible)

The Mutiny on the Bounty

1. The legendary 1789 mutiny on the British ship *Bounty* was the apparent result of <u>controversy</u> between Captian Bligh and his First Mate Fletcher Christian.
   dissension

2. Many writers and filmmakers have <u>devised</u> their own stories using the imagined and reported events of what happened on the *Bounty* 200 years ago.
   concocted

3. Fletcher Christian was unquestionably <u>deserving of blame</u> of staging the mutiny, but he claimed that he was forced to rebel against Bligh's ruthless tyranny.
   culpable

4. Christian and the mutineers set Bligh and his loyal crewmates adrift in the South Pacific in an open boat. Bligh survived these <u>stern</u> conditions for seven weeks until he finally reached Timor.
   austere

5. It is said that Captain Bligh was <u>lacking in resistance</u> to bouts of cruelty and arrogance, and often verbally attacked his crew.
   susceptible

6. In his defense, Bligh said that Christian made <u>seemingly grand</u> plans to form a society in the South Pacific, and it was for this reason that he mutinied.
   grandiose

7. Following the mutiny on the *Bounty*, Fletcher Christian and eight of his <u>strong supporters</u> fled to tiny and remote Pitcairn Island, where groups of their descendants live on to this day.
   stalwarts

Cumulative Review II

Analogies — In each of the following, circle the item that best completes the comparison.

See pages T38–T48 for explanations of answers.

1. **novice** is to **callow** as
   a. (slob is to slovenly)
   b. crony is to acrimonious
   c. brigand is to unctuous
   d. arbiter is to brusque

2. **evanescent** is to **transient** as
   a. unwieldy is to manageable
   b. austere is to opulent
   c. (immutable is to invariable)
   d. stalwart is to irresolute

3. **marauder** is to **pillage** as
   a. insurgent is to expostulate
   b. (embezzler is to peculate)
   c. archetype is to desecrate
   d. critic is to repudiate

4. **sangfroid** is to **consternation** as
   a. umbrage is to resentment
   b. avarice is to penury
   c. (aplomb is to clumsiness)
   d. ferment is to turmoil

5. **supposition** is to **hypothetical** as
   a. (equivocation is to nebulous)
   b. innuendo is to scathing
   c. gossamer is to inscrutable
   d. precept is to circuitous

6. **assuage** is to **mitigate** as
   a. reverberate is to enjoin
   b. flout is to filch
   c. (concoct is to contrive)
   d. transgress is to relegate

7. **astute** is to **acumen** as
   a. dispassionate is to foresight
   b. fractious is to wisdom
   c. ignoble is to skill
   d. (erudite is to learning)

8. **punctilious** is to **details** as
   a. insular is to possessions
   b. intrinsic is to value
   c. (straitlaced is to morals)
   d. meritorious is to awards

9. **crass** is to **grossness** as
   a. dilatory is to speediness
   b. succinct is to firmness
   c. (vapid is to dullness)
   d. tenuous is to forcefulness

10. **debase** is to **worse** as
    a. permeate is to better
    b. simulate is to worse
    c. (ameliorate is to better)
    d. transcend is to worse

Choosing the Right Meaning — Read each sentence carefully. Then circle the item that best completes the statement below the sentence.

See pages T38–T48 for explanations of answers.

"Americans are proud of the great waterways of our nation," the senator said, "and don't wish to see them desecrated by industrial waste and other contaminants." (2)

1. The word **desecrated** in line 2 is best defined as
   a. profaned   b. exhausted   c. (polluted)   d. misused

"Or is it that some Force, too wise, too strong,
Even for yourselves to conquer or beguile, (2)
Sweeps earth and heaven, and men, and gods along
Like the broad volume of the insurgent Nile?" (4)
   (Matthew Arnold, "Mycerinus," 37–40)

2. The best meaning for the word **insurgent** in line 4 is
   a. muddy   b. (rushing)   c. rebellious   d. salty

114 ■ Cumulative Review II

CUMULATIVE REVIEW II

For years the feelings and experiences of Proust's youth fermented in his brain before
they distilled out in one of the world's greatest works, *A la récherche du temps perdu*. (2)

3. The word **fermented** in line 1 most nearly means
   a. lay dormant   b. cluttered   c. jostled about   (d. brewed)

The views and values typically inculcated by the gang mindset usually precipitate
themselves in various concrete behavior patterns, some of which are decidedly (2)
antisocial.

4. The best meaning for the word **precipitate** in line 1 is
   (a. embody)   b. hurry   c. provoke   d. rain

Two-Word Completions

Circle the pair of words that best complete the meaning of each of the following sentences.

See pages T38–T48 for explanations of answers.

1. To the rather _____ and squeamish Victorians, some of
Shakespeare's language was so objectionable that they would only read his plays in
_____ versions, such as those produced by Thomas Bowdler.
   a. jaded . . . ameliorated   c. erudite . . . disabused
   (b. straitlaced . . . expurgated)   d. crass . . . expedited

2. Since all forms of idolatry were _____ to the Old Testament
prophets, they _____ relentlessly against such abhorrent
practices and castigated the people who persisted in adhering to them.
   a. heinous . . . expurgated   (c. anathema . . . inveighed)
   b. salutary . . . expostulated   d. axiomatic . . . remonstrated

3. Since no salary or _____ of any kind was attached to the job,
election to the Roman consulship eventually became the special _____
of a small group of wealthy nobles, who could afford the privilege of serving their
country for a year without pay.
   a. aura . . . sinecure   c. amnesty . . . proclivity
   b. contraband . . . epitome   (d. compensation . . . prerogative)

4. Like a summer thundershower, whose violence quickly _____
and is forgotten, his fits of temper were intense but _____.
   a. intercedes . . . tenuous   c. resuscitates . . . brusque
   (b. abates . . . transient)   d. dissipates . . . immutable

5. Attila the Hun soon came to be called "the _____ of God" because
the terror and devastation he wrought were looked upon as divine retribution for the
_____ of a wayward and recalcitrant Roman people.
   (a. Scourge . . . transgressions) c. Fetter . . . infringements
   b. Aura . . . infractions   d. Hiatus . . . exhortations

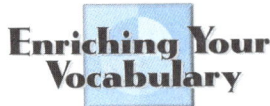

Enriching Your Vocabulary

Read the passage below. Then complete the exercise at the bottom of the page.

Animal Words

With much of the energy of their living counterparts, animal words and expressions scamper, flock, and swim across our language. Sometimes, we juxtapose animal words against human behaviors in order to liken ourselves to animal appearances or behaviors. In other cases, it is the contrast between animal and human behavior that makes these words or phrases relevant. And still other times, these words and phrases have taken on meanings far removed from their origins.

"Hungry as a bear"

Picture a cow lumbering slowly in an open field. She lies down and starts to graze, seemingly without a care in the world. Scientists classify the cow as a bovine. We therefore use *bovine* (Unit 8) to describe someone who is as placid and stolid as a cow. Nicknames or terms of endearment often derive from the playful characteristics of animals. We might call a young child a "pussycat," "bunny rabbit," or "lamb," or a very mischievous child a "monkey." Someone who is very busy can be called a "busy bee" or an "eager beaver."

These expressions are part of our political vocabulary as well. "Hawks" and "doves" have opposing attitudes towards war, but "bulls" and "bears" describe the downward or upward progression of the stock market. An unknown candidate is a "dark horse," and an official soon to leave office is a "lame duck."

In Column A below are 10 more animal phrases. With or without a dictionary, match each phrase with its scientific animal term in Column B.

Column A

- __h__ 1. sly as a fox
- __e__ 2. proud as a lion
- __f__ 3. horsing around
- __d__ 4. catty behavior
- __i__ 5. lovesick puppy
- __j__ 6. bullheaded
- __g__ 7. pigheaded
- __a__ 8. hungry as a bear
- __c__ 9. snake-eyes
- __b__ 10. never cry wolf

Column B

- **a.** ursine
- **b.** lupine
- **c.** ophidian
- **d.** feline
- **e.** leonine
- **f.** equine
- **g.** porcine
- **h.** vulpine
- **i.** canine
- **j.** taurine

🎧 See page T21 for information.

UNIT 10

Note carefully the spelling, pronunciation, part(s) of speech, and definition(s) of each of the following words. Then write the word in the blank space(s) in the illustrative sentence(s) following. Finally, study the lists of synonyms and antonyms given at the end of each entry.

1. accrue
(ə krü′)

(*v.*) to grow or accumulate over time; to happen as a natural result

We allowed the interest to __accrue__ on the account until it turned into a small fortune.

SYNONYMS: collect, accumulate, proceed from
ANTONYMS: dwindle, decrease, diminish, lessen

2. annotation
(an ə tā′ shən)

(*n.*) a critical or explanatory note or comment, especially for a literary work

Laurence Stern's novel *Tristram Shandy* has almost as many __annotations__ as lines of text.

3. bedlam
(bed′ ləm)

(*n.*) a state or scene of uproar and confusion

Is this the same band that caused mob scenes and virtual __bedlam__ on their first tour?

SYNONYMS: commotion, pandemonium, chaos, anarchy
ANTONYMS: peace and quiet, order, tranquility

4. covert
(kō′ vert)

(*adj.*) hidden, disguised, purposefully kept secret; sheltered, secluded; (*n.*) a sheltered place, a hiding place

Napoleon was an expert at making __covert__ preparations to attack unsuspecting opponents.

The bear made a lunge from her __covert__ before we realized she was nearby.

SYNONYMS: (*adj.*) undercover, clandestine, sub-rosa
ANTONYMS: (*adj.*) open, overt, undisguised

5. debonair
(deb ə nâr′)

(*adj.*) pleasant, courteous, lighthearted; smooth and polished in manner and appearance

Quite a few __debonair__ young men asked my cousin to dance.

SYNONYMS: carefree, jaunty, gracious, suave, urbane
ANTONYMS: distraught, agitated, boorish, churlish

6. dun
(dən)

(*v.*) to demand insistently, especially in payment of a debt; (*n.*) a creditor; (*adj.*) dark, dull, drab, dingy

Many of Charles Dickens' characters are __dunned__ by creditors because of their large debts.

SYNONYMS: (*v.*) hound, pester, harass, nag

7. efficacious
(ef ə kā′ shəs)

(*adj.*) effective, producing results
Not the most charming of senators, he nevertheless wielded the most _____efficacious_____ knowledge of statecraft.
SYNONYMS: effectual, efficient, potent, powerful
ANTONYMS: ineffective, worthless, useless

8. equanimity
(ek wə nim′ ə tē)

(*n.*) calmness, composure, refusal to panic
Injustice always sent him into a rage, but he could endure misfortune with _____equanimity_____.
SYNONYMS: tranquility, imperturbability
ANTONYMS: excitability, flappability, agitation

9. fortuitous
(fôr tü′ ə təs)

(*adj.*) accidental, occurring by a happy chance
Due to a _____fortuitous_____ drop in oil prices, the shipping company showed healthy profits for the year.
SYNONYMS: unintentional, unplanned, random, lucky
ANTONYMS: intentional, deliberate, premeditated

10. gist
(jist)

(*n.*) the essential part, main point, or essence
Would the talented fellow who keeps the back row in stitches please repeat the _____gist_____ of what I said?
SYNONYMS: substance, core, nucleus

11. gratuitous
(grə tü′ ə təs)

(*adj.*) freely given; not called for by circumstances, unwarranted
Though she had hoped to leave the lecture early, several members of the audience asked _____gratuitous_____ questions, delaying her by an hour.
SYNONYMS: voluntary, unjustified, uncalled-for
ANTONYMS: justified, warranted

12. imperious
(im pir′ ē əs)

(*adj.*) overbearing, arrogant; seeking to dominate; pressing, compelling
The Wizard of Oz's _____imperious_____ manner failed him when he revealed himself as a fussy little man behind a curtain.
SYNONYMS: domineering, magisterial, urgent, imperative
ANTONYMS: fawning, obsequious, humble, unassuming

13. invective
(in vek′ tiv)

(*n.*) a strong denunciation or condemnation; abusive language; (*adj.*) abusive, vituperative
It was his usual hail of _____invectives_____, a sort of furious, harmless shower that left the air a bit clearer.
As _____invective_____ speeches go, this one displayed originality, vigor, and, here and there, some wit.
SYNONYMS: (*n.*) vituperation, abuse, diatribe, philippic
ANTONYMS: (*n.*) tribute, panegyric, encomium

14. motley
(mät′ lē)

(*adj.*) showing great variety; composed of different elements or many colors; (*n.*) a jester's costume; a jester

Tall and short, thick and young, old and young, we share the family name but are a __motley__ bunch indeed.

To "put on __motley__" is to say what only a king's jester would dare to say.

SYNONYMS: (*adj.*) variegated, heterogeneous, diverse; (*n.*) fool
ANTONYMS: (*adj.*) uniform, homogenous, monochromatic

15. munificent
(myü nif′ ə sənt)

(*adj.*) extremely generous, lavish

Nothing the volunteers said could save the program until our anonymous friend donated a __munificent__ sum.

SYNONYMS: bounteous, liberal
ANTONYMS: stingy, miserly, tightfisted, parsimonious

16. procrastinate
(prə kras′ tə nāt)

(*v.*) to delay, put off until later

We all want to __procrastinate__ when a task is no fun, but some people make delaying a way of life.

SYNONYMS: stall, temporize, dillydally

17. provocative
(prə väk′ ə tiv)

(*adj.*) tending to produce a strong feeling or response; arousing desire or appetite; irritating, annoying

The ideas discussed in the film were so __provocative__ that I thought about them long after I left the theater.

SYNONYMS: stimulating, arousing, vexing, galling
ANTONYMS: dull, insipid, bland, unstimulating

18. recondite
(rek′ ən dīt)

(*adj.*) exceeding ordinary knowledge and understanding

The theories of relativity can seem __recondite__, even for people who are well versed in the sciences.

SYNONYMS: esoteric, arcane, profound, abstruse
ANTONYMS: simple, uncomplicated

19. reprobate
(rep′ rə bāt)

(*n.*) a depraved, vicious, or unprincipled person, scoundrel; (*adj.*) wicked, corrupt, or unprincipled; (*v.*) to disapprove of, condemn

__Reprobates__ are usually more charming, funny, or thrilling in fiction than they are in life.

SYNONYMS: (*n.*) scoundrel, blackguard; (*adj.*) immoral, corrupt
ANTONYMS: (*n.*) saint; (*adj.*) upright, virtuous, moral

20. sedentary
(sed′ ən ter ē)

(*adj.*) characterized by or calling for continued sitting; remaining in one place

She exchanged her __sedentary__ job for a position as a swimming instructor.

SYNONYMS: seated, stationary, static
ANTONYMS: active, peripatetic, migratory

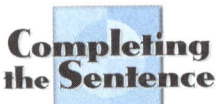

Completing the Sentence

From the words for this unit, choose the one that best completes each of the following sentences. Write the word in the space provided.

1. It will be helpful if you can state the _____gist_____ of his arguments in a few sentences.

2. It is up to the courts to decide how far police authorities may go in making use of _____covert_____ means of surveillance to catch criminals.

3. In view of the fact that I have been driving for many years without having a single accident, his advice on how to handle a car seemed entirely _____gratuitous_____.

4. My opponent's last speech was filled with such wild charges, acrimonious language, and bitter _____invectives_____ that I walked out of the room without even trying to reply.

5. His elegant appearance was matched by the _____debonair_____ ease and polish of his manners.

6. Our meeting seemed at the time to be entirely _____fortuitous_____, but I learned later that it was the result of a careful plan.

7. We have seen her accept victory with grace; now can she face defeat with _____equanimity_____?

8. Think of the great advantages that will _____accrue_____ for all of us if we can carry out a truly effective program to conserve and maintain our natural resources.

9. Anyone who _____procrastinates_____ when the opportunity to make a very profitable deal presents itself is not going to be notably successful in the business world.

10. The kinds of books I enjoy reading range from light and airy comedies to _____recondite_____ studies of social and philosophical problems.

11. As the British writer W. S. Maugham once observed, human nature is a(n) _____motley_____ collection of strengths and weaknesses, foibles and follies.

12. Daily exercise is recommended particularly for people whose occupations are, for the most part, _____sedentary_____.

13. Although their language was deliberately _____provocative_____, I did not allow it to cause me to lose my self-control.

14. The _____munificent_____ gift of the Mellon family made it possible to set up the National Gallery of Art in Washington, D.C.

15. No sooner had the incorrigible old _____reprobate_____ gotten out of jail than he returned to the wicked ways that had landed him there in the first place.

16. _____Bedlam_____ broke out in the meeting hall as the speaker tried vainly to be heard over the angry shouting of the audience.

17. If you resent being _____dunned_____ by tradespeople, why not try paying your bills on time?

18. She is a leader who can command loyalty and instant obedience without resorting to abusive language, threats, or a(n) __imperious__ manner.
19. This research program is entirely devoted to developing a drug that will be __efficacious__ in the treatment of arthritis.
20. Next day, the instructor returned my theme with a number of comments, queries, and other __annotations__ penciled in the margin.

Synonyms

*Choose the word from this unit that is **the same** or **most nearly the same** in meaning as the **boldface** word or expression in the given phrase. Write the word on the line provided.*

1. **pestering** her for overdue payments — dunning
2. added **notes** to the text — annotations
3. the **pandemonium** of a battlefield — bedlam
4. the **core** of her complaint — gist
5. a **diverse** group of volunteers — motley
6. a film with **uncalled-for** scenes of violence — gratuitous
7. an angry **diatribe** — invective
8. another excuse to **stall** — procrastinate
9. an explanation too **esoteric** to follow — recondite
10. a **random** encounter that changed his life — fortuitous
11. a brief and **clandestine** meeting — covert
12. a **suave** greeting from our host — debonair
13. facing the challenge with **imperturbability** — equanimity
14. **stimulating** words that perked things up — provocative
15. a **scoundrel** in her business methods — reprobate

Antonyms

*Choose the word from this unit that is **most nearly opposite** in meaning to the **boldface** word or expression in the given phrase. Write the word on the line provided.*

16. as the level of snow **diminished** — accrued
17. a **humble** plea for order — imperious
18. **tightfisted** when it came to gift-giving — munificent
19. preferred being **active** after dinner — sedentary
20. **worthless** as a cold remedy — efficacious

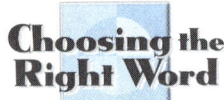

Choosing the Right Word

Circle the **boldface** word that more satisfactorily completes each of the following sentences.

1. Instead of relying on facts and logic, she used all kinds of rhetorical tricks and slashing (**invective**, equanimity) to attack her opponent.
2. I am convinced that some substantial advantages will surely (**accrue**, procrastinate) to me if I complete my college education.
3. It is generally agreed that we urgently need more (**efficacious**, reprobate) methods of handling criminals, both for their own benefit and for that of the public.
4. What good will it do you to (**dun**, procrastinate) me so mercilessly when you know that I am flat broke?
5. This new book is a(n) (imperious, **provocative**) examination of our school system that may upset some of your most cherished ideas about higher education.
6. To bear evils with (invective, **equanimity**) doesn't mean that you should make no effort to correct them.
7. Scientists believe that everything in nature occurs in accordance with invariable laws and that nothing is truly (imperious, **fortuitous**).
8. The scholars who compiled the notes and (**annotations**, provocations) for my portable edition of Chaucer did a superb job of clarifying obscure or puzzling words and passages.
9. The proverb "Make haste slowly" endorses prudence—not (invective, **procrastination**).
10. The crass and (**reprobate**, fortuitous) conduct of those responsible for the scandal deserved public censure.
11. During the war, soldiers assigned to desk jobs were sometimes sarcastically called the "chairbound infantry" or the "(**sedentary**, recondite) commandos."
12. Things were already hectic in our tiny apartment, but when my sister arrived with two very excited dogs, the place was thrown into absolute (**bedlam**, annotation).
13. Instead of that highly involved and (**recondite**, debonair) discussion of the nation's energy needs, why don't you simply tell us what we can do to help solve the problem?
14. My sad story is that after working for three hours in the hot sun cleaning up the yard, I received the (imperious, **munificent**) sum of $1.75.
15. He tried to make it appear that he was speaking in a friendly spirit, but I detected the (recondite, **covert**) malice beneath his "harmless" remarks.
16. Only a genius could have converted such a (**motley**, gratuitous) group of individuals, drawn from all walks of life, into a disciplined and efficient organization.
17. His tone of voice was so (munificent, **imperious**) that I wasn't sure if he was asking me for a loan or demanding payment of tribute.
18. We appreciated the services he furnished (**gratuitously**, debonairly), but we soon came to see that it would have been cheaper to pay for a really professional job.
19. The difficult stage part called for an actress to gradually change from a morose introvert to a(n) (**debonair**, efficacious) charmer during the course of the play.
20. Although they claimed that their summary gave us the (bedlam, **gist**) of the resolution, the fact is that it omitted important details.

Vocabulary in Context

*Read the following passage, in which some of the words you have studied in this unit appear in **boldface** type. Then complete each statement given below the passage by circling the letter of the item that is **the same** or **almost the same** in meaning as the highlighted word.*

Mahalia's Music

(Line)

Together, Mahalia Jackson and gospel music moved through the twentieth century like one irresistible force. Both were formed in African-American churches and influenced by hymns and spirituals. Both rocked to the rhymes of old slave work-songs, and to the preacher's rhythmical call and the congregation's
(5) response. Jackson, born in 1911, was the daughter of a longshoreman who doubled as a barber and preacher, and she grew up in segregated New Orleans in the musical **bedlam** of waterfront streets. There, jazz and blues from phonographs and radios resounded through open windows, and marching bands played
(10) on their way back from burials. On weekends she sang hymns and spirituals at her Baptist church. But from the church down the street she heard a different music. "They had a beat," she remembered, "a powerful beat, a
(15) rhythm we held on to from slavery days, and their music was so strong . . . it used to bring the tears to my eyes." From this same **motley** fabric of music, gospel songs were being pieced together and joyously sung. They
(20) **accrued** in Jackson's memory, and, at the age of sixteen, she took them to Chicago.

Jackson at the Newport Jazz Festival, 1957

While working odd jobs, she began to make a name for herself by singing in African-American churches. Soon, her singing career took off, and she began touring the
(25) country. Always, she refused others' urging that she train her huge contralto voice to sing blues or to sing opera—to sing anything that was more commercial than the gospel she adored. She turned it all down with **equanimity**. Before she died in 1972, she had taken her **munificent** talent to Carnegie Hall, to large recording companies (with whom she could be **imperious** about money), and on tours of Europe and
(30) Asia. She almost always sang gospel, which she called "the songs of hope."

---

1. The meaning of **bedlam** (line 7) is
  a. echoes   (c.) commotion
  b. lessons   d. restfulness

2. Motley (line 17) most nearly means
  a. uniform   c. expensive
  (b.) variegated   d. inexpensive

3. Accrued (line 20) is best defined as
  a. slipped through c. played
  (b.) collected   d. repeated

4. The meaning of **equanimity** (line 27) is
  (a.) tranquility   c. regret
  b. pleasure   d. thoughtlessness

5. Munificent (line 28) most nearly means
  (a.) bounteous   c. overwhelming
  b. expensive   d. well-trained

6. Imperious (line 29) most nearly means
  a. cagey   (c.) domineering
  b. happy   d. timid

UNIT 11

 See page T21 for information.

Note carefully the spelling, pronunciation, part(s) of speech, and definition(s) of each of the following words. Then write the word in the blank space(s) in the illustrative sentence(s) following. Finally, study the lists of synonyms and antonyms given at the end of each entry.

1. **abstemious**
(ab stē′ mē əs)

   (*adj.*) moderate, sparing (as in eating and drinking); characterized by abstinence and self-discipline

   She came from a long line of quiet, thrifty, and _____ **abstemious** _____ farming folk.

   SYNONYMS: temperate, sober, moderate
   ANTONYMS: indulgent, immoderate, intemperate

2. **censurable**
(sen′ shər ə bəl)

   (*adj.*) deserving of blame or correction

   Because he was unaware of what he had done, we decided that his behavior was not _____ **censurable** _____.

   SYNONYMS: blameworthy, discreditable, reprehensible
   ANTONYMS: commendable, laudable, meritorious

3. **contingent**
(kən tin′ jənt)

   (*adj.*) likely but not certain to happen, possible; dependent on uncertain events or conditions; happening by chance; (*n.*) a representative group forming part of a larger body

   _____ **Contingent** _____ on our parents' approval, we plan to take a trip through Alaska next summer.

   The meeting was delayed due to the late arrival of the California _____ **contingent** _____.

   SYNONYMS: (*adj.*) conditional, dependent; (*n.*) a detachment
   ANTONYMS: (*adj.*) independent of, unconnected with, certain

4. **corroborate**
(kə räb′ ə rāt)

   (*v.*) to confirm, make more certain, bolster, substantiate, verify

   He could tell the court where I was and for how long, but he still needed a witness to _____ **corroborate** _____ his statements.

   ANTONYMS: (*adj.*) refute, contradict, undermine, discredit

5. **denizen**
(den′ ə zən)

   (*n.*) an inhabitant, resident; one who frequents a place

   A lover of marine life, she knew all the names of the scaly _____ **denizens** _____ of our lake.

   SYNONYMS: resident, dweller, habitué
   ANTONYMS: alien, outsider, stranger, foreigner

6. **discursive**
(dis kər′ siv)

   (*adj.*) passing aimlessly from one place or subject to another, rambling, roving, nomadic

   Within the _____ **discursive** _____ account of his life, there was a fairly complete history of the whole village.

   SYNONYMS: digressive, diffuse, wandering, episodic
   ANTONYMS: short and to the point, succinct

7. disseminate
(di sem′ ə nāt)

(*v.*) to scatter or spread widely

I decided that it was a bad idea to use my position in order to __disseminate__ my personal views.

SYNONYMS: disperse, publicize, broadcast, circulate
ANTONYMS: bring together, concentrate, muster, conceal, hide

8. dowdy
(daü′ dē)

(*adj.*) poorly dressed, shabby; lacking smartness and good taste

The actor wore __dowdy__ clothing and sunglasses so that no one would recognize him.

SYNONYMS: frumpy, tacky, frowsy, drab
ANTONYMS: chic, stylish, elegant, fashionable

9. florid
(flär′ id)

(*adj.*) highly colored, reddish; excessively ornate, showy

The __florid__ style of architecture in the old part of town was a welcome change from the grim, newer blocks we had seen.

SYNONYMS: flushed, ruddy, flowery, frilly, flamboyant
ANTONYMS: pale, ashen, pallid, sallow, austere, stark

10. foist
(foist)

(*v.*) to impose by fraud; to pass off as worthy or genuine; to bring about by stealth, dishonesty, or coercion

During the 19th century the unscrupulous Jay Gould __foisted__ thousands of worthless railroad shares on an unsuspecting public.

SYNONYMS: pass off, palm off, fob off

11. gauche
(gōsh)

(*adj.*) awkward, lacking in social graces, tactless, clumsy

Though he was sincere when he thanked his guest for having stayed an extra week, his comment was considered __gauche__.

SYNONYMS: inept, uncouth, maladroit
ANTONYMS: adroit, tactful, diplomatic, politic

12. heresy
(her′ ə sē)

(*n.*) an opinion different from accepted belief; the denial of an idea that is generally held sacred

Saving money to accumulate interest seems to be a form of __heresy__ in these days of instant credit.

SYNONYMS: unorthodox belief, heterodoxy
ANTONYM: orthodoxy

13. inculcate
(in′ kəl kāt)

(*v.*) to impress on the mind by repetition, teach persistently and earnestly

It is important to __inculcate__ a healthy respect for authority into army recruits.

SYNONYMS: instill, implant, infuse, ingrain, imbue
ANTONYMS: efface, extirpate, root out

14. palpable
(pal′ pə bəl)

(*adj.*) capable of being touched or felt; easily seen, heard, or recognized

The excitement in the room was almost ____**palpable**____.

SYNONYMS: tangible, plain, obvious, manifest
ANTONYMS: intangible, insubstantial, incorporeal

15. perceptive
(pər sep′ tiv)

(*adj.*) having sympathetic insight or understanding, capable of keen appreciation

His ____**perceptive**____ eye went at once through the roomful of noisy children to the child who was most ill at ease.

SYNONYMS: insightful, discerning, observant
ANTONYMS: dense, thick, obtuse, dim-witted

16. pernicious
(per nish′ əs)

(*adj.*) extremely harmful; deadly, fatal

Night air was once thought to have a ____**pernicious**____ effect on infants who were in poor health.

SYNONYMS: injurious, deleterious, baleful, noxious
ANTONYMS: harmless, innocuous, salutary, salubrious

17. salient
(sāl′ yənt)

(*adj.*) leaping, jumping, or springing forth; prominent, standing out, conspicuous; (*n.*) a projection or bulge, a land form that projects upward or outward

I think the most ____**salient**____ feature of the new plan is its similarity to the old plan.

Our forces occupied a ____**salient**____ that was extremely vulnerable to attack.

SYNONYMS: (*adj.*) striking, notable, protrusive, obvious
ANTONYMS: (*adj.*) inconspicuous, recessive

18. satiate
(*v.*, sā′ shē āt;
adj., sā′ shē it)

(*v.*) to satisfy completely; to fill to excess; (*adj.*) full, satisfied

Nothing will ____**satiate**____ my hunger.

The ____**satiate**____ brown bear had a good sleep after raiding the honey-laden beehives.

SYNONYMS: (*v.*) gratify, cloy, surfeit, gorge
ANTONYMS: (*v.*) starve, deprive entirely of

19. sear
(sir)

(*v.*) to make or become dry and withered; to char or scorch the surface of; to harden or make unfeeling; to parch, dessicate, singe

We wanted to serve grilled vegetables, but I ____**seared**____ them, and they tasted like leather.

20. specious
(spē′ shəs)

(*adj.*) deceptive, apparently good or valid but lacking real merit

Though her resume looked very impressive, her claims of vast experience in the field were ____**specious**____.

SYNONYMS: deceptively plausible, sophistic, casuistic
ANTONYMS: valid, sound, solid, genuine

Completing the Sentence

From the words for this unit, choose the one that best completes each of the following sentences. Write the word in the space provided.

1. Is there any need for me to describe at length the **pernicious** effects of smoking?

2. Though this may not be the smartest-looking blouse I own, I thought to myself, it certainly doesn't make me look **dowdy**!

3. A(n) **salient** characteristic of every great athlete is the ability to perform at maximum efficiency when under extreme pressure.

4. The old fellow did indeed look like a typical **denizen** of the racetrack, as described in Damon Runyon's famous stories.

5. No honest mechanic will try to **foist** inferior replacement parts on his customers.

6. If I had the time, I could point out many flaws in the **specious** arguments you find so impressive.

7. When I referred to her favorite singer as an "untalented, overpaid, and conceited lout," she looked at me in shock, as though I had been guilty of **heresy**.

8. Unless you can produce witnesses to **corroborate** your claim that you stopped at the red light, the mere assertion will have little or no effect on the jury.

9. Psychologists tell us that the years of early childhood are the best time to **inculcate** basic concepts of right and wrong.

10. The stubborn refusal to give me a chance to compete for the scholarship on the same basis as everyone else is a(n) **palpable** injustice to the whole idea of fair play.

11. Among all those pale and sallow people, her highly **florid** complexion stood out like a beacon.

12. I don't like to criticize your behavior, but I feel obliged to tell you that your discourtesy to that confused tourist was highly **censurable**.

13. After the long summer vacation, I was **satiated** with loafing and eager to return to school!

14. The purpose of this program is to **disseminate** throughout the community information about job-training opportunities for young people.

15. It is hard to believe that people coming from such a refined social milieu could be so **gauche** and boorish in their behavior.

16. His talk on world affairs was so disorganized and **discursive** that it left us more confused than ever.

17. Eudora Welty is considered one of the most **perceptive** and insightful American writers of her time.

18. Her good health in old age is due in large part to the __abstemious__ habits of her younger years.
19. Since we wished our group to have some say in the town council's final decision, we sent a small __contingent__ of our most articulate and convincing speakers to the hearings.
20. If you wish to seal in the juices and bring out the flavor of your pot roast, __sear__ it briefly in a hot pan before you put it in the oven.

Synonyms

Choose the word from this unit that is **the same** or **most nearly the same** in meaning as the **boldface** word or expression in the given phrase. Write the word on the line provided.

1. a long and **digressive** novel — discursive
2. **tacky** window decorations — dowdy
3. an impulsive and **awkward** embrace — gauche
4. to **singe** the marshmallows over a campfire — sear
5. **substantiate** an old rumor — corroborate
6. a **flowery** introduction — florid
7. a **tangible** change in the mood of the crowd — palpable
8. few but **discerning** remarks — perceptive
9. **gratify** the appetite for gossip — satiate
10. an **habitué** of the public library — denizen
11. **broadcast** the child's baby pictures — disseminate
12. **implant** a strong dislike — inculcate
13. ignored the **injurious** rumors — pernicious
14. **palm off** fake diamonds — foist
15. a **temperate** use of such words — abstemious

Antonyms

Choose the word from this unit that is **most nearly opposite** in meaning to the **boldface** word or expression in the given phrase. Write the word on the line provided.

16. judged the actions as **commendable** — censurable
17. a steadfast commitment to **orthodoxy** — heresy
18. an **inconspicuous** feature — salient
19. payment **independent of** need — contingent on
20. **genuine** grounds for complaint — specious

Choosing the Right Word

Circle the **boldface** word that more satisfactorily completes each of the following sentences.

1. In a series of (**searing**, contingent) attacks now known as the *Philippics,* Cicero launched his entire battery of political invective against the hapless Mark Anthony.

2. The most tragic aspect of a forest fire is its destructive effects on the innumerable plant and animal (**denizens**, heresies) of that environment.

3. Some English queens were strikingly elegant and imposing figures; others were somewhat (specious, **dowdy**) and unprepossessing.

4. Modern nutritionists emphasize that there is a(n) (palpable, **abstemious**) difference between "eating to live" and "living to eat."

5. Let's not allow them to (**foist**, satiate) on us ideas and programs that have been proved failures in other countries!

6. The study of history teaches us that many ideas regarded as (**heresies**, disseminations) by one generation are accepted as sound and orthodox by the next.

7. No doubt his efforts to advance his own interests were (**censurable**, florid), but let's try to keep a sense of proportion and not condemn him too much.

8. Before we start out to (**inculcate**, foist) certain principles in our young people, let's be very sure that these principles are truly desirable for them and their society.

9. Her (perceptive, **florid**) writing style, abounding in adjectives and fancy metaphors, is far from suitable for factual newspaper stories.

10. Although the Declaration of Independence was framed only to justify a revolution in the British colonies in North America, its ideas and ideals have been (**disseminated**, seared) throughout the world.

11. We are most likely to fall victim to (discursive, **specious**) reasoning when we have an emotional desire to believe what we are being told.

12. All the available evidence (**corroborates**, foists) my theory that the theft was planned by someone familiar with the layout of the house.

13. Children are often remarkably (discursive, **perceptive**) in understanding how adults feel about them.

14. Out of all the endless flow of dull verbiage in that long lecture, we could recognize only two or three (gauche, **salient**) points.

15. As the Scottish poet Robert Burns aptly suggests, even the best laid plans are often entirely (palpable, **contingent**) on events over which we have no earthly control.

16. Although the essays are highly (**discursive**, dowdy), covering a wide range of topics, they are written with such clarity and grace that they are easy to follow.

17. She was so (palpable, **abstemious**) that she extended her self-control even to her beloved books, and read them no more than an hour each day.

18. Though I rather like the better TV game shows, I find that after a certain point, I'm (**satiated**, inculcated) and ready for more substantial fare.

19. He thought he was being witty and charming, but I regard his conduct at the party as altogether (abstemious, **gauche**).

20. The more we studied the drug problem, the more we became aware of its (florid, **pernicious**) influence on the American people today.

Vocabulary in Context

*Read the following passage, in which some of the words you have studied in this unit appear in **boldface** type. Then complete each statement given below the passage by circling the letter of the item that is **the same** or **almost the same** in meaning as the highlighted word.*

War at Home
(Line)

We often hear that the United States was the only great nation never to be invaded during the Second World War (1939–1945). All the same, the war transformed American life on the Home Front. Once rationing limited the amount of meat, sugar, coffee, butter, and canned goods they could buy each month, families often ate **abstemious** meals. Blue and red ration coupons, **disseminated** to households, had (5) to be counted into grocers' hands along with the money for a given product. If there were no coupons, the families did not receive goods until the next month. In addition, ships transporting foreign goods like coffee and sugar were often turned over to the military. The tin in tin cans was made into weapons. Even shoes were rationed, as (10) leather was needed for military gear.

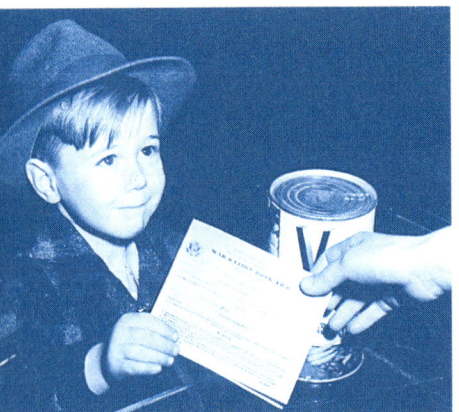

School boy using ration coupons, 1943

On the roads gas, too, was rationed. No new cars were made, and the family car became **dowdy**. Ordinary motorists could buy between three and five gallons a week, (15) **contingent** on supplies. Commuters could buy slightly more, and only farmers, the police, the clergy, and some politicians could buy as much gasoline as they wanted. Trains were crammed full of commuters, (20) while aging cars rested at home.

It is also somewhat **specious** to say that the U.S. was never bombed or invaded. In 1942 Nazi Germany landed four agents on Long Island and four more on the Florida coast. Trained and equipped to blow up (25) factories, these **gauche** invaders were picked up in no time, secretly tried, and punished. Wartime secrecy kept their story quiet, just as it silenced the story of the Japanese plane that failed to set fire to West Coast forests and the fleet of balloon-borne time bombs with which the Japanese started some random fires. And so, though no battles were fought on American soil during WWII, rationing and the threat of (30) invasion forever changed the American perspective of the world beyond its shores.

---

1. The meaning of **abstemious** (line 5) is
   a. amazing
   b. huge
   c. temperate ⓒ
   d. bizarre

2. **Disseminated** (line 5) most nearly means
   a. sold
   b. advertised
   c. circulated ⓒ
   d. e-mailed

3. **Dowdy** (line 14) is best defined as
   a. valuable
   b. shabby ⓑ
   c. crowded
   d. beloved

4. The meaning of **contingent** (line 16) is
   a. conditional ⓐ
   b. cheating
   c. regardless of
   d. imposing

5. **Specious** (line 22) most nearly means
   a. deceptive ⓐ
   b. ridiculous
   c. bizarre
   d. fussy

6. **Gauche** (line 26) is best defined as
   a. sneaky
   b. dangerous
   c. frightened
   d. maladroit ⓓ

See page T21 for information.

UNIT 12

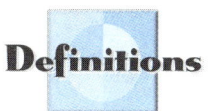 **Definitions**

Note carefully the spelling, pronunciation, part(s) of speech, and definition(s) of each of the following words. Then write the word in the blank space(s) in the illustrative sentence(s) following. Finally, study the lists of synonyms and antonyms given at the end of each entry.

1. absolve
(ab zälv′)

(*v.*) to clear from blame, responsibility, or guilt

They assumed that their alibi would __absolve__ them of suspicion.

SYNONYMS: acquit, exonerate, vindicate, excuse, pardon
ANTONYMS: condemn, convict, incriminate, inculpate

2. caricature
(kar′ i kə chür)

(*n.*) a representation (especially a drawing) in which the subject's characteristic features are deliberately exaggerated; (*v.*) to present someone or something in a deliberately distorted way

What began as a hasty newspaper __caricature__ soon turned up on coffee mugs, T-shirts, and sweatshirts.

The satiric television program __caricatured__ the movie star and made him seem more clumsy than he really was.

SYNONYMS: (*n.*) cartoon, burlesque, parody, lampoon

3. clangor
(klang′ ər)

(*n.*) a loud ringing sound; (*v.*) to make a loud ringing noise

For more than a century, American grade schools summoned children to school with the __clangor__ of a bell.

SYNONYMS: (*n.*) din, clamor, uproar
ANTONYMS: (*n.*) silence, stillness, peace and quiet

4. contiguous
(kən tig′ yü əs)

(*adj.*) side by side, touching; near; adjacent in time

Trouble arose over who should control the weeds and bushes that rioted in the lot __contiguous__ to ours.

SYNONYMS: adjoining, abutting, next door to
ANTONYMS: detached, apart, distant, remote

5. cupidity
(kyü pid′ ə tē)

(*n.*) an eager desire for something; greed

You say that these catalogue prices show the quality of the goods, but I say they show the seller's __cupidity__.

SYNONYMS: avarice, rapacity, craving, lust
ANTONYMS: generosity, contentment, satiation, gratification

6. deleterious
(del ə tir′ ē əs)

(*adj.*) harmful, injurious

Wishing can give zest and purpose to anyone's life, but wishful thinking can have a __deleterious__ effect.

SYNONYMS: detrimental, destructive, pernicious, damaging
ANTONYMS: helpful, beneficial, harmless, innocuous

7. **enhance**
(en hans′)
(v.) to raise to a higher degree; to increase the value or desirability of

She sanded and varnished the old table in order to _____enhance_____ its appearance and value.

SYNONYMS: improve, magnify, heighten, elevate
ANTONYMS: diminish, reduce, lessen, degrade

8. **enthrall**
(en thrôl′)
(v.) to captivate, charm, hold spellbound; to enslave; to imprison

All the critics were _____enthralled_____ by the performance and wrote rave reviews.

SYNONYMS: fascinate, enchant, attract, bewitch
ANTONYMS: bore to tears, repel, put someone off

9. **extenuate**
(ek sten′ yü āt)
(v.) to lessen the seriousness or magnitude of an offense by making partial excuses

Because hunger caused the novel's young hero to steal the bread, the jurors believed that the crime had been committed under _____extenuating_____ circumstances.

SYNONYMS: moderate, mitigate, diminish, downplay
ANTONYMS: intensify, aggravate, worsen, exacerbate

10. **implicit**
(im plis′ it)
(adj.) implied or understood though unexpressed; without doubts or reservations, unquestioning; potentially contained in

Though she never said so, it was _____implicit_____ that she did not like to have long conversations before her morning coffee.

SYNONYMS: inferred, tacit, unspoken, unconditional
ANTONYMS: explicit, expressed, stated, revealed

11. **incisive**
(in sī′ siv)
(adj.) sharp, keen, penetrating (with a suggestion of decisiveness and effectiveness)

I am truly thankful for your _____incisive_____ remarks about my report.

SYNONYMS: acute, cutting, perceptive, trenchant

12. **ostentatious**
(äs ten tā′ shəs)
(adj.) marked by conspicuous or pretentious display, showy

The inside of the restaurant was so _____ostentatious_____ that the meager meal, when it came, seemed only a hasty afterthought.

SYNONYMS: flashy, overdone, affected, flamboyant
ANTONYMS: modest, plain, simple, demure, retiring

13. **paragon**
(par′ ə gän)
(n.) a model of excellence or perfection

I may not be a _____paragon_____ of scholarship, but I do try my best.

SYNONYMS: exemplar, ideal, paradigm, model, good example

14. paraphrase
(par' ə frāz)

(v.) to restate in other words; (n.) a statement that presents a given idea in new language

You can _____paraphrase_____ "The Gettysburg Address," but in doing so you will diminish its force.

SYNONYMS: (v.) reword, rephrase; (n.) a rendition, version
ANTONYMS: (v.) repeat verbatim, duplicate, quote

15. politic
(päl' ə tik)

(adj.) prudent, shrewdly conceived and developed; artful, expedient

In your angry state I think it would be _____politic_____ to say nothing, at least until you have calmed down.

SYNONYMS: tactful, diplomatic, judicious, circumspect
ANTONYMS: unwise, injudicious, imprudent, rash

16. prosaic
(prō zā' ik)

(adj.) dull, lacking in distinction and originality; matter-of-fact, straightforward; characteristic of prose, not poetic

I remember his singing voice as being on key and clear but also _____prosaic_____.

SYNONYMS: commonplace, humdrum, literal, pedestrian
ANTONYMS: remarkable, distinctive, poetic, inspired

17. redundant
(ri dən' dənt)

(adj.) extra, excess, more than is needed; wordy, repetitive; profuse, lush

Some _____redundant_____ expressions, such as "hollow tubing," are considered an acceptable part of the English language.

SYNONYMS: unnecessary, superfluous, verbose, prolix
ANTONYMS: succinct, terse, laconic, scarce, inadequate

18. sanctimonious
(saŋk tə mō' nē əs)

(adj.) making a show of virtue or righteousness; hypocritically moralistic or pious, self-righteous, canting, holier-than-thou

Cautionary tales that take on a _____sanctimonious_____ tone often achieve the opposite of the desired result.

ANTONYMS: heartfelt, sincere, humble

19. scintillating
(sin' tə lāt iŋ)

(adj., part.) sparkling, twinkling, exceptionally brilliant (applied to mental or personal qualities)

She was known for her _____scintillating_____ conversation.

SYNONYMS: stimulating, lively, glittering, flashing
ANTONYMS: dull, boring, insipid, flat, tame, vapid

20. winsome
(win' səm)

(adj.) charming, attractive, pleasing (often suggesting a childlike charm and innocence)

When my little brother wanted something badly, he became as _____winsome_____ as a puppy.

SYNONYMS: winning, engaging, delightful, prepossessing
ANTONYMS: unattractive, unappealing, repulsive

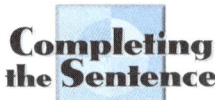

Completing the Sentence

From the words for this unit, choose the one that best completes each of the following sentences. Write the word in the space provided.

1. Her new hairstyle greatly _____enhances_____ her appearance.

2. The jury may have found him not guilty, but the "court of public opinion" will never _____absolve_____ him of responsibility for the crime.

3. Detective stories seem to _____enthrall_____ her to such a degree that she reads virtually nothing else.

4. Until he rose to speak, the meeting had been dull, but he immediately enlivened it with his _____scintillating_____ wit.

5. We resented his _____sanctimonious_____ self-assurance that he was morally superior to everyone else.

6. She did her work so quietly that it took us time to realize that she was a veritable _____paragon_____ of efficiency and diligence.

7. His highly technical discussion will have to be _____paraphrased_____ if it is to be understood by most readers.

8. How can anyone be so foolish as to develop a smoking habit when it has been proven that cigarettes are _____deleterious_____ to health?

9. Since we had been told the new TV series was original and witty, we were disappointed by the obvious and _____prosaic_____ situation comedy that unfolded on our screen.

10. The fact that he had hungry children at home does not justify what he did, but it does _____extenuate_____ his crime.

11. With that one _____incisive_____ comment, she brought an end to all the aimless talk and directed our attention to the real problem facing us.

12. "Evening dress is far too _____ostentatious_____ for such an informal occasion," I thought to myself as I tried to decide what to wear that night.

13. In most contracts there are _____implicit_____ duties and obligations that must be fulfilled even though they aren't expressed in so many words.

14. There are some situations in life when it is _____politic_____ to remain quiet and wait for a better opportunity to assert yourself.

15. To characterize the literary style of Edgar Allan Poe as "unique and one of a kind" is certainly _____redundant_____.

16. The _____clangor_____ of the fire bells as they echoed through the night filled our hearts with terror.

17. His long nose and prominent teeth give the candidate the kind of face that cartoonists love to _____caricature_____.

18. Marie's engaging personality and charming manner make her quite ____winsome____.

19. Since the gym is ____contiguous____ to the library, it is easy for me to shift from academic to athletic activities.

20. His normal desire for financial security was eventually distorted into a boundless ____cupidity____.

Synonyms

Choose the word from this unit that is **the same** or **most nearly the same** in meaning as the **boldface** word or expression in the given phrase. Write the word on the line provided.

1. a **din** of cowbells from the bleachers — clangor
2. to **improve** the sound of the chorus — enhance
3. an **exemplar** of team spirit — paragon
4. a **trenchant** report — incisive
5. a **lively** play of wit — scintillating
6. the **commonplace** routines of housework — prosaic
7. a **parody** of his behavior — caricature
8. a book with the power to **enchant** — enthrall
9. a **hypocritical** accusation — sanctimonious
10. an **engaging** smile — winsome
11. a **flashy** new car — ostentatious
12. a **detrimental** effect on the harvest — deleterious
13. an **unspoken** but lifelong loyalty — implicit
14. a **judicious** decision — politic
15. bought lots that were **adjoining** — contiguous

Antonyms

Choose the word from this unit that is **most nearly opposite** in meaning to the **boldface** word or expression in the given phrase. Write the word on the line provided.

16. never exhibited **generosity** — cupidity
17. evidence to **incriminate** — absolve
18. charges **aggravated** by circumstances — extenuated
19. issuing **succinct** instructions — redundant
20. to **quote** her memorable words — paraphrase

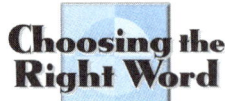

Choosing the Right Word

Circle the **boldface** word that more satisfactorily completes each of the following sentences.

1. What we do now to remedy the evils in our society will determine whether or not we are to be (**absolved**, **paraphrased**) of blame for the injustices of the past.
2. Is it logical to conclude that because this substance has had a (**prosaic**, **deleterious**) effect on some test animals, it is not at all safe for human consumption?
3. When he demanded that I immediately "return back" the money I owed him, I found him not merely unpleasant but (**redundant**, **winsome**).
4. I will try to tell the story in a balanced way, without either exaggerating or (**extenuating**, **scintilating**) his responsibility for those sad events.
5. It is hardly (**politic**, **clangorous**) for someone who hopes to win a popularity contest to go about making such brutally frank remarks.
6. Words about "tolerance" are empty and (**sanctimonious**, **contiguous**) when they come from one who has shown no concern about civil liberties.
7. As long as we are (**enthralled**, **extenuated**) by the idea that it is possible to get something for nothing, we will not be able to come up with a sound economic program.
8. "In seeking to discredit me," I replied, "my opponent has deliberately (**caricatured**, **paraphrased**) my ideas, making them seem simplistic and unrealistic."
9. She delivered her lines with such artistry and verve that she made the rather commonplace dialogue seem (**scintillating**, **deleterious**).
10. In the Lincoln-Douglas debates, Lincoln asked a few (**incisive**, **prosaic**) questions that showed up the fatal weaknesses in his opponent's position.
11. The aspiring salesperson stood in front of the mirror for hours, practicing a (**winsome**, **redundant**) smile.
12. A fresh coat of paint and some attention to the lawn would greatly (**enhance**, **absolve**) the appearance of our bungalow.
13. He was the type of officer who expected (**ostentatious**, **implicit**) obedience from the troops he commanded. When he gave an order, he assumed it would be carried out.
14. She tried to convince me that the proposed advertisement would be "dynamic" and a "real eye-catcher," but I found it utterly (**politic**, **prosaic**).
15. I realized I was being kept awake not by the (**paragon**, **clangor**) of the city traffic but by a gnawing fear that I had done the wrong thing.
16. The Gettysburg Address is so concise, so lucid, and so beautiful, that it would be folly to attempt to (**paraphrase**, **enthrall**) it.
17. My parents set up my older brother as such a (**caricature**, **paragon**) that I despaired of ever being able to follow in his footsteps.
18. Isn't it rather (**ostentatious**, **redundant**) to wear a Phi Beta Kappa key on a chain around your neck?
19. We wanted to find a house that was near that of my parents, but not (**contiguous**, **prosaic**) to it.
20. The rumors of "easy money" and "lush profits" to be made in the stock market aroused the (**clangor**, **cupidity**) of many small investors.

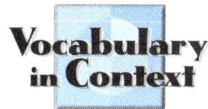

Vocabulary in Context

*Read the following passage, in which some of the words you have studied in this unit appear in **boldface** type. Then complete each statement given below the passage by circling the letter of the item that is **the same** or **almost the same** in meaning as the highlighted word.*

Truffles

(Line)

The truffle, considered by gourmets to be a **paragon** among foods, grows underground but cannot be planted, is hunted by dogs and fed to royalty, costs a small fortune, and looks like a battered golf ball. No less famous for its mystery than for its flavor, the truffle has **enthralled**
(5) cooks and growers of food since 1800 B.C. Because it reproduces by spores that cannot be seen by the naked eye, people once thought that truffles only grew in soil struck by
(10) lightning. Today experts tell a less **ostentatious** story; they say that white truffles can be found near small oak trees in chalky soil in northern Italy and black ones in the South of
(15) France in similar patches of oaks.

Like a mushroom, the truffle is a fungus—but one that grows under the ground, sometimes inches deep. Unlike a carrot or radish, it
(20) sends up no **winsome** little plume of

Man and pet harvesting truffles in France

green leaves to announce its location. Only its scent gives the truffle away, and that scent is much too faint for a human to perceive. Pigs have long been said to lead hunters to the treasure —but pigs will in fact eat the truffles they find. Trained dogs are content to track them, then leave them for the hunter
(25) to collect.

Though many parts of the world boast of local truffles, cooks find most too mundane to eat, let alone hunt. By contrast, the French black truffle has been called "the black diamond." American chefs cook it in sauces made with eggs, cream, and cheese, and sometimes add it to pastries. The white they cut in little
(30) pieces and sprinkle on finished dishes to **enhance** them. One experienced diner, when asked how he preferred his truffles, gave an **incisive** reply: "In great quantity."

---

1. The meaning of **paragon** (line 1) is
 a. most fattening   c. prettiest
 b. most nutritious (d.) ideal

2. Enthralled (line 4) most nearly means
 a. repulsed   c. defeated
 (b.) bewitched d. distressed

3. Ostentatious (line 11) is best defined as
 a. hackneyed   c. frightening
 (b.) flamboyant d. foolish

4. The meaning of **winsome** (line 20) is
 a. waving   c. victorious
 b. tangled   (d.) delightful

5. Enhance (line 30) most nearly means
 a. cover   c. disguise
 (b.) improve d. cool

6. Incisive (line 31) is best defined as
 a. unpleasant (c.) trenchant
 b. puzzling   d. greedy

Review Units 10–12

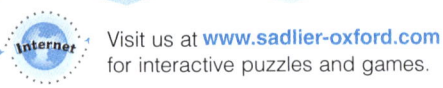

Visit us at www.sadlier-oxford.com
for interactive puzzles and games.

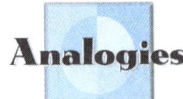

Analogies — In each of the following, circle the item that best completes the comparison.

See pages T38–T48 for explanations of answers.

1. **palpable** is to **feel** as
   a. **visible is to see**
   b. audible is to listen
   c. tangible is to smell
   d. edible is to taste

2. **dowdy** is to **appearance** as
   a. imperious is to background
   b. **gauche is to behavior**
   c. sedentary is to beauty
   d. debonair is to build

3. **hypocrite** is to **sanctimonious** as
   a. **showoff is to ostentatious**
   b. glutton is to abstemious
   c. pauper is to munificent
   d. drunkard is to winsome

4. **tirade** is to **invective** as
   a. paraphrase is to provocation
   b. **panegyric is to praise**
   c. encomium is to gist
   d. harangue is to annotation

5. **prosaic** is to **scintillating** as
   a. repetitive is to redundant
   b. culpable is to censurable
   c. arcane is to recondite
   d. **homely is to winsome**

6. **bedlam** is to **raucous** as
   a. clangor is to contiguous
   b. contingent is to implicit
   c. conflagration is to sonorous
   d. **chaos is to turbulent**

7. **caricature** is to **drawing** as
   a. **parody is to writing**
   b. opera is to singing
   c. jeté is to dancing
   d. palette is to painting

8. **enhance** is to **more** as
   a. accrue is to less
   b. absolve is to more
   c. **extenuate is to less**
   d. dun is to more

9. **incisive** is to **cut** as
   a. enthralling is to burn
   b. **searing is to scorch**
   c. corroborating is to singe
   d. procrastinating is to char

10. **jester** is to **motley** as
    a. shepherd is to crook
    b. soldier is to rifle
    c. tailor is to clothing
    d. **ballerina is to tutu**

11. **enhance** is to **exacerbate** as
    a. ostentatious is to opulent
    b. **absolve is to indict**
    c. paragon is to redundant
    d. incisive is to perceptive

12. **efficacious** is to **favorable** as
    a. fortuitous is to unfavorable
    b. pernicious is to favorable
    c. **deleterious is to unfavorable**
    d. ostentatious is to favorable

13. **miser** is to **cupidity** as
    a. humanitarian is to greed
    b. **stoic is to equanimity**
    c. saint is to heresy
    d. curmudgeon is to valor

14. **perceptive** is to **insight** as
    a. salient is to force
    b. specious is to nutrition
    c. obtuse is to intelligence
    d. **adroit is to skill**

15. **inculcate** is to **in** as
    a. instill is to out
    b. disseminate is to in
    c. **efface is to out**
    d. absolve is to in

16. **florid** is to **complexion** as
    a. discursive is to appearance
    b. gratuitous is to bearing
    c. **ornate is to style**
    d. motley is to manner

17. **paragon** is to **exemplary** as
    a. denizen is to extinct
    b. **reprobate is to incorrigible**
    c. heretic is to orthodox
    d. klutz is to politic

18. **dunned** is to **annoyance** as
    a. **absolved is to relief**
    b. enthralled is to puzzlement
    c. satiated is to interest
    d. enhanced is to contentment

REVIEW UNITS 10-12

Word Associations

In each of the following groups, circle the word that is best defined or suggested by the given phrase.

1. confirm a report
   a. satiate   b. foist   c. accrue   **d. corroborate**
2. the ringing of the fire alarm
   a. invective   **b. clangor**   c. dun   d. bedlam
3. a tendency to delay
   a. pernicious   b. satiate   c. enthrall   **d. procrastinate**
4. a courteous and gracious host
   a. debonair   b. gauche   c. munificent   d. discursive
5. a harmful effect
   a. deleterious   b. motley   c. palpable   d. winsome
6. an abstruse report
   a. florid   b. covert   **c. recondite**   d. abstemious
7. a prudent decision
   a. politic   b. gauche   c. debonair   d. fortuitous
8. broadcast the news
   a. disseminate   b. inculcate   c. foist   d. satiate
9. passing rhinestones off as diamonds
   a. accrue   **b. foist**   c. extenuate   d. sear
10. instill a desire for success
    a. procrastinate   **b. inculcate**   c. imperious   d. contingent
11. a representative group
    a. salient   b. gratuitous   c. imperious   **d. contingent**
12. a wordy expression
    a. motley   **b. redundant**   c. incisive   d. efficacious
13. effective remedies
    a. specious   b. deleterious   **c. efficacious**   d. pernicious
14. the gist of the story
    a. paragon   **b. paraphrase**   c. heresy   d. politic
15. gaudy display of opulence
    a. winsome   b. provocative   c. scintillating   **d. ostentatious**
16. an unstated agreement
    a. gratuitous   **b. implicit**   c. covert   d. redundant
17. a meager meal
    a. satiate   **b. abstemious**   c. winsome   d. fortuitous
18. collect over time
    a. absolve   b. procrastinate   c. dun   **d. accrue**
19. unwarranted violence on television
    a. censurable   **b. gratuitous**   c. provocative   d. dowdy
20. harmful rumors that caused much pain
    a. scintillating   **b. pernicious**   c. invective   d. reprobate

Vocabulary in Context

*Read the following passage, in which some of the words you have studied in Units 10–12 appear in **boldface** type. Then complete each statement given below the passage by circling the item that is **the same** or **almost the same** in meaning as the highlighted word.*

Mapping It Out

(Line)

Modern maps record **palpable** scientific measurements, but in the Middle Ages maps drew upon the excited and imprecise recollections of
(5) hired explorers. Employed to aggrandize a nation's wealth by finding new colonies and better trade routes to the riches of India, these explorers were driven more by their
(10) clients' **cupidity** than by a thirst for scientific knowledge. Thus, they came to some **gratuitous** assumptions and made some big mistakes.

Most commonly, explorers
(15) misjudged the size and shape of North and South America while searching the seas for Cathay. So intent was Columbus on reaching the East that he thought that Cuba, when
(20) he saw it, was actually Japan and that the coast of Central America was the shore of southern Asia. In 1525 Giovanni da Verrazano, sailing south of New England, "discovered"
(25) and named the "Sea of Verrazano"— which cartographers dutifully included on their maps for the next hundred years. This grand waterway led, said Verrazano, to India and
(30) China; more likely it was the wet doorstep to North Carolina.

Eventually, rough sizes and shapes for North and South America— **caricatures**, really—were determined.
(35) But the ocean beyond them continued to be overlooked by European eyes fastened on Asia; for years the Pacific was mapped as a narrow strait between North America and Japan.
(40) Harder to explain is why California changed from being part of the mainland on some maps to an island on others.

Juan Ponce de León, discovering
(45) Florida in 1513, reported that it, too, was an island (this was clearly not **corroborated** by the facts). But he didn't call it "land of flowers" (*flores* in Spanish), as some current **denizens**
(50) of the state might suppose. He found it on Easter, which the Spaniards called Pascua Florida for the flowers displayed in their churches. Ponce was honoring Easter.

(55) Very old place names can also be confusing. North and South Carolina, once a single British colony, pay tribute to no one named Caroline. Instead, they honor King Charles I of
(60) England, who set up the colony and whose name in Latin was Carolus.

---

1. Palpable (line 1) most nearly means
a. tangible   c. odd
b. large   d. puzzling

2. The meaning of **cupidity** (line 10) is
a. thrift   c. avarice
b. affection   d. stupidity

3. Gratuitous (line 12) is best defined as
a. leafy   c. welcoming
b. beautiful   d. uncalled-for

4. The meaning of **caricatures** (line 34) is
a. cartoons   c. maps
b. copies   d. photographs

5. Corroborated (line 47) most nearly means
a. contradicted   c. reported
b. substantiated   d. described

6. Denizens (line 49) is best defined as
a. critics   c. readers
b. students   d. habitués

REVIEW UNITS 10–12

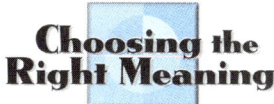
Choosing the Right Meaning

Read each sentence carefully. Then circle the item that best completes the statement below the sentence.

See pages T38–T48 for explanations of answers.

Though the enemy line held on the flanks, it fell back in the center, producing a large salient, of which our commander was quick to take advantage.

1. In line 2 the word **salient** may best be defined as
   a. bulge (circled)   b. gap   c. bottleneck   d. spread

"Alas! 'tis true I have gone here and there,
And made myself a motley to the view,
Gor'd mine own thoughts, sold cheap what is most dear
Made old offenses of affections new."
    (Shakespeare, Sonnet 110, 1–4)

2. The best meaning for the word **motley** in line 2 is
   a. mixture of odd elements   c. brightly colored uniform
   b. jester (circled)   d. gaudy fabric

When Hamlet sourly observes:
    "Thrift, thrift, Horatio. The funeral baked meats
    did coldly furnish forth the marriage tables,"
he is essentially registering his disapproval of the fact that the funeral of his father and the remarriage of his mother were so contiguous.

3. The best definition for the word **contiguous** in line 5 is
   a. close in size   b. related in blood   c. near in time (circled)   d. adjacent in space

During the "Neolithic Revolution," as it is called, human beings exchanged the highly discursive lifestyle of the hunter/gatherer for the more sedentary one of the farmer.

4. In line 2 the word **discursive** is used to mean
   a. primitive   b. digressive   c. episodic   d. nomadic (circled)

Antonyms

In each of the following groups, circle the word or expression that is most nearly the **opposite** of the word in **boldface** type.

1. **censurable**
   a. laudable (circled)
   b. conscientious
   c. puzzling
   d. habitual

2. **specious**
   a. special
   b. strange
   c. valid (circled)
   d. deceptive

3. **extenuating**
   a. poor
   b. aggravating (circled)
   c. unexpected
   d. mitigating

4. **munificent**
   a. generous
   b. stingy (circled)
   c. thoughtful
   d. sensible

5. **satiated**
   a. horrified
   b. bored
   c. angered
   d. unsatisfied (circled)

6. **florid**
   a. unadorned (circled)
   b. truthful
   c. effective
   d. dull

7. **palpable**
   a. careless
   b. unnoticeable (circled)
   c. obvious
   d. significant

8. **pernicious**
   a. contagious
   b. painful
   c. destructive
   d. harmless (circled)

Review Units 10–12 ■ 141

9. **heresy**
a. orthodoxy ✓
b. fear
c. bravery
d. belief

10. **scintillating**
a. humorous
b. dull ✓
c. taped
d. impromptu

11. **dowdy**
a. drab
b. ruddy
c. chic ✓
d. conspicuous

12. **fortuitous**
a. unexpected
b. chance
c. prearranged ✓
d. longed for

13. **silence**
a. dun
b. clangor ✓
c. salient
d. bedlam

14. **politic**
a. wise
b. imprudent ✓
c. prosaic
d. digressive

15. **foreigner**
a. salient
b. denizen ✓
c. gist
d. covert

16. **inconspicuous**
a. munificent
b. imperious
c. prosaic
d. salient ✓

Word Families

A. On the line provided, write the word you have learned in Units 10–12 that is related to each of the following nouns.

EXAMPLE: provocation—**provocative**

#	Noun	Answer
1.	dowdiness	dowdy
2.	inculcation, inculcator	inculcate
3.	gaucheness, gaucherie	gauche
4.	abstemiousness	abstemious
5.	fortuity, fortuitousness	fortuitous
6.	efficacy, efficaciousness	efficacious
7.	imperiousness	imperious
8.	munificence	munificent
9.	gratuity, gratuitousness	gratuitous
10.	corroboration	corroborate
11.	dissemination	disseminate
12.	satiation	satiate
13.	inculcation	inculcate
14.	censure	censurable
15.	discourse	discursive

B. On the line provided, write the word you have learned in Units 10–12 that is related to each of the following verbs.

EXAMPLE: clang—**clangor**

#	Verb	Answer
16.	scintillate	scintillating
17.	annotate	annotation
18.	perceive	perceptive
19.	imply	implicit
20.	provoke	provocative

REVIEW UNITS 10–12

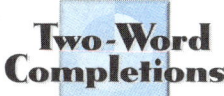

Two-Word Completions

Circle the pair of words that best complete the meaning of each of the following passages.

See pages T38–T48 for explanations of answers.

1. Office workers usually lead relatively _____ lives between nine and five. For that reason, many a "desk jockey" finds a weekly trip to the gym a(n) _____ way to keep fit.
   a. covert . . . gratuitous
   b. ostentatious . . . provocative
   c. sedentary . . . efficacious
   d. prosaic . . . pernicious

2. "The flamboyant plumage of the male of the species has always struck me as overly _____," the ornithologist observed. "By contrast, the female looks so drab and _____ in her somber browns and grays."
   a. debonair . . . censurable
   b. specious . . . gauche
   c. prosaic . . . scintillating
   d. ostentatious . . . dowdy

3. In a series of _____ attacks, chock-full of the most withering political _____, the famous orator Demosthenes fulminated against King Philip of Macedon's nefarious efforts to curtail Greek rights and liberties.
   a. scintillating . . . heresies
   b. gratuitous . . . clangor
   c. searing . . . invective
   d. motley . . . annotations

4. Most of the adults seemed to find Kal's Kiddie Karnival a bit of a bore, but their children were _____. Though the grown-ups had clearly had enough halfway through the performance, the youngsters' appetites for the kind of fare that Kal served up were by no means _____ when the show was over.
   a. enhanced . . . accentuated
   b. enthralled . . . satiated
   c. seared . . . absolved
   d. exuded . . . extenuated

5. Florida Fats and the other _____ of McDuffy's Billiard Emporium seem to come from every walk of life. One is unlikely to find such a(n) _____ crew under any other roof in town.
   a. denizens . . . motley
   b. caricatures . . . abstemious
   c. paragons . . . fortuitous
   d. reprobate . . . contiguous

6. "We must take immediate steps to counteract this highly dangerous development," the new President told his advisors, "for the longer we _____, the more _____ its effects will be."
   a. procrastinate . . . pernicious
   b. quail . . . prosaic
   c. disseminate . . . deleterious
   d. accrue . . . inimical

Building with Classical Roots

equa, equi, ega, iqui—equal

This root appears in **equanimity** (page 118), literally "equal-mindedness." The word now means "composure, evenness of mind or temper." Other words based on the same root are listed below.

| egalitarian | equate | equilibrium | iniquitous |
| equable | equidistant | inequity | unequivocal |

From the list of words above, choose the one that corresponds to each of the brief definitions below. Write the word in the blank space in the illustrative sentence below the definition.

1. uniform, marked by lack of noticeable or extreme variation; steady
   Los Angeles is famous for its __**equable**__ climate.

2. to regard or treat as equivalent; to make equal, equalize
   It's a mistake to __**equate**__ politeness with kindness.

3. clear, plain, absolute, certain
   There was no mistaking his __**unequivocal**__ refusal to compromise.

4. wicked, very unjust, vicious
   The former dictator was tried for __**iniquitous**__ deeds.

5. asserting or promoting social, political, or economic equality; advocating the removal of inequalities among people
   Most utopian societies are envisioned as __**egalitarian**__.

6. balance ("equal balance")
   It's not easy to maintain one's __**equilibrium**__ in a difficult situation.

7. an act or situation of injustice and unfairness
   A society based on __**inequity**__ is ripe for revolution.

8. equally separated from a given point or location
   The two suburbs are __**equidistant**__ from St. Louis.

From the list of words above, choose the one that best completes each of the following sentences. Write the word in the space provided.

1. The __**egalitarian**__ principles of Lafayette led him to fight for the rights of a people thousands of miles from his homeland.
2. The company agreed to set up a committee that would correct any __**inequities**__ in their hiring practices.

REVIEW UNITS 10–12

3. All points on the circumference of a circle are **equidistant** from its center.
4. A wise leader does not **equate** disagreement with disloyalty.
5. Will yoga exercises help maintain my emotional **equilibrium** during periods of stress?
6. The evidence in favor of her innocence is so **unequivocal** that I am sure she will be acquitted.
7. Anyone who is going to be your companion on a long and exhausting backpacking trip should have not only the right physical attributes, but a(n) **equable** disposition as well.
8. In any just society, the persecution of racial, ethnic, or religious minorities must be condemned as **iniquitous**.

Circle the **boldface** word that more satisfactorily completes each of the following sentences.

1. Fair-minded judges do not (**equate**, **equivocate**) justice with retribution.
2. The Senator's objection to the proposed increase in the federal minimum wage was (**equidistant**, **unequivocal**).
3. The union attacked the blatant (**inequity**, **equilibrium**) of raising management's salaries while freezing worker's wages.
4. The (**equable**, **egalitarian**) values of Abraham Lincoln had their origin in his own experience of rising from obscurity to the Presidency.
5. The international human rights organization condemned the (**equable**, **iniquitous**) practice of imprisoning and torturing political dissidents.
6. The delicate (**equilibrium**, **inequity**) in the region was disturbed when the discovery of oil promised to make one country very rich.
7. The fountain in the middle of the garden is (**unequivocal**, **equidistant**) from each of the trellised entrances.
8. Because the father's will called for a(n) (**equable**, **iniquitous**) distribution of his wealth among all his children, there was no squabbling after his death.

Read the following sentences, paying special attention to the words and phrases underlined. From the words in the box below, find better choices for these underlined words and phrases. Then use these choices to rewrite the sentences.

WORD BANK

abstemious	dun	foist	procrastinate	salient
contiguous	efficacious	gauche	prosaic	sedentary
contingent	enthrall	gist	recondite	specious
corroborate	florid	inculcate	redundant	winsome

What Are Tangrams?

1. A simple and remarkably versatile geometric puzzle from China has been said to hold spellbound children and adults for generations.
enthrall

2. The nucleus of solving *tangram* puzzles is to arrange all the pieces in the set—five triangles, a parallelogram, and a square—to form different figures.
gist

3. The basic rule for tangram solvers is to set all pieces so that they share an edge or boundary to one another in any arrangement that creates a recognizable figure—a letter, an animal, a boat, a flower, whatever!
contiguous

4. In 1903, American puzzle master Sam Loyd wrote an epic and difficult to understand by virtue of its abstruse nature study of tangrams, called *The Seven Books of Tan*.
recondite

5. In this charming yet seemingly sound but actually lacking in merit work, Loyd claimed that tangrams were invented 4000 years ago by the Chinese god Tan.
specious

6. Loyd effectively passed off his delightful work on the puzzle-loving public, who were dazzled by the intricate but harmless joke.
foisted

7. Serious mathematicians, anthropologists, and historians have been unable to attest to the accuracy of the true origin of tangrams. Still, tangrams can provide hours of entertainment and challenge.
corroborate

CUMULATIVE REVIEW III

Analogies

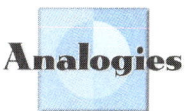

In each of the following, circle the item that best completes the comparison.

See pages T38–T48 for explanations of answers.

1. **fortuitous** is to **adventitious** as
   a. egregious is to inconsequential
   b. callow is to unctuous
   c. cadaverous is to florid
   d. recondite is to arcane

2. **salutary** is to **deleterious** as
   a. vitriolic is to acrimonious
   b. abstemious is to intemperate
   c. pernicious is to seditious
   d. insular is to provincial

3. **precept** is to **inculcate** as
   a. caveat is to enjoin
   b. aspersion is to enliven
   c. exhortation is to urge
   d. allegation is to corroborate

4. **succinct** is to **discursive** as
   a. prosaic is to hackneyed
   b. scurrilous is to nebulous
   c. bombastic is to pretentious
   d. incisive is to vapid

5. **skinflint** is to **munificent** as
   a. ignoramus is to erudite
   b. workaholic is to sedulous
   c. showoff is to ostentatious
   d. spy is to covert

6. **ferment** is to **agitation** as
   a. clangor is to serenity
   b. drivel is to effervescence
   c. bedlam is to noise
   d. lassitude is to petulance

7. **beneficent** is to **inimical** as
   a. meritorious is to censurable
   b. inscrutable is to irrevocable
   c. intrinsic is to implicit
   d. vulnerable is to susceptible

8. **bovine** is to **disposition** as
   a. soporific is to background
   b. corpulent is to personality
   c. sedentary is to lifestyle
   d. sepulchral is to attitude

9. **affable** is to **debonair** as
   a. fractious is to equitable
   b. anomalous is to amorphous
   c. sleazy is to dark
   d. transient is to evanescent

10. **sagacity** is to **astute** as
    a. wisdom is to provocative
    b. prejudice is to dispassionate
    c. discernment is to perceptive
    d. intelligence is to efficacious

11. **dilatory** is to **procrastination** as
    a. querulous is to commiseration
    b. straitlaced is to dissipation
    c. noncommittal is to equivocation
    d. crass is to peculation

12. **avarice** is to **cupidity** as
    a. sangfroid is to equanimity
    b. innuendo is to supposition
    c. annotation is to coalition
    d. heresy is to penury

13. **satiate** is to **jaded** as
    a. absolve is to culpable
    b. disabuse is to fatigued
    c. dun is to grateful
    d. whet is to stimulated

14. **mitigate** is to **extenuate** as
    a. foist is to expiate
    b. infer is to erudite
    c. relegate is to infringe
    d. remonstrate is to expostulate

15. **enthrall** is to **disconcert** as
    a. avouch is to repudiate
    b. scourge is to flout
    c. resound is to reverberate
    d. fetter is to shackle

16. **aplomb** is to **gauche** as
    a. ennui is to bored
    b. elegance is to lackluster
    c. megalomania is to grandiose
    d. aura is to awkward

17. **tyrant** is to **imperious** as
    a. diplomat is to brusque
    b. lackey is to subservient
    c. spendthrift is to austere
    d. hero is to ignoble

18. **sear** is to **fire** as
    a. scald is to steam
    b. scintillate is to water
    c. wheedle is to air
    d. filch is to dirt

19. scholar is to **erudite** as
a. greenhorn is to callow
b. curmudgeon is to unctuous
c. orator is to bombastic
d. parent is to straitlaced

20. infer is to **surmise** as
a. blazon is to conceal
b. assuage is to intensify
c. filch is to swipe
d. fetter is to liberate

Choosing the Right Meaning

Read each sentence carefully. Then circle the item that best completes the statement below the sentence.

See pages T38–T48 for explanations of answers.

"Our feathered friend the thrush chirrups his beauteous song
Above the crocus beds, whose fragrant denizens (2)
Lie nestled snugly in the umbrage of the pine."
  (A.E. Glug, "Alexandrines in a Country Churchyard," 5–7)

1. In line 3, the word **umbrage** most nearly means
  a. branches   b. resentment   c. power   d. shade

           "Come, thick night,
And pall thee in the dunnest smoke of hell (2)
That my keen knife see not the wound it makes,
Nor heaven peep through the blanket of the dark (4)
To cry, '"Hold, hold!"'
  (Shakespeare, *Macbeth*, I, V, 49–53)

2. The word **dunnest** in line 2 most nearly means
  a. smelliest   b. blackest   c. dullest   d. thickest

Far from fulfilling the bright promise of this early years, the hero drivels away his life
by the teaspoonful in meaningless social pastimes. (2)

3. The best meaning for the word **drivels** in line 1 is
  a. slavers   b. hastens   c. fritters   d. baby talks

A true child of the Marshalsea Prison, Tip Dorrit soon finds himself employment
in one or another of the sleazier forms of human enterprise. (2)

4. The word **sleazier** in line 2 may best be defined as
  a. socially lower   c. physically thinner
  b. ethically meaner   d. financially cheaper

The oil spill had been so devastating that centuries, rather than years, would be
needed to effect the restitution of the environments and ecologies affected, one (2)
eminent conservationist wrote.

5. The best meaning for the word **restitution** in line 2 is
  a. restoration   b. compensation   c. reimbursement   d. indemnification

CUMULATIVE REVIEW III

"In order to protect the confidentiality of my sources," the reporter replied, "I often abate all mention of their names in the articles I write." (2)

6. The word **abate** in line 2 may best be defined as
a. deduct
b. nullify
(c. omit)
d. decrease

Two-Word Completions

Circle the pair of words that best complete the meaning of each of the following sentences.

See pages T38–T48 for explanations of answers.

1. Modern scientists smile in bemusement at the faulty methodology and _____ reasoning behind the medieval alchemists' vain endeavors to _____ base metals such as iron or copper into gold and silver.
(a. specious . . . transmute)
b. irrevocable . . . aggrandize
c. anomalous . . . debase
d. hypothetical . . . relegate

2. "The large cache of _____ drugs we found in the suspect's possession clearly _____ the charges of smuggling that we have brought against him," the chief of detectives observed with an air of satisfaction.
(a. contraband . . . corroborates)
b. covert . . . dissipates
c. surreptitious . . . mitigates
d. occult . . . abets

3. "The girl may not be Einstein," I remarked, "but her comments on life are often quite _____ and show that she possesses a(n) _____ store of common sense."
a. soporific . . . ignoble
b. equitable . . . enigmatic
c. vapid . . . contiguous
(d. astute . . . redoubtable)

4. In earlier times, people who professed views that conflicted with the official teachings of their religion were often forced to _____ their ideas publicly or face charges of _____.
a. disavow . . . decadence
b. abominate . . . cupidity
(c. repudiate . . . heresy)
d. disseminate . . . perfidy

5. The lead paragraph of any newspaper article provides a kind of _____ of events in that it gives the reader only the most _____ features of a story in language that is as clear and concise as possible.
a. gist . . . lurid
b. collation . . . inconsequential
c. caricature . . . provocative
(d. epitome . . . salient)

6. It must take a lifetime to acquire the vast _____ needed to compile the kind of scholarly notes and comments that one meets with at the foot of every page of an _____ edition of Shakespeare.
a. megalomania . . . ameliorated
(b. erudition . . . annotated)
c. avarice . . . expurgated
d. acculturation . . . enhanced

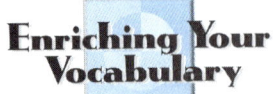

Enriching Your Vocabulary

Read the passage below. Then complete the exercise at the bottom of the page.

Words from Place Names

Certain words and phrases in the English language are derived from place names. For example the word *ascot*, a tie-like scarf, comes from the town of Ascot, England, where the item originated. Often as time passes, these words lose their association with their original place names, and are adapted into the English language as words in their own right. Studying the meaning and manner in which these words and phrases slowly became incorporated into common English usage often reveals historical and cultural information about the society from which they came.

In addition to nouns associated with particular places, such as *Boston cream pie*, *Philadelphia cheese steak*, and *Texas chili*, there are words such as *bedlam* that also tell a story. *Bedlam* (Unit 10), meaning "noisy uproar, chaos, or confusion," is a corruption of Bethlehem, from the St. Mary of Bethlehem Insane Asylum in north London, the oldest mental institution in the world. Though it began by admitting the poor and destitute, it soon took in "lunatics," as they were called, in the 1300s. By the 1700s the patients were seriously mistreated, and staff members sold admission tickets to the wealthy so that they could see the mentally ill up close.

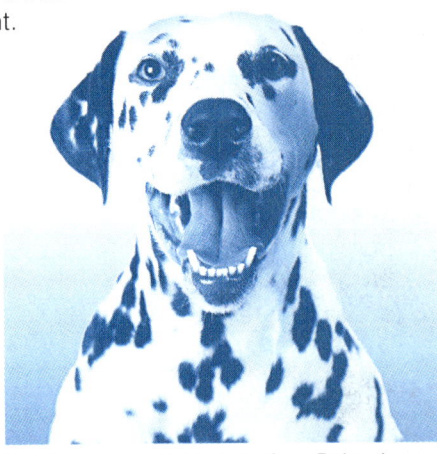

The Dalmatian gets its name from Dalmatia, Yugoslavia.

In Column A below are 10 more place name words. With or without a dictionary, match the words to the professions or descriptions associated with them in Column B.

Column A

- __e__ 1. academy
- __c__ 2. cologne
- __a__ 3. limerick
- __d__ 4. varnish
- __g__ 5. sybaritic
- __h__ 6. limousine
- __b__ 7. blarney
- __i__ 8. hackneyed
- __f__ 9. mecca
- __j__ 10. sardonic

Column B

- **a.** poet
- **b.** liar; exaggerator
- **c.** perfume
- **d.** carpenter
- **e.** professor; student
- **f.** pilgrim
- **g.** hedonist, epicure
- **h.** driver
- **i.** cliché
- **j.** poisonous plant; mocking, cynical

🎧 See page T21 for information.

UNIT 13

Note carefully the spelling, pronunciation, part(s) of speech, and definition(s) of each of the following words. Then write the word in the blank space(s) in the illustrative sentence(s) following. Finally, study the lists of synonyms and antonyms given at the end of each entry.

1. abet
(ə bet′)

(*v.*) to encourage, assist, aid, support (especially in something wrong or unworthy)

To allow a man in his condition behind the wheel of a car is to _____**abet**_____ a potential crime.

ANTONYMS: hamper, hinder, impede, frustrate

2. aver
(ə vər′)

(*v.*) to affirm, declare confidently

I will _____**aver**_____ your fitness to do the work to any prospective employer who inquires.

SYNONYMS: assert, asseverate, avouch
ANTONYMS: deny, disavow, repudiate, disclaim

3. blatant
(blāt′ ənt)

(*adj.*) noisy in a coarse, offensive way; obvious or conspicuous, especially in an unfavorable sense

Your comments showed a _____**blatant**_____ disregard for my feelings.

SYNONYMS: flagrant, glaring, egregious, disagreeably loud
ANTONYMS: inconsequential, trifling, piddling, petty

4. broach
(brōch)

(*v.*) to bring up or begin to talk about (a subject); to announce, introduce; to break the surface of the water; to turn sideways to the wind and waves; to pierce (a keg or cask) in order to draw off liquid; (*n.*) a spit for roasting; a tool for tapping casks

Though he did not like scrambled eggs, he opted not to _____**broach**_____ the subject for fear of insulting his hosts.

5. buttress
(bə′ trəs)

(*v.*) to support, prop up, strengthen; (*n.*) a supporting structure

He has read so widely and in such depth that he can produce facts to _____**buttress**_____ any argument he advances.

I had to add _____**buttresses**_____ on either side of my rickety shed to keep it from collapsing.

SYNONYMS: (*v.*) bolster, reinforce, brace, shore up
ANTONYMS: (*v.*) undermine, weaken, impair

6. carousal
(kə raù′ zəl)

(*n.*) noisy revelry or merrymaking (often with a suggestion of heavy drinking)

Vikings are notorious for having enjoyed a _____**carousal**_____ after each of their battles.

SYNONYMS: drinking bout, drunken revel, binge

7. collate
(kō′ lāt)

(*v.*) to compare critically in order to note differences, similarities, etc.; to arrange in order for some specific purpose

We decided to _____**collate**_____ the recipes according to how complicated they are.

SYNONYMS: sort out, cross-check, rearrange

8. connoisseur
(kän ə sər′)

(*n.*) an expert; one who is well qualified to pass critical judgments, especially in one of the fine arts

She was a _____**connoisseur**_____ of both music and film.

SYNONYMS: authority, savant, pundit
ANTONYMS: ignoramus, philistine, yahoo

9. disconsolate
(dis kän′ sə lət)

(*adj.*) deeply unhappy or dejected; without hope, beyond consolation

Shakespeare's Macbeth hardly seems _____**disconsolate**_____ when his wife dies, and bluntly says he has no time to grieve.

SYNONYMS: grief-stricken, inconsolable, comfortless
ANTONYMS: cheerful, blithe, buoyant, jaunty

10. encumber
(in kəm′ bər)

(*v.*) to weigh down or burden (with difficulties, cares, debt, etc.); to fill up, block up, hinder

I feared that joining another club would _____**encumber**_____ me with too many obligations.

SYNONYMS: overload, saddle, hamper, clog
ANTONYMS: unburden, unload, relieve

11. foment
(fō ment′)

(*v.*) to promote trouble or rebellion; to apply warm liquids to, warm

Toward the end of the film, the peasant leader attempts to _____**foment**_____ a storming of the scientist's castle.

SYNONYMS: instigate, incite, stir up
ANTONYMS: quell, quash, squelch, suppress

12. grisly
(griz′ lē)

(*adj.*) frightful, horrible, ghastly

Katherine Anne Porter's "Pale Horse, Pale Rider" reveals the _____**grisly**_____ effects of the influenza virus during the epidemic that followed World War I.

SYNONYMS: gruesome, gory, hideous
ANTONYMS: pleasant, delightful, attractive

13. herculean
(hər kyü lē′ ən)

(*adj.*) (*capital H*) relating to Hercules; (*lowercase h*) characterized by great strength; very hard to do in the sense of requiring unusual strength

We carried the desk into the house successfully but saw that getting it up the stairs would require a _____**herculean**_____ effort.

SYNONYMS: mighty, powerful, arduous, onerous, colossal
ANTONYMS: puny, Lilliputian, bantam

14. impassive
(im pas′ iv)

(*adj.*) showing no feeling or emotion; inanimate; motionless
Since nervous laughter is the sign of an inexperienced actor, I tried to adopt an _____**impassive**_____ expression on stage.
SYNONYMS: emotionless, stoical, unemotional, insensible
ANTONYMS: emotional, passionate, excitable

15. inauspicious
(in ô spish′ əs)

(*adj.*) unfavorable, unlucky, suggesting bad luck for the future
Our road trip got off to an _____**inauspicious**_____ start when we ran out of gas within five miles of home.
SYNONYMS: unpropitious, unpromising, untimely
ANTONYMS: propitious, favorable

16. incontrovertible
(in kän trə vər′ tə bəl)

(*adj.*) unquestionable, beyond dispute
The document was remarkable for its tact yet also _____**incontrovertible**_____ in its facts.
SYNONYMS: incontestable, indisputable, indubitable
ANTONYMS: debatable, dubious, open to question

17. nonplussed
(nän pləst′)

(*adj., part.*) puzzled, not knowing what to do, at a loss
Prepared as she thought she was for all contingencies, she found herself _____**nonplussed**_____ by the surprising turn of events.
SYNONYMS: perplexed, baffled, stumped, flabbergasted
ANTONYMS: poised, confident, assured

18. opportune
(äp ər tün′)

(*adj.*) suitable or convenient for a particular purpose; occurring at an appropriate time
If you intend to give that dog a bath, you had better pick an _____**opportune**_____ moment, and then pounce!
SYNONYMS: timely, appropriate, felicitous
ANTONYMS: untimely, inconvenient, inappropriate

19. prolific
(pro lif′ ik)

(*adj.*) abundantly productive; abundant, profuse
Haydn was a more _____**prolific**_____ composer than Mozart, in part because he lived much longer.
SYNONYMS: fruitful, fecund, proliferous
ANTONYMS: barren, unproductive, sterile, sparse

20. rejoinder
(ri join′ dər)

(*n.*) a reply to a reply, especially from the defendant in a legal suit
When he explained where he had been and what he had done, her _____**rejoinder**_____ was sharp and critical.
SYNONYMS: answer, reply, response, riposte, retort

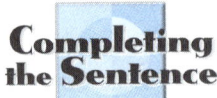

Completing the Sentence

From the words for this unit, choose the one that best completes each of the following sentences. Write the word in the space provided.

1. I don't think you can really accuse the producers of _____**blatant**_____ favoritism simply because they chose a friend for the title role.

2. I will not in any way _____**abet**_____ their plans to play a cruel and humiliating trick on an unoffending person.

3. "When I first _____**broached**_____ this topic two years ago," I observed, "my ideas were met by a very indifferent reception."

4. Aren't you exaggerating when you suggest that the job of stock clerk calls for someone with _____**herculean**_____ strength?

5. If the pages aren't _____**collated**_____ properly, they'll be out of proper sequence when our class magazine is bound.

6. The mangled bodies of the victims told their own _____**grisly**_____ story of what had happened.

7. When I saw the worried expression on the face of my employer, I realized that it wasn't a(n) _____**opportune**_____ time to ask for a raise.

8. One need not be a(n) _____**connoisseur**_____ of modern dance to recognize that Martha is exceptionally talented in that field.

9. The New Year's Eve party started off quietly enough, but it soon became a full-fledged _____**carousal**_____.

10. The testimony of three different witnesses, all confirming the same basic facts, made the guilt of the accused _____**incontrovertible**_____.

11. He is such a(n) _____**prolific**_____ writer that his books occupy almost an entire shelf in the school library.

12. The big game had a truly _____**inauspicious**_____ start for us when our star quarterback fumbled and lost the ball on the first play.

13. She is so _____**encumbered**_____ with family obligations that she rarely has a free moment for herself.

14. Although we have had our disagreements, I will _____**aver**_____ now that she was always been scrupulously honest in her dealings with me.

15. Although she remained outwardly _____**impassive**_____ during the trial, I could sense the emotional turmoil beneath the surface.

16. I know you are really disappointed at not getting that job, but don't allow yourself to feel so _____**disconsolate**_____ that you won't have the energy to look for another.

17. The towering walls of many medieval cathedrals are prevented from falling down by huge "flying _____**buttresses**_____" on the outsides of the buildings.

18. I was utterly ____nonplussed____ when I realized that football practice and the rehearsal for the class show were at the same time.

19. It would be impossible to ____foment____ racial discord in a school where students of different backgrounds understand and respect one another.

20. Now that you mention it, I don't think that "Sez you" was a particularly effective ____rejoinder____ to her trenchant and insightful criticisms of your proposal.

Synonyms

Choose the word from this unit that is **the same** or **most nearly the same** in meaning as the **boldface** word or expression in the given phrase. Write the word on the line provided.

1. **introduce** a complete change of plan — broach
2. was **grief-stricken** after the tragedy — disconsolate
3. gave a conciliatory **reply** — rejoinder
4. **support** her sleazy scheme — abet
5. an **unpromising** beginning — inauspicious
6. **baffled** by the answer — nonplussed
7. woken by the **drunken revel** — carousal
8. **overloaded** with cares and troubles — encumbered
9. a **colossal** challenge — herculean
10. a **timely** moment to act — opportune
11. **shore up** their declining popularity — buttress
12. **sort out** in order of relevance — collate
13. **gruesome** evidence of the wreck — grisly
14. **stir up** fury in the crowd — foment
15. **indisputable** proof of innocence — incontrovertible

Antonyms

Choose the word from this unit that is **most nearly opposite** in meaning to the **boldface** word or expression in the given phrase. Write the word on the line provided.

16. going through an **unproductive** period — prolific
17. an **inconsequential** error — blatant
18. a disturbingly **excitable** nature — impassive
19. a **philistine's** appreciation of food — connoisseur's
20. **disavow** an earlier statement — aver

Choosing the Right Word Circle the **boldface** word that more satisfactorily completes each of the following sentences.

1. Dr. Slavin's original diagnosis, although questioned by several colleagues, was strongly (**buttressed, fomented**) by the results of the laboratory tests.
2. I like a good time as much as anyone, but I don't think that the celebration of our nation's birthday should become a rowdy (**carousal, rejoinder**).
3. Well-meaning but misguided friends (**abetted, averred**) his plans to run away to Hollywood and "become a movie star."
4. You will never be able to complete this hike if you (**encumber, collate**) yourself with so much "essential equipment."
5. What could be more (**disconsolate, herculean**) than the long drive home on a rainy night after we had lost the championship game by one point!
6. His parents are such sensitive people that I'm not at all sure how I should (**broach, foment**) the news of his untimely death to them.
7. In spite of her long and (**grisly, prolific**) career, her reputation today rests entirely on one great play.
8. Cleaning up the old beach house seemed an almost impossible task, but she attacked it with (**herculean, disconsolate**) energy.
9. Psychologists tell us that people who seem to be unusually (**impassive, blatant**) are often the ones most likely to lose control of their emotions in times of stress.
10. I wasn't so much surprised at not getting the job as I was (**nonplussed, encumbered**) by his strange explanation that I was "overqualified."
11. The speaker's inept replies to questions from the floor were met with a barrage of indignant (**carousals, rejoinders**).
12. When they offered to help him, he proudly (**averred, abetted**) that he could handle the situation entirely on his own.
13. If you are going to wait for an occasion that seems (**opportune, grisly**) in *every* respect, then in all probability you will have to wait forever.
14. I don't know anything about quiches and soufflés, but I'm a true (**buttress, connoisseur**) when it comes to pizza.
15. I know that he is wealthy and comes from a "prominent" family, but does that excuse his (**blatant, impassive**) disregard of good manners?
16. I truly felt that reality could never be as horrible as the (**prolific, grisly**) phantoms that were disturbing my dreams.
17. The opening of our show took place most (**inauspiciously, opportunely**) in the midst of a transit strike and a record-breaking snowstorm.
18. Isn't it ridiculous to say that the disorder was (**fomented, nonplussed**) by "outsiders" when we all know that it resulted from bad conditions inside the institution?
19. With tireless patience, the wily detective (**encumbered, collated**) bits and pieces of evidence until he gained an insight into how the crime had been committed.
20. What we need is not opinions or "educated guesses" but (**impassive, incontrovertible**) proof that can stand up under the closest examination.

Vocabulary in Context

Read the following passage, in which some of the words you have studied in this unit appear in **boldface** type. Then complete each statement given below the passage by circling the letter of the item that is **the same** or **almost the same** in meaning as the highlighted word.

Risky Business

(Line)

John Peter Zenger entered history when he was locked in a New York jail by the British Colonial Government in 1734. Twenty-four years earlier, the British Crown had paid his fare as an immigrant German boy seeking a home in America. Eager for colonists the Crown had not known what it was getting in Zenger.

(5) Young Zenger apprenticed for a New York printer named Bradford in a shop that published the city's first newspaper, the *New-York Gazette*. After eight years Zenger became Bradford's partner but, seeking independence, Zenger quit the shop one year later in order
(10) to open a store of his own.

Competing with his former master and partner, a man of many connections, proved a **herculean** task. Zenger published stories in
(15) Dutch for the Dutch community and hoped to **buttress** his publishing endeavor with a Dutch arithmetic book. But the choice proved **inauspicious**; the shop was not
(20) **prolific**. Only when he began printing leaflets from a party that opposed the policies of a new

18th century print room workers

colonial governor did Zenger find an **opportune** alliance; he started representing an opposition party with a newspaper of his own. The new governor remained
(25) a target, and Zenger was soon jailed for printing what was characterized as dangerous libel. The Crown did its **blatant** worst, trying him a second time when the first jury failed to convict him. Just in time, a Philadelphian named Hamilton, brought by Zenger's friends, took over the case. He made the novel argument that no true statement can be libelous—and that what Zenger had published was true.
(30) In minutes, the jury aquitted the defendant. Zenger's name has ever since been an emblem for freedom of the press in the United States.

1. The meaning of **herculean** (line 13) is
a. peculiar   c. arduous
b. memorable   d. unpopular

2. Buttress (line 16) most nearly means
a. to explain   c. to advertise
b. to bolster   d. to outsell

3. Inauspicious (line 19) is best defined as
a. unfavorable   c. unwieldy
b. unusual   d. little known

4. The meaning of **prolific** (line 20) is
a. healthy   c. popular
b. productive   d. pleasant

5. Opportune (line 23) most nearly means
a. secret   c. desperate
b. exciting   d. timely

6. Blatant (line 26) is best defined as
a. flagrant   c. usual
b. timid   d. silly

Unit 14

 See page T21 for information.

Note carefully the spelling, pronunciation, part(s) of speech, and definition(s) of each of the following words. Then write the word in the blank space(s) in the illustrative sentence(s) following. Finally, study the lists of synonyms and antonyms given at the end of each entry.

1. amenable
(ə mē′ nə bəl)

(*adj.*) willing to follow advice or authority, tractable, submissive; responsive; liable to be held responsible

They will be _____amenable_____ to your instructions as long as what you say makes sense.
SYNONYMS: agreeable, compliant, docile
ANTONYMS: unresponsive, resistant, recalcitrant

2. berate
(bi rāt′)

(*v.*) to scold sharply

He removed the dog from obedience school when he discovered that they had _____berated_____ it too harshly.
SYNONYMS: chide, rebuke, reprove, reprimand
ANTONYMS: praise, compliment, pat on the back

3. carnage
(kär′ nəj)

(*n.*) large-scale slaughter or loss of life

Until television broadcast film footage of it, the _____carnage_____ of war was rarely made real to far-off civilian populations.
SYNONYMS: butchery, bloodbath, massacre

4. credulous
(krej′ ə ləs)

(*adj.*) too ready to believe, easily deceived

Though he was no dolt, his _____credulous_____ nature and desire to believe the best of people made him easy to deceive.
SYNONYM: gullible
ANTONYMS: dubious, skeptical

5. criterion
(*pl.,* **criteria**)
(krī tir′ ē ən)

(*n.*) a rule, test; a standard for judgment or evaluation

She was disturbed to discover that the _____criterion_____ for the award was based on style, not substance.
SYNONYMS: yardstick, touchstone, gauge, canon

6. deplete
(di plēt′)

(*v.*) to use up as a result of spending or consumption; to diminish greatly

Dwelling on all that could go wrong with your project will _____deplete_____ your energy and courage.
SYNONYMS: exhaust, empty, drain, bankrupt
ANTONYMS: replenish, refill, restock, resupply

7. expatiate
(ek spā′ shē āt)

(v.) to expand on, write or talk at length or in detail; to move about freely

We would like you to _____**expatiate**_____ on the interesting matters you only touched upon earlier today.

SYNONYMS: elaborate, enlarge, descant, wander, roam
ANTONYMS: sketch roughly, summarize, condense, adumbrate

8. extraneous
(ek strā′ nē əs)

(adj.) coming from the outside, foreign; present but not essential, irrelevant

One handy way to dodge a difficult question is to earnestly begin talking about something _____**extraneous**_____ to it.

SYNONYMS: incidental, extrinsic
ANTONYMS: intrinsic, relevant, pertinent, germane

9. inception
(in sep′ shən)

(n.) the beginning, start, earliest stage of some process, institution, etc.

He has worked here quietly and steadily since the firm's _____**inception**_____, and knows how to do everybody's job.

SYNONYMS: commencement, inauguration, outset
ANTONYMS: completion, conclusion, termination

10. infirmity
(in fərm′ ə tē)

(n.) a weakness or ailment (physical, mental, moral, etc.)

Was his "deafness" an _____**infirmity**_____ of old age, or a lack of interest in the conversation?

SYNONYMS: affliction, malady, defect

11. jejune
(ji jün′)

(adj.) lacking in nutritive value; lacking in interest or substance; immature, juvenile

My favorite teacher turned history from a _____**jejune**_____ study of the distant past into a relevant topic of discussion.

SYNONYMS: vapid, insipid, puerile, childish
ANTONYMS: stimulating, mature

12. obdurate
(äb′ dyü rət)

(adj.) stubborn, unyielding

Vincent van Gogh was _____**obdurate**_____ in painting whatever he wished, despite the fact that no one would buy his pictures.

SYNONYMS: obstinate, adamant
ANTONYMS: yielding, tractable, flexible

13. potpourri
(pō pü rē′)

(n.) A collection of diverse or miscellaneous items; a general mixture; petals mixed with spices for scent

The furniture was a _____**potpourri**_____ of hand-me-downs from my father's parents and my stepmother's uncle and aunt.

SYNONYMS: hodgepodge, mélange, farrago, medley
ANTONYMS: homogenous or uniform group

14. precocious
(pri kō' shəs)

(*adj.*) showing unusually early development (especially in talents and mental capacity)

She showed a _____**precocious**_____ talent for science.

SYNONYMS: forward, gifted, advanced
ANTONYMS: backward, retarded, slow

15. sadistic
(sə dis' tik)

(*adj.*) delighting in cruelty, excessively cruel

The Geneva Convention of 1949 outlawed torture and _____**sadistic**_____ treatment of prisoners of war.

SYNONYMS: brutal, vicious, inhuman, fiendish
ANTONYMS: masochistic, clement, humane, merciful

16. sententious
(sen ten' shəs)

(*adj.*) self-righteous, characterized by moralizing; given to use of maxims or adages; saying much in few words, pithy

The _____**sententious**_____ advice, though wise, was too general to help their particular situation.

SYNONYMS: aphoristic, epigrammatic, moralistic
ANTONYMS: discursive, diffuse, episodic

17. supplicate
(səp' lə kāt)

(*v.*) to beg earnestly and humbly

He chose to _____**supplicate**_____ for mercy not on his own account, but so that his wife would not suffer.

SYNONYMS: plead, petition, implore, entreat

18. surfeit
(sər' fət)

(*n.*) an excess or overindulgence, as in eating or drinking, causing disgust; (*v.*) to feed or supply with anything to excess

A _____**surfeit**_____ of food, drink, and clowning puts Shakespeare's Falstaff in disgrace with the King.

SYNONYMS: (*n.*) excess, glut; (*v.*) cloy, satiate
ANTONYMS: (*n.*) dearth, paucity, lack

19. tortuous
(tôr' chü əs)

(*adj.*) winding, twisted, crooked; highly involved, complex; devious

The cameras had to be portable in order to follow the athletes up the narrow and _____**tortuous**_____ path to the summit.

SYNONYMS: circuitous, serpentine, labyrinthine
ANTONYMS: direct, straight, straightforward

20. turgid
(tər' jid)

(*adj.*) swollen, bloated, filled to excess; overdecorated or excessive in language

The heavy rains turned the fields swampy and the river _____**turgid**_____ .

SYNONYMS: inflated, pompous, bombastic, overblown
ANTONYMS: muted, understated, unadorned, austere

Completing the Sentence

From the words for this unit, choose the one that best completes each of the following sentences. Write the word in the space provided.

1. Any child who can read at the age of four must be considered remarkably __precocious__.

2. Her instructions told me exactly what I wanted to know, without a single __extraneous__ detail.

3. In spite of all our efforts to appeal to whatever human sympathies the kidnappers might have, they remained __obdurate__.

4. At the very __inception__ of his administration, the new President announced a list of the objectives he hoped to accomplish.

5. When my stubborn younger brother proved so __amenable__ to my request, I began to suspect that he had some special reason for wanting to please me.

6. Although I ask no special consideration for myself, I am not too proud to __supplicate__ on behalf of my children.

7. The simple and austere prose of the Gettysburg Address stands in stark contrast to the __turgid__ and overblown rhetoric of a great many other 19th-century orations.

8. Wouldn't you agree that TV has been __surfeited__ lately with sitcoms and soap operas?

9. The more __credulous__ you are, the easier it will be for swindlers and con artists to hoodwink you.

10. "How do you expect your mind to grow when you feed it solely on the __jejune__ pap that comes out of the boob tube?" I asked him pointedly.

11. The stream followed a(n) __tortuous__ course as it twisted through the broken countryside.

12. Usefulness is not the only __criterion__ for including words in this book, but it is the primary one.

13. Our reading program this term is a delightful __potpourri__ of stories, essays, poetry, and drama from many different periods.

14. My last date turned out to be such an expensive affair that my funds were sadly __depleted__ for the rest of the month.

15. When I asked him why he wasn't going to the prom, he answered in his usual __sententious__ style, "No dough, no dance!"

16. It's painful to have to listen to him __expatiate__ on his own virtues when I'm dying to give some fascinating details about my own life and accomplishments.

17. One of the many benefits that I derived from my summer job in the new hospital was learning to be patient with people suffering from various types of __infirmities__.

18. You deserve to be severely __berated__ for your misbehavior during such a solemn ceremony.
19. It is difficult to imagine the __carnage__ that would result from an all-out war fought with nuclear weapons.
20. Although he announces piously how much it hurts him to punish people, I think he takes a(n) __sadistic__ pleasure in it.

Synonyms

Choose the word from this unit that is **the same** or **most nearly the same** in meaning as the **boldface** word or expression in the given phrase. Write the word on the line provided.

1. **exhaust** his supply of good stories — deplete
2. **adamant** in refusing to join in — obdurate
3. **entreat** the captain on behalf of her son — supplicate
4. a **serpentine**, complicated plot — tortuous
5. always full of **moralistic** advice — sententious
6. an **affliction** of aging dancers — infirmity
7. a **mélange** of spices — potpourri
8. was present at the **outset** — inception
9. not **agreeable** to that idea — amenable
10. too **gullible** to perceive trickery — credulous
11. to **elaborate** on her years in Chicago — expatiate
12. a **vicious** love of teasing — sadistic
13. a **gauge** by which to judge — criterion
14. a **massacre** of the English language — carnage
15. quicker to **rebuke** than to praise — berate

Antonyms

Choose the word from this unit that is **most nearly opposite** in meaning to the **boldface** word or expression in the given phrase. Write the word on the line provided.

16. a **relevant** comment — extraneous
17. a **stimulating** discussion — jejune
18. a **backward** capability — precocious
19. thought the decor **muted** — turgid
20. a **dearth** of good things to eat — surfeit

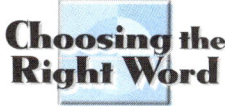

Choosing the Right Word

Circle the **boldface** word that more satisfactorily completes each of the following sentences.

1. You cannot dismiss everything he says as (**obdurate, jejune**) simply because he is young and lacks experience of the world.
2. "The Lord hath heard my (**expatiation, supplication**); the Lord will receive my prayer."—PSALMS
3. In his efforts to impress moral principles on the children, he made use of (**sententious, tortuous**) formulas, such as "To be good, do good."
4. Instead of constantly (**berating, depleting**) the children, why don't you try to explain quietly and clearly how you expect them to behave?
5. The sales manager said she would apply only one (**criterion, carnage**) to my plan for an advertising campaign: "Will it sell more mouthwash?"
6. Given the kinds of tools the ancient Egyptians had to work with, the raising of the pyramids was an extraordinarily (**precocious, jejune**) feat of engineering.
7. I think the class show will be much more effective if it has a constant theme running through it, instead of being just a (**potpourri, surfeit**) of songs, dances, and sketches.
8. Many students feel that our dean is a strict disciplinarian, but I have always found her (**amenable, turgid**) to reasonable requests.
9. Although he is not given to physical maltreatment, I think there is a truly (**sadistic, precocious**) element in his willingness to humiliate people by belittling them in public.
10. I have had my (**surfeit, carnage**) of excuses and evasions; now I want action.
11. My rules for effective writing are: "Emphasize what is essential, play down what is secondary, eliminate what is (**extraneous, turgid**)."
12. She tried to justify the lies she had told us, but I was unable to follow her (**tortuous, amenable**) explanation.
13. Vic is so (**sententious, credulous**) that he actually believed me when I said that I had invented an automatic composition-writing machine.
14. Although he (**expatiates, supplicates**) fluently on the need for a new community action program, I have yet to see him do anything to bring it about.
15. His (**turgid, extraneous**) conversation, with its exaggerated adjectives and far-fetched figures of speech, made me realize once and for all the virtues of simplicity in language.
16. The (**infirmity, carnage**) caused on our streets and highways each year by careless driving has become a major national scandal.
17. The prolonged drought has so (**depleted, berated**) the supplies in our reservoir that we may have to consider rationing water.
18. Few things are more tragic than to see a great mind fall victim to a serious (**inception, infirmity**).
19. What disturbs the coach is not that Tom called the wrong play but he refuses (**obdurately, precociously**) to admit that he made a mistake.
20. At the very (**inception, criterion**) of my career, I set the goals and adopted the basic strategies that were to guide me through many years of outstanding success.

Vocabulary in Context

Read the following passage, in which some of the words you have studied in this unit appear in **boldface** type. Then complete each statement given below the passage by circling the letter of the item that is **the same** or **almost the same** in meaning as the highlighted word.

Marking Time

(Line)

In mid-nineteenth-century America, riding the shiny new railroads across the United States was a nightmare of time-travel and a **tortuous** search among differing schedules and clocks in each town and city. Those who wanted to reform this confusing system had to combat the outrage of many Americans who believed that human beings did not have sovereignty over time. (5)

In the 1840s rail lines had rapidly multiplied and vastly extended their reach. And yet, every city and town marked 12 o'clock noon by when the sun stood straight overhead, regardless of the fact that the sun was not overhead and it was still a little before noon in the next town to the west. Add to (10) this nationwide **potpourri** of local times the fact that each railroad pegged its own timetable to the clocks in the city where its headquarters stood. Imagine boarding the New York Central line in (15) Stamford, Connecticut: you would read Stamford time on the watch in your pocket, New York City time on the station clock and the conductor's watch, and a different time in each town the train (20) passed through. Try changing trains in yet

Modern Amtrak Superliner Train

another city and you'd better find out what time it is there. For unwitting travelers who found themselves stranded in far-off cities, this might seem a **sadistic** ordeal indeed!

Soon the idea was advanced of giving up local times altogether—of dividing the country by four longitudinal zones, the hour to be the same within each. But (25) thousands of **obdurate** citizens viewed their local time with strong civic pride. Many others gave it the same reverence they felt for the sun and the stars.

Furious letter-writers **berated** the railroads for trying to usurp power from Nature itself. It took years to persuade city governments to adopt the change. Its **inception** came on November 18, 1883, at noon. Thirty-five years later, the new daylight saving (30) time set off the same storm once more.

---

1. The meaning of **tortuous** (line 2) is
   a. torturing   c. comical
   b. labyrinthine   d. boring

2. Potpourri (line 11) is best defined as
   a. hodgepodge   c. history
   b. system   d. disaster

3. Sadistic (line 23) most nearly means
   a. satisfying   c. careless
   b. brutal   d. unnecessary

4. The meaning of **obdurate** (line 26) is
   a. disorderly   c. obstinate
   b. organized   d. educated

5. Berated (line 28) most nearly means
   a. congratulated   c. sued
   b. fired upon   d. rebuked

6. Inception (line 29) is best defined as
   a. commencement   c. high point
   b. success   d. defeat

🎧 See page T21 for information.

UNIT 15

Note carefully the spelling, pronunciation, part(s) of speech, and definition(s) of each of the following words. Then write the word in the blank space(s) in the illustrative sentence(s) following. Finally, study the lists of synonyms and antonyms given at the end of each entry.

1. adamant
(ad' ə mənt)

(*adj.*) firm in purpose or opinion, unyielding, obdurate, implacable, inflexible; (*n.*) an extremely hard substance

The government was __**adamant**__ in its refusal to negotiate with terrorists.

By what they called __**adamant**__, writers centuries ago sometimes meant diamonds and sometimes magnetized iron.
ANTONYMS: (*adj.*) yielding, flexible, pliable

2. brouhaha
(brü' hä hä)

(*n.*) a confused hodgepodge of sounds, hubbub; an uproar or commotion that goes far beyond what is justified

After the __**brouhaha**__ had finally subsided, we asked the group to give us a written list of all their complaints.
SYNONYMS: furor, hullabaloo, tumult, pandemonium

3. bulwark
(bəl' wərk)

(*n.*) a strong defense or protection, a solid wall-like structure for defense; (*v.*) to provide such defense or protection

The only remaining evidence of a once thriving civilization is this __**bulwark**__ against the encroachments of the sea.

His staff had to __**bulwark**__ him against fans who wanted to get near him.
SYNONYMS: (*n.*) stronghold, citadel, bastion, rampart
ANTONYMS: (*n.*) breach, weak point in the defense

4. choleric
(käl' ər ik)

(*adj.*) easily made angry, bad-tempered

His __**choleric**__ temperament and erratic behavior made him an ineffective ruler.
SYNONYMS: irascible, testy, splenetic, bilious
ANTONYMS: affable, genial, even-tempered

5. cloy
(kloi)

(*v.*) to spoil or destroy an appetite by too much indulgence, especially in sweet or rich things; to glut, satiate, surfeit

A steady diet of TV began to __**cloy**__, and I was glad to begin a book.
ANTONYMS: stimulate, whet

6. curtail
(kər tāl')

(*v.*) to cut short, bring to a halt or end sooner than expected; to reduce

It is time yet again to __**curtail**__ the flow of unsolicited nonsense that somehow reaches me as e-mail.
SYNONYMS: limit, abbreviate, abridge, contract
ANTONYMS: protract, extend

Unit 15 ■ 165

7. deference
(def′ ər əns)

(*n.*) courteous yielding to the wishes and ideas of another person; great respect marked by submission, as to a superior

Some moderate _____**deference**_____ is due the boss, but too much can seem to conceal other motives.

SYNONYMS: respect, consideration, courtesy
ANTONYMS: contempt, disrespect, scorn, disdain

8. definitive
(də fin′ ə tiv)

(*adj.*) conclusive, final, representing the limit of what can be done

She is working on what she hopes will be the ___**definitive**___ biography of Emily Dickenson.

SYNONYMS: exhaustive, authoritative
ANTONYMS: tentative, inconclusive

9. demeanor
(di mē′ nər)

(*n.*) the way a person behaves, overall impression made by comportment, manner, etc.; facial appearance, mien

Charles Dickens' Mr. Pickwick has such a cheerful and sympathetic _____**demeanor**_____ that few can resist him.

SYNONYMS: conduct, behavior, bearing, carriage

10. enigmatic
(en ig mat′ ik)

(*adj.*) puzzling, perplexing, inexplicable, not easily understood

He was staring me straight in the eye, neither pleased nor displeased, his expression _____**enigmatic**_____.

SYNONYMS: baffling, mysterious, inexplicable
ANTONYMS: intelligible, understandable, fathomable

11. impromptu
(im prämp′ tü)

(*adj., adv.*) without preparation, offhand, suddenly or hastily done; (*n.*) an extemporaneous composition or remark; a minimal piece suggestive of improvisation

His _____**impromptu**_____ speech allowed him to express not only what he was thinking but what he was feeling.

At first, an _____**impromptu**_____ by Schubert may not stun you, but hours later you'll find that you haven't forgotten it.

SYNONYMS: (*adj.*) spontaneous, improvised, unrehearsed
ANTONYMS: (*adj.*) rehearsed, planned, prepared, premeditated

12. mawkish
(mô′ kish)

(*adj.*) excessively and objectionably sentimental; having a mildly sickening flavor

In *It's a Wonderful Life,* Jimmy Stewart was praised for making his character poignant without being ___**mawkish**___.

SYNONYMS: sentimentalized, maudlin, mushy, nauseating
ANTONYMS: unsentimental, callous, insensitive

13. mollify
(mäl′ ə fī)

(*v.*) to soften, make gentle, pacify; to calm, allay (as an emotion), assuage, appease, placate; to reduce in intensity

The Senator hoped to _____**mollify**_____ her angry public, but nothing she said was likely to get her reelected.

ANTONYMS: enrage, anger, aggravate, exacerbate

14. **onus**
    (ō′ nəs)
    (*n.*) something that is heavy or burdensome (especially an unwelcome responsibility); a stigma; blame
    If the _____onus_____ for a defective product is placed on the consumer, some complicated legal and ethical questions are sure to arise.
    SYNONYMS: burden, obligation, duty, stigma

15. **presentiment**
    (pre zen′ tə ment)
    (*n.*) a vague sense of approaching misfortune
    It was a strange irony that in denying their __presentiments__, they made their worst fears come true.
    SYNONYMS: foreboding, premonition, hunch

16. **profligate**
    (präf′ lə gət)
    (*adj.*) given over to dissipation and self-indulgence, immoral; recklessly extravagant; (*n.*) a person given to self-indulgent and wild spending
    This was the _____profligate_____ son in the family, the one who could charm, the one of whom nothing was expected.
    She was a _____profligate_____, and no matter how much money she earned, she always spent more than she had.
    SYNONYMS: (*adj.*) prodigal, improvident; (*n.*) spendthrift
    ANTONYMS: (*adj.*) penny-pinching, frugal, economical

17. **remit**
    (ri mit′)
    (*v.*) to send or hand in (as money); to cancel (as a penalty or punishment), forgive, pardon; to lessen, diminish; to put off, postpone, defer
    They would _____remit_____ a certain sum each year to a local charity.
    SYNONYMS: pay, absolve, subside, abate

18. **requisite**
    (rek′ wə zit)
    (*adj.*) needed, necessary, regarded as essential or indispensable
    If you have the _____requisite_____ physical strength and an ear for music, I'll pay for your first year of dance instruction.
    SYNONYMS: required, obligatory, incumbent
    ANTONYMS: nonessential, superfluous, optional

19. **sartorial**
    (sär tôr′ ē əl)
    (*adj.*) of or pertaining to a tailor or his work; having to do with clothes or dress (especially men's)
    Paging through historical picture books is a fascinating study in _____sartorial_____ standards through the years.

20. **thwart**
    (thwôrt)
    (*v.*) to oppose successfully; to prevent, frustrate
    Our dog's friendliness would _____thwart_____ the sternest efforts of the most expensive guard-dog trainer.
    SYNONYMS: foil, baffle
    ANTONYMS: aid, assist, abet, further

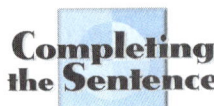

Completing the Sentence

From the words for this unit, choose the one that best completes each of the following sentences. Write the word in the space provided.

1. I was surprised that so trivial an incident should have provided such a fearful __**brouhaha**__ in the popular press.

2. The circumstances surrounding the death are so __**enigmatic**__ that the police are not even sure that a crime was committed.

3. By talking so much about your __**presentiment**__ that "we're going to have an accident," you are simply making me nervous and preventing me from driving properly.

4. I see no point in your applying for that job when it is perfectly clear that you lack the __**requisite**__ qualifications.

5. He was so __**profligate**__ with his inheritance that he consumed in a few years the fortune it had taken his parents a lifetime to accumulate.

6. By getting the students to apologize for their thoughtless discourtesy, we __**mollified**__ the anger of the elderly elevator operator.

7. I think that the phrase "having a short fuse" aptly describes my new boss's __**choleric**__ and curmudgeonly disposition.

8. Somehow, whenever more money is needed for our club activities, the __**onus**__ of raising it always seems to fall on me.

9. We are still looking for a(n) __**definitive**__ answer to the question of whether or not our prisons can rehabilitate as well as punish.

10. At first, I was glad to see my old classmate again, but he embarrassed me with his __**mawkish**__ talk about "those wonderful, golden school days."

11. In his plaid jacket, light gray slacks, and tailored sport shirt, he was a model of __**sartorial**__ elegance.

12. Although we must have armed forces to protect the country, the most important __**bulwark**__ of national security is the devotion of the people to our democratic institutions.

13. How can you watch those silly soap operas day after day without being __**cloyed**__ by their gooey sentimentality?

14. Throughout the trial she maintained a(n) __**demeanor**__ of quiet dignity and confidence that made a favorable impression on the jury.

15. He was willing to compromise on many issues, but elimination of the "Male Only" requirements for those jobs was the one point on which he was absolutely __**adamant**__.

16. The candidate seems much more human and appealing when she delivers a(n) __**impromptu**__ speech than when she reads a prepared text.

17. In __**deference**__ to the wishes of the widow, the funeral services will be brief, and no eulogy will be delivered.

18. When the chairperson saw that the speakers were becoming more heated, without offering any new facts or ideas to clarify the situation, she decided to __curtail__ the discussion period.

19. We heard that the South High fans were planning to "kidnap" our mascot before the game, and we were determined to __thwart__ them.

20. Attached to every bill for the merchandise was a brief notice asking the customer to __remit__ payment promptly.

Synonyms

Choose the word from this unit that is **the same** or **most nearly the same** in meaning as the **boldface** word or expression in the given phrase. Write the word on the line provided.

1. a clearly expressed yet **mystifying** statement — enigmatic
2. a weighty and mournful **bearing** — demeanor
3. a heavy **burden** — onus
4. **pay** the fine — remit
5. visited by a **premonition** — presentiment
6. **foil** a complicated plot — thwart
7. a **sentimentalized** love story — mawkish
8. the **furor** over the court's decision — brouhaha
9. felt protected inside the **citadel** — bulwark
10. to **surfeit** my taste for ice cream — cloy
11. **improvident** with her energies — profligate
12. not owning the **obligatory** dark suit — requisite
13. **implacable** in the face of conflict — adamant
14. **abridge** the length of the working day — curtail
15. a store for all your **tailoring** needs — sartorial

Antonyms

Choose the word from this unit that is **most nearly opposite** in meaning to the **boldface** word or expression in the given phrase. Write the word on the line provided.

16. draw up a **tentative** agreement — definitive
17. show **disrespect** for the leader — deference
18. a **prepared** statement for the press — impromptu
19. an explanation that will **anger** them — mollify
20. a **genial** reply to the question — choleric

Choosing the Right Word

Circle the **boldface** word that more satisfactorily completes each of the following sentences.

1. His bitter anger was eventually (**mollified**, **thwarted**) by the effects of time and by our skillful appeals to his vanity.
2. Expressing his mystification at the Soviet Union, Churchill referred to it as a "riddle wrapped in a mystery inside a(n) (**enigma**, **presentiment**)."
3. Scholastic proficiency, emotional stability, and a genuine interest in young people are the (**requisites**, **profligates**) for a good teacher.
4. The special privileges extended to members of the senior class have not been entirely withdrawn, but they have been sharply (**thwarted**, **curtailed**) for the rest of the term.
5. I am a great admirer of Dickens, but even I must admit that the death of Little Nell in *The Old Curiosity Shop* is too (**sartorial**, **mawkish**) to be truly effective.
6. We all admired her (**demeanor**, **presentiment**), which was dignified without any suggestion of superiority or stuffiness.
7. Their efforts to win the game by a last-minute trick play were (**thwarted**, **remitted**) when our alert safety intercepted the deep pass.
8. The recent (**presentiment**, **brouhaha**) over the choice of a host for our local beauty pageant seemed to me nothing more than a "tempest in a teapot."
9. The cancer from which she was suffering went into (**remission**, **deference**).
10. Let us place the (**presentiment**, **onus**) for the defeat where it belongs—on each and every of us!
11. Her unvarying sweetness, like a diet composed entirely of desserts, does become (**cloying**, **choleric**) after a while.
12. He delivered his speech poorly, but since he was the best dressed man on the dais that afternoon, he enjoyed a (**sartorial**, **profligate**) if not an oratorical triumph.
13. His constant blustering and (**definitive**, **choleric**) behavior may be no more than an unconscious attempt to conceal his lack of self-confidence.
14. I came to realize that the demure little woman who never raised her voice had a will of pure (**adamant**, **deference**).
15. Scientific knowledge and the scientific method stand as a(n) (**bulwark**, **onus**) against the tides of irrationality, superstition, and wishful thinking.
16. Far from being (**impromptu**, **profligate**), all those jokes and wisecracks you hear on TV talk shows are usually prepared by professional writers and are carefully rehearsed.
17. There are so many aspects to Shakespeare that there will never be a truly (**definitive**, **bumptious**) study of his work.
18. I am really surprised that he now shows such exaggerated (**deference**, **adamant**) to people whose "aristocratic" pretensions he has always regarded with contempt.
19. According to psychologists, when you have an "uncanny" feeling that something is about to happen, you may unconsciously act in a way that will help the (**forbearance**, **presentiment**) to come true.
20. After years of (**profligate**, **enigmatic**) living, he experienced a religious conversion and devoted the rest of his life to serving mankind.

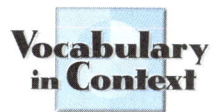

Vocabulary in Context

*Read the following passage, in which some of the words you have studied in this unit appear in **boldface** type. Then complete each statement given below the passage by circling the letter of the item that is **the same** or **almost the same** in meaning as the highlighted word.*

Looking at Laughter

(Line)

Stop and think about laughter and you'll begin to see why psychologists want to study it. This seemingly automatic action, a sudden exhaling of single syllables ("ha-ha-ha" or "huh-huh-huh") expresses no concrete meaning and yet it peppers our everyday conversations. One psychologist found ordinary laughter so **enigmatic** that he spent
(5) years investigating how, when, and why we do it. What he found was surprising.

It goes without saying that laugher's **demeanor** often expresses some degree of cheer or amusement. But the study found that what sets off the laugh is most often neither funny nor intended to be. The **requisite** condition for a laugh is simply the
(10) presence of another person. When people are alone and lacking such substitutes for company as television, radio, or reading, they almost never laugh. (Similarly, you cannot tickle yourself.) Very often when two
(15) or more people *are* together, a remark as simple as "I've got to go now" can trigger an **impromptu** laugh. And the one who laughs, the study found, is far more often the speaker than the person who is spoken to.

Laughing at danger on a rollercoaster

(20) All this suggests two things about comedy programs on television. First, the laughter of a studio audience is greatly helped by the fact that its members sit sociably together in the studio. Second, the recorded laughter—the "laugh
(25) track"—that is broadcast for programs without a studio audience really does stimulate people watching at home to laugh.

The study also confirmed that laughter can be a sign of **deference** or an attempt by the laugher to **mollify** someone with greater power or higher social standing—a charming defense we all use. Though the psychological intricacies of
(30) laughter have not been fully determined, it is clear that laughter is a healthy expression of joy as well as a tool used to form human connections.

---

1. The meaning of **enigmatic** (line 4) is
a. distracting   c. mystifying
b. ridiculous   d. obvious

2. Demeanor (line 6) most nearly means
a. embarrassment   c. state of mind
b. behavior   d. background

3. Requisite (line 9) is best defined as
a. obligatory   c. surprising
b. pleasantest   d. funny

4. The meaning of **impromptu** (line 17) is
a. extreme   c. prepared
b. spontaneous   d. inappropriate

5. Deference (line 27) most nearly means
a. stalling   c. respect
b. high spirits   d. distraction

6. Mollify (line 28) is best defined as
a. amuse   c. disturb
b. distract   d. placate

Review Units 13–15

Visit us at www.sadlier-oxford.com
for interactive puzzles and games.

Analogies

In each of the following, circle the item that best completes the comparison.

See pages T38–T48 for explanations of answers.

1. **burden** is to **encumber** as
   a. onus is to assist
   b. presentiment is to gladden
   c. **infirmity is to weaken**
   d. buttress is to repel

2. **jejune** is to **unfavorable** as
   a. blatant is to favorable
   b. requisite is to unfavorable
   c. **providential is to favorable**
   d. precocious is to unfavorable

3. **monkey** is to **agile** as
   a. donkey is to sadistic
   b. horse is to herculean
   c. zebra is to profligate
   d. **mule is to obdurate**

4. **passive** is to **act** as
   a. **adamant is to yield**
   b. credulous is to trust
   c. ostensible is to appear
   d. amenable is to comply

5. **skeptical** is to **doubt** as
   a. disconsolate is to hope
   b. **credulous is to believe**
   c. choleric is to trust
   d. jejune is to deny

6. **profligate** is to **squander** as
   a. skinflint is to invest
   b. debtor is to dun
   c. banker is to embezzle
   d. **miser is to hoard**

7. **inanimate** is to **life** as
   a. **impassive is to emotion**
   b. incontrovertible is to talent
   c. inauspicious is to money
   d. impromptu is to class

8. **incontrovertible** is to **dispute** as
   a. incredible is to refute
   b. **incalculable is to compute**
   c. immaculate is to pollute
   d. incoherent is to salute

9. **quandary** is to **nonplus** as
   a. onus is to amuse
   b. criterion is to sadden
   c. **enigma is to puzzle**
   d. brouhaha is to delight

10. **cloy** is to **palate** as
    a. surfeit is to demeanor
    b. intrigue is to imagination
    c. **nauseate is to stomach**
    d. whet is to appetite

11. **abet** is to **thwart** as
    a. **foment is to quell**
    b. aver is to avow
    c. collate is to annotate
    d. berate is to rebuke

12. **herculean** is to **strength** as
    a. **titanic is to size**
    b. laconic is to volume
    c. spartan is to wealth
    d. stentorian is to length

13. **amenable** is to **compliant** as
    a. disruptive is to impassive
    b. grisly is to cloying
    c. obdurate is to pliant
    d. **precocious is to advanced**

14. **saccharine** is to **sweetness** as
    a. turgid is to clarity
    b. sententious is to coherence
    c. tortuous is to simplicity
    d. **mawkish is to sentiment**

15. **criterion** is to **judge** as
    a. gauge is to balance
    b. scale is to estimate
    c. yardstick is to weigh
    d. **ruler is to measure**

16. **sartorial** is to **tailor** as
    a. sacerdotal is to cobbler
    b. **tonsorial is to barber**
    c. vestigial is to couturier
    d. juridical is to connoisseur

17. **solace** is to **disconsolate** as
    a. broach is to mawkish
    b. incense is to choleric
    c. **budge is to adamant**
    d. supplicate is to clement

18. **protract** is to **curtail** as
    a. aver is to affirm
    b. **replenish is to deplete**
    c. placate is to mollify
    d. expatiate is to immigrate

REVIEW UNITS 13-15

In each of the following groups, circle the word that is best defined or suggested by the given phrase.

1. assuage her guilt
   a. buttress   b. foment   **c. mollify**   d. aver
2. at the beginning of the journey
   a. inception   b. presentiment   c. brouhaha   d. rejoinder
3. an unpromising set of circumstances
   a. amenable   **b. inauspicious**   c. enigmatic   d. herculean
4. perplexed by their reaction
   a. thwarted   **b. nonplussed**   c. fomented   d. mollified
5. not too proud to beg
   a. berate   **b. supplicate**   c. remit   d. buttress
6. support the cause
   a. deplete   b. foment   c. mollify   **d. buttress**
7. a bastion of civilization
   a. requisite   **b. bulwark**   c. onus   d. inception
8. testimony unrelated to the case
   a. mawkish   **b. extraneous**   c. remitting   d. broaching
9. too much information to process
   a. turgid   b. onus   **c. surfeit**   d. requisite
10. a noted expert
    a. onus   **b. connoisseur**   c. supplicant   d. impromptu
11. an announcement that incited a furor
    a. brouhaha   b. choleric   c. potpourri   d. lassitude
12. the grief-stricken victim
    a. nonplussed   b. obdurate   c. credulous   **d. disconsolate**
13. a self-indulgent lifestyle
    a. definitive   b. blatant   **c. profligate**   d. extraneous
14. remain unyielding
    a. jejune   **b. obdurate**   c. tortuous   d. sadistic
15. pay a penalty
    a. supplicate   b. thwart   **c. remit**   d. mollify
16. a heavy burden
    a. rejoinder   b. demeanor   **c. onus**   d. buttress
17. a foreboding dream
    a. surfeit   **b. presentiment**   c. onus   d. carnage
18. a quick retort
    a. rejoinder   b. surfeit   c. presentiment   d. inception
19. an aphoristic speech
    a. sententious   b. turgid   c. tortuous   d. obdurate
20. an advanced student
    a. sartorial   b. sadistic   c. profligate   **d. precocious**

Vocabulary in Context

*Read the following passage, in which some of the words you have studied in Units 13–15 appear in **boldface** type. Then complete each statement given below the passage by circling the item that is **the same** or **almost the same** in meaning as the highlighted word.*

When Stumps Were Stumps

(Line)

Before the birth of the modern media, staging a campaign to elect an American President was a scattered, street-level affair. Professional poll-
(5) takers, convention planners, and spin doctors did not yet exist and the task of drawing attention to a candidate's name and platform was relegated to party members and neighborhood
(10) volunteers.

The very idea of campaigning would have **nonplussed** the first Presidential candidate. George Washington, running without an opponent, was
(15) unanimously elected president. He fulfilled two terms in office purely out of a sense of duty. Having led an amateur army to defeat the British Empire, this tall, **impassive**, and dignified hero
(20) seemed, by any **criterion**, a national leader beyond compare.

But when the right to vote was extended, political parties formed. These parties needed to promulgate
(25) their ideas in order to stir up party sentiment and attract new members. Colorful banners were unfurled in public places, blazoning a candidate's virtues and ideology. Citizens were
(30) encouraged to **broach** their party loyalty by wearing it where one could see it—on cheap badges hung from around the neck or else from printed ribbons hung from a pin. (Campaign
(35) buttons with pins on the back, still produced today, did not appear until 1896.) All such attention-getters (they included printed bandanas) bore the candidate's name or nickname—and a
(40) slogan if there was room. Slogans were hugely popular. Campaigners for William Henry Harrison rolled enormous metal spheres, painted with slogans, through city streets.

(45) From Andrew Jackson's second campaign onward, rowdy picnics, barbecues, and loud parades were used to attract the voters, much as they are used in primary-election
(50) campaigns today. Even Abraham Lincoln had his carnival-like supporters who contributed to the general **brouhaha**: the Wide-Awakes, as they called themselves (awake to
(55) **thwart** the enemy, slavery), marched in closely drilled formations, sporting shiny hats and capes.

In addition, countless speeches were made and handbills printed—
(60) but first and last the message was simply: "Look here, look here!"

1. The meaning of **nonplussed** (line 12) is
a. perplexed   c. amused
b. outraged   d. excited

2. Impassive (line 19) most nearly means
a. proud   c. conceited
b. stoical   d. hard-working

3. Criterion (line 20) is best defined as
a. yardstick   c. opinion
b. vote   d. luck

4. The meaning of **broach** (line 30) is
a. make fun of   c. conceal
b. present   d. enhance

5. Brouhaha (line 53) most nearly means
a. cheerfulness   c. crowd
b. anger   d. hullaballoo

6. Thwart (line 55) is best defined as
a. capture   c. foil
b. destroy   d. puzzle

REVIEW UNITS 13–15

 Choosing the Right Meaning

Read each sentence carefully. Then circle the item that best completes the statement below the sentence.

See pages T38–T48 for explanations of answers.

"They hove the wheel up just in time to save her from broaching to. (Richard Henry Dana, *Two Years Before the Mast*, Ch. 32) (1)

1. The best meaning for the phrase **broaching to** in line 1 is
   - **a. turning sideways to the wind** ✓
   - b. tapping a cask of rum
   - c. breaking the surface of the water
   - d. striking a hidden reef

"We can load up a piece of amber . . . with the greatest possible excess of negative charge, and still it remains absolutely impassive in the presence of a magnet." (K.K. Darrow) (2)

2. The word **impassive** in line 2 most nearly means
   - a. stoical
   - b. insensible
   - c. unemotional
   - **d. motionless** ✓

Try as I might, I simply could not swallow the mawkish-tasting medicine without gagging. (2)

3. The term **mawkish-tasting** in line 1 most nearly means
   - a. insipid
   - b. excessively sentimental
   - **c. nauseating** ✓
   - d. mushy

As I was dusting the sideboard, I accidentally knocked against the potpourri and spilled it all over the new rug. (2)

4. The word **potpourri** in line 1 may best be defined as
   - a. meat-and-potato stew
   - **b. jar of mixed petals and spices** ✓
   - c. album of family photos
   - d. collection of sheet music

 Antonyms

In each of the following groups, circle the word or expression that is most nearly the **opposite** of the word in **boldface** type.

1. **grisly**
   a. spectacular
   b. horrible
   c. pleasant ✓
   d. natural

2. **mollify**
   a. arouse ✓
   b. quiet
   c. amuse
   d. disperse

3. **infirmities**
   a. strengths ✓
   b. intentions
   c. vices
   d. misconceptions

4. **impromptu**
   a. prepared ✓
   b. amusing
   c. spontaneous
   d. praiseworthy

5. **averred**
   a. proved
   b. denied ✓
   c. predicted
   d. proclaimed

6. **berate**
   a. expel
   b. praise ✓
   c. lecture
   d. join

7. **definitive**
   a. critical
   b. logical
   c. unreliable ✓
   d. new

8. **deference**
   a. fear
   b. disrespect ✓
   c. impulse
   d. reverence

Review Units 13–15 ■ 175

9. thwart
a. facilitate ✓
b. criticize
c. evaluate
d. consider

10. encumbered
a. unburdened ✓
b. sensitized
c. cautioned
d. tortured

11. tortuous
a. tricky
b. straightforward ✓
c. circuitous
d. bizarre

12. curtail
a. enjoy
b. plan
c. lengthen ✓
d. pay for

13. turgid
a. austere ✓
b. cloying
c. thick
d. ornate

14. sadistic
a. excessive
b. humane ✓
c. supine
d. understated

15. foment
a. excite
b. forage
c. suppress ✓
d. disguise

16. jejune
a. serious
b. stimulating ✓
c. irrelevant
d. essential

A. On the line provided, write the word you have learned in Units 13–15 that is related to each of the following nouns.

EXAMPLE: remission—**remit**

1. opportuneness, opportunist, opportunism — **opportune**
2. supplication, supplicant, suppliant, suppliance — **supplicate**
3. turgidity, turgidness — **turgid**
4. precocity, precociousness — **precocious**
5. expatiation — **expatiate**
6. mawkishness — **mawkish**
7. obdurateness, obduracy — **obdurate**
8. credulity, credulousness — **credulous**
9. sadism, sadist — **sadistic**
10. collation, collator — **collate**
11. depletion — **deplete**
12. impassiveness, impassivity — **impassive**
13. encumbrance, encumbrancer — **encumber**
14. choler — **choleric**

B. On the line provided, write the word you have learned in Units 13–15 that is related to each of the following verbs.

EXAMPLE: controvert—**incontrovertible**

15. proliferate — **prolific**
16. console — **disconsolate**
17. carouse — **carousal**
18. defer — **deference**
19. require — **requisite**
20. demean — **demeanor**

REVIEW UNITS 13–15

Two-Word Completions

Circle the pair of words that best complete the meaning of each of the following passages.

See pages T38–T48 for explanations of answers.

1. Mozart was a(n) _____ youngster who wrote his first opera at the age of eleven. Though he was never as _____ a composer of theater music as some of his contemporaries, his output of stage works was by no means negligible.
   a. precocious . . . prolific
   b. sententious . . . incontrovertible
   c. credulous . . . profligate
   d. enigmatic . . . blatant

2. Friends hoped that the tearful _____ of the mother would soften the king's heart toward the young reprobates, but the dour old man _____ refused to yield to her entreaties.
   a. presentiments . . . obdurately
   b. demeanor . . . mawkishly
   c. supplications . . . adamantly
   d. deference . . . floridly

3. Though one of his parents reacted to the unexpected news of his death with a(n) _____ display of emotion, the other received it with all the _____ and restraint of a true stoic.
   a. enigmatic . . . credulity
   b. mawkish . . . choler
   c. sadistic . . . deference
   d. blatant . . . impassivity

4. During the battle, the _____ had been horrendous. Where the fighting had been the fiercest, the bodies were piled three deep. It took days to complete the _____ task of burying the dead.
   a. surfeit . . . turgid
   b. brouhaha . . . herculean
   c. carnage . . . grisly
   d. onus . . . mawkish

5. Once our fossil-fuel reserves are exhausted, they are gone forever. For that reason, we should try to _____ our use of these precious resources so that they are not _____ too quickly.
   a. abet . . . nonplussed
   b. curtail . . . depleted
   c. remit . . . expatiated
   d. mollify . . . buttressed

6. No matter how much protective consumer legislation we pass in order to _____ would-be swindlers and con artists, there probably will always be _____ people around for them to prey on.
   a. buttress . . . adamant
   b. thwart . . . credulous
   c. abet . . . jejune
   d. curtail . . . precocious

Building with Classical Roots

quer, ques, quis—to seek, ask

This root appears in **requisite** (page 167), which means "essential, necessary." Other words based on the same root are listed below.

| disquisition | inquisition | perquisite | query |
| inquest | inquisitive | prerequisite | requisition |

From the list of words above, choose the one that corresponds to each of the brief definitions below. Write the word in the blank space in the illustrative sentence below the definition.

1. to ask, ask about, inquire into; to express doubts about; a question or inquiry
   If you have a question about that newspaper article, **query** the editor.

2. eager for knowledge; given to inquiry or research, curious; nosy, prying
   A good detective needs a(n) **inquisitive** mind.

3. a demand or application made in an authoritative way; to demand or call for with authority
   The department made a(n) **requisition** for ten additional trucks.

4. an extra payment; anything received for work besides regular compensation (*"that which is sought"*)
   She enjoyed the **perquisites** of her office.

5. a legal inquiry before a jury (*"asking into"*)
   The family of the victim attend the coroner's **inquest**.

6. that which is necessary beforehand; a qualification (as for enrolling in a course)
   Beginning Spanish is a(n) **prerequisite** for advanced Spanish.

7. a long and formal speech or writing about a subject
   The scientist prepared a scholarly **disquisition** on her findings.

8. a severe investigation; an official inquiry conducted with little regard for human rights
   The zealous reporter turned a simple interview into a(n) **inquisition**.

From the list of words above, choose the one that best completes each of the following sentences. Write the word in the blank space provided.

1. The pay for this job is not very good, but the **perquisites**, such as free housing and use of a car, make it attractive.

2. Can you understand why she is being so **inquisitive** about matters that are really none of her concern?

REVIEW UNITS 13–15

3. Her long __disquisition__ on the need for personal values and standards was so abstract that I found little in it that I could relate to.

4. A law degree is the minimum __prerequisite__ for this job.

5. Because of the suspicious circumstances surrounding her sudden death, the body was exhumed and a(n) __inquest__ held.

6. We objected strenuously to his questioning, which we felt had turned into a(n) __inquisition__ into our behavior.

7. The public library is prepared to answer __queries__ on a wide variety of subjects.

8. We can issue no supplies without a properly executed __requisition__.

Circle the **boldface** word that more satisfactorily completes each of the following sentences.

1. American citizenship is among the few (**perquisites**, **prerequisites**) for running for the Presidency of the United States.

2. The school administration plans to (**query**, **inquire**) all parents about the inoculation histories of their children.

3. The secret police conducted illegal (**disquistions**, **inquisitions**) of those whom they suspected of having anti-government views.

4. The parents had a difficult time keeping anything, especially presents, hidden from their (**inquisitive**, **requisite**) three-year-old.

5. The teacher submitted a(n) (**requisition**, **inquest**) to the principal for more painting and drawing supplies for her preschool classes.

6. The company officers offered stock options as (**prerequisites**, **perquisites**) to those executives whom they were particularly eager to recruit.

7. The (**inquest**, **disquisition**) into the sudden death of the young schoolteacher resulted in a finding of death from natural causes.

8. The anthropologist delivered a detailed (**requisition**, **disquisition**) on the culture of the Mayans, which he has studied for many years.

Writer's Challenge

Read the following sentences, paying special attention to the words and phrases underlined. From the words in the box below, find better choices for these underlined words and phrases. Then use these choices to rewrite the sentences.

WORD BANK				
abet	curtail	encumber	infirmity	sadistic
adamant	deference	extraneous	jejune	surfeit
berate	definitive	grisly	opportune	thwart
choleric	deplete	herculean	rejoinder	turgid

At the Cottage at Mount McGregor

1. In his later years, former Civil War general and 18th president Ulysses S. Grant made some poor business deals that <u>emptied</u> his once significant wealth.
depleted

2. He decided to write his memoirs, the profits from which he hoped would <u>baffle</u> his family's otherwise certain financial ruin.
thwart

3. But this goal was far more than a writing task; it became a <u>very hard to do in the sense of requiring unusual strength</u> effort to beat the fiercest opponent of Grant's life: terminal throat cancer.
herculean

4. Grant <u>cut short</u> his other activities to focus on his final mission, which he completed in a mountain cottage in upstate New York.
curtailed

5. Despite growing weakness, Grant remained <u>as firm and unyielding as a rock</u> about finishing the book.
adamant

6. He spent the last days of his <u>disability</u> unable to speak, but doggedly struggling to finish his manuscript. He did so, just days before his death on July 23, 1885.
infirmity

7. *Personal Memoirs of U.S. Grant* became one of the <u>finally determining</u> books of the late 19th century and, as he had hoped, earned his family ample profits—equivalent to nearly $40 million today.
definitive

Cumulative Review IV

Analogies

In each of the following, circle the item that best completes the comparison.

See pages T38–T48 for explanations of answers.

1. **thwart** is to **expedite** as
   a. contrive is to concoct
   b. expostulate is to remonstrate
   c. aver is to repudiate
   d. surmise is to infer

2. **impromptu** is to **improvise** as
   a. bizarre is to precipitate
   b. resilient is to sear
   c. anomalous is to enhance
   d. synthetic is to fabricate

3. **hoodwink** is to **credulous** as
   a. persuade is to adamant
   b. touch is to callous
   c. incense is to choleric
   d. manage is to fractious

4. **adage** is to **sententious** as
   a. caveat is to hypothetical
   b. cliché is to hackneyed
   c. precept is to recondite
   d. axiom is to nebulous

5. **connoisseur** is to **erudite** as
   a. novice is to callow
   b. interloper is to querulous
   c. paragon is to heinous
   d. demagogue is to surreptitious

6. **beaver** is to **sedulous** as
   a. sheep is to obdurate
   b. cow is to imperious
   c. horse is to politic
   d. pig is to slovenly

7. **abstemious** is to **forbear** as
   a. intemperate is to peculate
   b. crass is to expatiate
   c. pretentious is to enjoin
   d. profligate is to dissipate

8. **cloy** is to **jaded** as
   a. surfeit is to satiated
   b. encumber is to absolved
   c. prate is to enthralled
   d. foist is to dunned

9. **contretemps** is to **disconcerted** as
   a. hiatus is to scourged
   b. dissension is to disabused
   c. dilemma is to nonplussed
   d. irony is to reproved

10. **buttress** is to **strength** as
    a. reverberate is to echo
    b. ameliorate is to improvement
    c. expiate is to sin
    d. debase is to quality

11. **irrevocable** is to **retract** as
    a. intrinsic is to resusitate
    b. incontrovertible is to impugn
    c. inadvertent is to deliberate
    d. irresolute is to waver

12. **enigmatic** is to **inscrutable** as
    a. definitive is to redoubtable
    b. dilatory is to punctilious
    c. pernicious is to deleterious
    d. subservient is to pretentious

13. **reprove** is to **reprimand** as
    a. prate is to captious
    b. abate is to continue
    c. restrain is to fetter
    d. satiate is to quell

14. **prodigy** is to **precocious** as
    a. denizen is to sanctimonious
    b. interloper is to unctuous
    c. reprobate is to astute
    d. insurgent is to seditious

15. **jejune** is to **substance** as
    a. brusque is to brevity
    b. vapid is to zest
    c. provocative is to interest
    d. efficacious is to effect

16. **berate** is to **castigate** as
    a. remit is to abate
    b. wheedle is to deplete
    c. equivocate is to wheedle
    d. broach is to elicit

17. **mollify** is to **assuage** as
    a. blazon is to flout
    b. collate is to wheedle
    c. extenuate is to mitigate
    d. permeate is to invoke

18. **torpid** is to **lassitude** as
    a. affable is to dissension
    b. noncommittal is to umbrage
    c. querulous is to approbation
    d. jaded is to ennui

19. cadaverous is to **corpse** as
  a. vitriolic is to cemetery
  (b. sepulchral is to grave)
  c. soporific is to funeral
  d. adventitious is to coffin

20. mawkish is to **sentiment** as
  a. sleazy is to sincerity
  b. grisly is to appeal
  c. tortuous is to direction
  (d. lurid is to sensation)

Choosing the Right Meaning

Read each sentence carefully. Then circle the item that best completes the statement below the sentence.

See pages T38–T48 for explanations of answers.

"Anon comes Pyramus, sweet youth and tall
  And finds his trusty Thisbe's mantle slain; (2)
Whereat with blade—with bloody, blameful blade—
  He bravely broached his boiling bloody breast." (4)
    (Shakespeare, *A Midsummer Night's Dream*, V, 1, 143–146)

1. The word **broached** in line 4 most nearly means
  a. brought up
  b. turned sideways
  (c. pierced)
  d. touched upon

"The bars survive the captive they enthrall." (1)
  (George Gordon, Lord Byron, *Childe Harold's Pilgrimage*)

2. The word **enthrall** in line 1 may best be defined as
  a. hold responsible
  (b. hold captive)
  c. hold hostage
  d. hold spellbound

At that memorable feast, we found ourselves surrounded by enough food to assuage the hunger of even the most ravenous guest. (2)

3. In line 2, the word **assuage** most nearly means
  a. whet acutely
  b. relieve moderately
  (c. satisfy thoroughly)
  d. ease slightly

The constant rocking of the great ship made me quite squeamish for the first few days of the voyage, but I soon got used to the motion and had no further trouble with my stomach. (2)

4. The word **squeamish** in line 1 most nearly means
  a. fastidious   (b. nauseous)   c. priggish   d. delicate

For several weeks after their birth, the callow young birds are completely helpless and must be fed, warmed, and protected constantly by their parents. (2)

5. The best meaning for the word **callow** in line 1 is
  (a. featherless)   b. numerous   c. unsophisticated   d. small

CUMULATIVE REVIEW IV

Two-Word Completions

Circle the pair of words that best complete the meaning of each of the following sentences.

See pages T38–T48 for explanations of answers.

1. In the eyes of the law, the accomplices who aid and _____ the commission of a crime are just as _____ as the actual perpetrator, even though they may not have been present when the deed was committed.
   a. expedite . . . nominal
   b. disavow . . . autonomous
   c. abet . . . culpable
   d. corroborate . . . scurrilous

2. An evening's fare at an old-fashioned vaudeville house consisted of a(n) _____ of circus and nightclub acts performed by a(n) _____ assortment of singers, dancers, comedians, and other entertainers.
   a. aura . . . ostentatious
   b. gauntlet . . . prolific
   c. onus . . . inadvertent
   d. potpourri . . . motley

3. _____ of crack troops drawn from the various branches of the armed forces were sent in to quell the riots and other disorders that a few malcontent firebrands had managed to _____ in the wake of the premier's assassination.
   a. Potpourris . . . exhort
   b. Contingents . . . foment
   c. Coalitions . . . simulate
   d. Infractions . . . transmute

4. Some of my friends are the epitome of _____ splendor; others always look as if they've slept in their clothes. Personally, I am neither as dapper as the first group nor as _____ as the second.
   a. provincial . . . mawkish
   b. herculean . . . sleazy
   c. sedulous . . . vapid
   d. sartorial . . . slovenly

5. The _____ fears and suspicions that had haunted his troubled dreams like so many shapeless ghosts _____ and vanished in the strong light of day.
   a. squeamish . . . curtailed
   b. nebulous . . . dissipated
   c. amorphous . . . relegated
   d. intemperate . . . absolved

6. Unfortunately for the accused, there was no possible _____ to the _____ evidence of guilt that the prosecution's airtight case laid before the jury.
   a. rejoinder . . . incontrovertible
   b. precept . . . specious
   c. repudiation . . . inconsequential
   d. caveat . . . bizarre

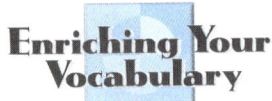

Enriching Your Vocabulary

Read the passage below. Then complete the exercise at the bottom of the page.

Words from Greek Mythology

Greek mythology, like a soap opera, is full of thwarted love, betrayal, ignoble acts, and Promethean feats of glory. Though many know that Zeus was the ruler of the gods, few remember that the gods overthrew their parents, the titans, in order to control Olympia. Zeus, Poseidon, and Hades drew lots to determine who would rule which provinces, and it was in this manner that Zeus, with his thunderbolt, became supreme ruler of the heavens and earth, Poseidon, with his pronged triton, controlled the seas, and Hades dwelled in the underworld of the dead.

The Olympian gods had many children, such as: Aphrodite, the goddess of beauty; Athena, the warlike goddess of Olympia; Apollo, the god of music and truth; the Muses; the Fates; and half-mortal children such as Hercules, Helen of Troy, and Perseus. There are many interesting myths that stem from these characters, such as the story of Hercules, mortal son of Zeus. At birth, Hercules strangled a serpent that had been sent to kill him, and became known as the strongest man in the world. The word *herculean* (Unit 13), meaning "strength," comes from the superhuman strength exhibited by Hercules in performing his tasks.

The Trojan Horse comes to Hollywood

In Column A below are 7 more words derived from Greek myths. With or without a dictionary, match each word with its definition in Column B.

Column A

__f__	1. Adonis
__g__	2. atlas
__d__	3. labyrinth
__c__	4. mentor
__b__	5. Odyssey
__a__	6. paean
__e__	7. stentorian

Column B

a. song of joyful praise; ancient Greek hymn of thanksgiving to the gods, especially Apollo

b. the second book of Homer's epic recounting the adventures of King Odysseus; long journey

c. wise and trusted advisor; Odysseus' trusted friend

d. maze in which the Minotaur, who was half man, half bull, was confined

e. extremely loud; a loud-voiced Greek messenger

f. handsome young man; a man loved by Aphrodite for his beauty

g. book of maps; a titan condemned to support the heavens on his shoulders

Final Mastery Test

Selecting Word Meanings

In each of the following groups, circle the word or expression that is **most nearly the same** in meaning as the word in **boldface** type in the given phrase.

1. **foment** disagreements
   - **a. cause** ✓
   - b. repress
   - c. take part in
   - d. solve
2. struggle for **autonomy**
   - a. recognition
   - b. honor
   - **c. independence** ✓
   - d. self-respect
3. **enthrall** the audience
   - **a. charm** ✓
   - b. horrify
   - c. expel
   - d. compensate
4. view with **approbation**
   - a. fear
   - b. distaste
   - c. indifference
   - **d. approval** ✓
5. **scintillating** company
   - a. discordant
   - **b. witty** ✓
   - c. international
   - d. dull
6. an awkward **hiatus**
   - **a. pause** ✓
   - b. disagreement
   - c. revival
   - d. situation
7. a **gauche** remark
   - **a. graceless** ✓
   - b. clever
   - c. humorous
   - d. bitter
8. filled with **lassitude**
   - a. eagerness
   - b. food
   - **c. weariness** ✓
   - d. sadness
9. a **motley** gathering
   - a. uniform
   - b. dull
   - **c. diverse** ✓
   - d. enthusiastic
10. **permeate** the area
    - **a. saturate** ✓
    - b. scour
    - c. destroy
    - d. cleanse
11. **recapitulate** the lesson
    - a. begin
    - b. end
    - **c. summarize** ✓
    - d. learn
12. an **implicit** agreement
    - a. overt
    - b. untrustworthy
    - **c. unstated** ✓
    - d. unhealthy
13. an act of **perfidy**
    - a. cowardice
    - b. valor
    - c. faith
    - **d. treachery** ✓
14. a **sanctimonious** attitude
    - a. intense
    - b. spontaneous
    - c. genuine
    - **d. hypocritical** ✓
15. a **grandiose** scheme
    - a. profitable
    - **b. extravagant** ✓
    - c. prudent
    - d. wicked
16. an **amorphous** mass of old papers
    - a. tidy
    - b. surprising
    - **c. shapeless** ✓
    - d. compact
17. a **bovine** temperament
    - a. angry
    - b. fearful
    - **c. placid** ✓
    - d. nervous
18. **aura** of respectability
    - a. result
    - b. cause
    - c. fear
    - **d. atmosphere** ✓
19. **disconcert** the players
    - a. criticize
    - b. replace
    - c. praise
    - **d. upset** ✓

20. wise **precepts**
    a. rulers   b. followers   c. actions   **(d. principles)**
21. the **adulation** of the crowd
    (a. admiration)   b. disorder   c. indifference   d. scorn
22. in the **sepulchral** gloom
    (a. gravelike)   b. sudden   c. nocturnal   d. surrounding
23. **blazoned** on the pages of history
    a. discovered   **(b. displayed)**   c. ignored   d. explained
24. **bizarre** findings
    a. expected   **(b. weird)**   c. disconcerting   d. lucky
25. **transmute** the economic system
    (a. change)   b. improve   c. disorganize   d. revive

Antonyms

*In each of the following groups, circle the **two** words that are **most nearly opposite** in meaning.*

26. a. collate   **(b. extricate)**   **(c. embroil)**   d. rearrange
27. **(a. hackneyed)**   b. provincial   **(c. novel)**   d. insular
28. a. vitriolic   **(b. deliberate)**   **(c. inadvertent)**   d. harsh
29. **(a. dissension)**   b. gossamer   c. simple   **(d. agreement)**
30. a. fractious   **(b. dilatory)**   c. expensive   **(d. prompt)**
31. a. infirmity   **(b. sadistic)**   c. decisive   **(d. humane)**
32. **(a. implicit)**   **(b. expressed)**   c. beneficent   d. constructive
33. **(a. politic)**   **(b. imprudent)**   c. abundant   d. resilient
34. a. unctuous   **(b. torpid)**   **(c. energetic)**   d. intellectual
35. a. impassive   **(b. imperious)**   c. remarkable   **(d. subservient)**
36. a. remit   **(b. mollify)**   c. profligate   **(d. irritate)**
37. a. produce   **(b. aver)**   **(c. disavow)**   d. paraphrase
38. **(a. abate)**   b. intercede   c. exorcise   **(d. resume)**
39. a. vicarious   **(b. surreptitious)**   **(c. overt)**   d. substitute
40. a. legendary   **(b. even-tempered)**   c. slovenly   **(d. petulant)**
41. a. adventitious   **(b. lenient)**   c. childish   **(d. stringent)**
42. a. paragon   **(b. contiguous)**   c. champion   **(d. remote)**
43. **(a. intelligible)**   b. contingent   c. egregious   **(d. inscrutable)**
44. **(a. salutary)**   b. vapid   **(c. pernicious)**   d. talkative
45. **(a. pallid)**   **(b. florid)**   c. discursive   d. unkempt

FINAL MASTERY TEST

Words Pairs

In the space before each pair of words, write:
S—if the words are synonyms or near-synonyms;
O—if the words are antonyms or near-antonyms;
N—if the words are unrelated in meaning.

__O__ 46. corpulent—cadaverous
__S__ 47. cajole—wheedle
__S__ 48. susceptible—vulnerable
__N__ 49. herculean—punctilious
__O__ 50. censurable—meritorious
__N__ 51. querulous—sartorial
__O__ 52. tenuous—palpable
__S__ 53. remonstrate—expostulate

__S__ 54. propensity—proclivity
__N__ 55. turgid—ignoble
__O__ 56. thwart—expedite
__S__ 57. circuitous—tortuous
__N__ 58. nominal—provincial
__N__ 59. recondite—heinous
__O__ 60. opportune—inauspicious

Words That Describe the Presentation of Ideas

Some words that describe the way arguments are developed and ideas are presented, in speech or writing, are listed below. Write the appropriate word on the line next to each of the following descriptive sentences.

nebulous	innuendo	extraneous	dispassionate
specious	rejoinder	hypothetical	caveat
incontrovertible	criteria	recondite	astute
erudite	redundant	provocative	precocious

61. He has unnecessarily repeated the same ideas over and over again, in slightly different language.   __redundant__

62. Rather than using something that had really happened, the speaker proved his point with an invented story.   __hypothetical__

63. In writing this article, the author has drawn on a vast store of learning, covering many different sciences and other specialties.   __erudite__

64. You have confused the issue by bringing in facts and ideas which have no bearing on the matter under discussion.   __extraneous__

65. The argument is so strongly backed by sound reasoning and verifiable data that it is really beyond dispute.   __incontrovertible__

66. The speaker raised a number of interesting questions that aroused the audience and led to a lively discussion.   __provocative__

67. Your line of reasoning is fallacious, and your conclusions don't stand up under careful analysis.   __specious__

68. The article was written for specialists in the field, and made little sense to the rest of us.   __recondite__

Final Mastery Test ■ 187

69. The ideas that emerge from the article are so vague and wispy that it is impossible to say if they are right or wrong. — **nebulous**

70. She used several standards for judgment in trying to decide whether the politician's speech had merit. — **criteria**

Using Verbs

Verbs are the "action words" that, more than any other part of speech, make language forceful and vivid. In the space before each verb in Column A, write the letter of the item in Column B that best identifies it.

	Column A	Column B
i	71. remonstrate	a. to encroach on the rights of another
b	72. dissipate	b. to live self-indulgently
d	73. wheedle	c. to spread far and wide
f	74. mitigate	d. to coax or flatter for a desired end
h	75. corroborate	e. to go beyond, surpass
a	76. infringe	f. to make less severe or painful
e	77. transcend	g. to reject, disown
g	78. repudiate	h. to confirm the truth of
j	79. scourge	i. to offer objections or protests
c	80. disseminate	j. to punish severely

Word Associations

*In each of the following, circle the word or expression that best completes the meaning of the sentence or answers the question, with particular reference to the meaning of the word in **boldface** type.*

81. A practitioner of the **occult** sciences might specialize in
    a. astronomy
    b. biology
    c. fortune-telling
    d. sociology

82. The distinguishing symptom of a person suffering from **megalomania** is
    a. chronic depression
    b. high blood pressure
    c. delusions of grandeur
    d. problem dandruff

83. Good advice to someone who is constantly being **dunned** is
    a. Go home!
    b. Keep your eye on the ball!
    c. Don't waste fuel!
    d. Pay your bills!

84. A scene of **carnage** would be most likely to occur in a
    a. collection of literary essays
    b. love story
    c. fairy tale
    d. novel about World War II

85. Taking **umbrage** would be a reasonable reaction when you are
    a. complimented
    b. insulted
    c. rewarded
    d. introduced to someone new

86. Which of the following is the best remedy for being **callow**?
    a. time and experience
    b. dancing lessons
    c. vitamins
    d. sun and surf

188 ■ Final Mastery Test

FINAL MASTERY TEST

87. If you are suffering from **penury**, you should look for
    a. new hobbies
    b. gainful employment
    c. medical advice
    d. a better mouthwash

88. The best thing to do with an **onus** is to
    a. ride it
    b. feed it
    c. show it off to your friends
    d. try to get rid of it

89. A person regarded as **squeamish** would probably be reluctant to
    a. visit an art museum
    b. dissect a frog in the biology lab
    c. play tennis
    d. prepare for final examinations

90. You would probably be **disconsolate** if you
    a. added all the words in this program to your active vocabulary
    b. ran across some of these words in the works of a favorite writer
    c. checked the word origins in a dictionary
    d. did poorly on this final mastery test

91. Which of the following reactions would best characterize someone suffering from **ennui**?
    a. a smile
    b. a wink
    c. a yawn
    d. a grimace

92. It's hard to behave with **equanimity** when
    a. nothing much is happening
    b. everything seems to be going wrong
    c. you're very drowsy
    d. you have just finished a good meal

93. A person who is the **epitome** of wit
    a. uses it maliciously
    b. is actually not very witty
    c. is an ideal example of wittiness
    d. employs wit in a strange way

94. You would **buttress** an argument if you wanted to
    a. incite it
    b. support it
    c. avoid it
    d. repudiate it

95. A person who has suffered an **egregious** defeat has lost
    a. gloriously
    b. conspicuously
    c. by a close score
    d. as a result of unfair tactics

96. Which of the following would by definition be guilty of **peculation**?
    a. a judge
    b. a coward
    c. an embezzler
    d. a philanthropist

97. The usual reason for **expurgating** a book is to
    a. get rid of objectionable material
    b. make it more readable
    c. translate it into a foreign language
    d. reissue it in paperback

98. To describe an author as **prolific** refers to
    a. nationality
    b. the size of the author's bank account
    c. relations with critics
    d. the number of books produced

99. If you receive a **noncommittal** reply to a request, you will probably be
    a. in a state of uncertainty
    b. deeply depressed
    c. overjoyed
    d. ready to fight

100. A famous literary character known for **avarice** is
     a. Ivanhoe
     b. Silas Marner
     c. David Copperfield
     d. Hester Prynne

INDEX

The following tabulation lists all the basic words taught in the various units of this workbook, as well as those introduced in the *Vocabulary of Vocabulary, Working with Analogies, Building with Classical Roots,* and *Enriching Your Vocabulary* sections. Words taught in the units are printed in **boldface** type. The number following each entry indicates the page on which the word is first introduced. Exercises and review materials in which the word also appears are not cited.

abate, 98
abet, 151
abominate, 35
absolve, 131
abstemious, 124
academy, 150
accede, 48
accessory, 48
accrue, 117
acculturation, 35
acrimonious, 91
adamant, 165
Adonis, 184
adulation, 98
adventitious, 35
affable, 51
aggrandize, 51
aggressive, 78
alma mater, 83
ameliorate, 28
amenable, 158
amnesty, 58
amorphous, 51
analogy, 11
anathema, 98
annotation, 117
anomalous, 65
anthropomorphic, 111
antonym, 8
aplomb, 28
approbation, 21
ascribe, 35
aspersion, 65
assuage, 21
astute, 98
atlas, 184
audience, 17
aura, 51
austere, 84
autonomy, 58
avarice, 98
aver, 151
axiomatic, 58

bases, 15
bedlam, 117
beneficent, 84
berate, 158
bizarre, 65
blatant, 151

blarney, 150
blazon, 58
bombastic, 28
bovine, 91
broach, 151
brouhaha, 165
brusque, 65
bulwark, 165
buttress, 151

cadaverous, 84
cajole, 65
callow, 28
canine, 116
caricature, 131
carnage, 158
carousal, 151
castigate, 65
caveat, 58
censurable, 124
cessation, 48
choleric, 165
circuitous, 35
clangor, 131
cloy, 165
coalition, 21
collate, 152
cologne, 150
commiserate, 35
concession, 48
concoct, 84
congress, 78
connoisseur, 152
connotation, 7
consternation, 91
context, 9
context clues, 9
contiguous, 131
contingent, 124
contraband, 51
contrast clue, 9
contrive, 66
corpulent, 91
corroborate, 124
covert, 117
crass, 84
credulous, 158
criterion, 158
culpable, 98
cupidity, 131

curtail, 165

debase, 84
debonair, 117
decadence, 21
decease, 48
de facto, 83
deference, 166
definitive, 166
deleterious, 131
demagogue, 66
demeanor, 166
denizen, 124
denotation, 7
deplete, 158
desecrate, 85
digress, 78
dilatory, 99
disabuse, 66
disavow, 91
disconcert, 85
disconsolate, 152
discursive, 124
dispassionate, 91
disquisition, 178
disseminate, 125
dissension, 92
dissipate, 92
dowdy, 125
drivel, 28
dun, 117

economy, 17
efficacious, 118
egalitarian, 144
egregious, 99
egress, 78
elicit, 21
encumber, 152
enhance, 132
enigmatic, 166
enjoin, 36
ennui, 66
enthrall, 132
epithet, 111
epitome, 28
equable, 144
equanimity, 118
equate, 144
equidistant, 144

equilibrium, 144
equine, 116
equitable, 58
equivocate, 99
erudite, 51
et cetera, 83
evanescent, 99
exhort, 29
ex officio, 29
expatiate, 159
expedite, 36
expiate, 36
ex post facto, 83
expostulate, 21
expurgate, 92
extenuate, 132
extraneous, 159
extricate, 58

feline, 116
ferment, 36
fetter, 66
figurative, 7
filch, 59
florid, 125
flout, 59
foist, 125
foment, 152
fortuitous, 118
fractious, 59

gauche, 125
gauntlet, 92
gist, 118
gossamer, 52
gradient, 78
gradualism, 78
grandiose, 85
gratuitous, 118
grisly, 152

habeas corpus, 83
hackneyed, 22
heinous, 66
herculean, 152
heresy, 125
hiatus, 22
hypothetical, 92

ignoble, 92
immutable, 66
impassive, 153

190 ▪ Index

imperious, 118
implicit, 132
impromptu, 166
impugn, 92
inadvertent, 36
inauspicious, 153
inception, 159
incisive, 132
inconsequential, 85
incontrovertible, 153
inculcate, 125
inequity, 144
infer, 52
inference clue, 10
infirmity, 159
infraction, 85
infringe, 29
ingratiate, 29
iniquitous, 144
innuendo, 22
inquest, 178
inquisition, 178
inquisitive, 178
inscrutable, 52
insular, 52
insurgent, 67
intemperate, 93
intercede, 22
interloper, 29
intrinsic, 29
invective, 118
inveigh, 29
irresolute, 99
irrevocable, 52

jaded, 22
jejune, 159

labyrinth, 184
lassitude, 29
leonine, 116
limerick, 150
limousine, 150
literal, 7
lupine, 116
lurid, 22

mawkish, 166
mecca, 150
megalomania, 67
mentor, 184
meritorious, 22
metamorphosis, 111

metaphorical, 7
millennium, 30
mitigate, 85
modus operandi, 83
mollify, 166
morphology, 111
motley, 119
munificent, 119

nebulous, 99
nominal, 36
noncommittal, 36
nonplussed, 153
novice, 99

obdurate, 159
occult, 30
odium, 93
Odyssey, 184
onus, 167
ophidian, 116
opportune, 153
ostentatious, 132

paean, 184
palpable, 126
paragon, 132
paraphrase, 133
parenthetical, 111
peculate, 37
penury, 100
perceptive, 126
perfidy, 93
permeate, 30
pernicious, 126
perquisite, 178
persona non grata, 83
petulant, 23
pillage, 85
politic, 133
porcine, 116
potpourri, 159
prate, 86
precedence, 48
precept, 59
precipitate, 30
precocious, 160
predecessor, 48
prerequisite, 178
prerogative, 23
presentiment, 167
pretentious, 100
pro tempore, 83

proclivity, 38
procrastinate, 119
profligate, 167
prolific, 153
propensity, 52
prosaic, 133
provincial, 23
provocative, 119
pseudomorph, 111
punctilious, 86
purpose, 17

querulous, 52
query, 178

recapitulate, 100
recession, 48
recondite, 119
redoubtable, 86
redundant, 133
regress, 78
rejoinder, 153
relegate, 93
remit, 167
remonstrate, 53
reprobate, 119
reprove, 86
repudiate, 53
requisite, 167
requisition, 178
resilient, 53
restatement clue, 9
restitution, 86
resuscitate, 100
retrograde, 78
reverberate, 53
roots, 15

sadistic, 160
salient, 126
salutary, 59
sanctimonious, 133
sangfroid, 38
sardonic, 150
sartorial, 167
satiate, 126
scathing, 59
scintillating, 133
scourge, 59
scurrilous, 53
sear, 126
sedentary, 119
seditious, 38
sedulous, 53

sententious, 160
sepulchral, 60
simulate, 23
sinecure, 67
sleazy, 53
slovenly, 100
soporific, 60
specious, 126
squeamish, 93
stalwart, 86
status quo, 83
stentorian, 184
straitlaced, 60
stringent, 30
structure, 9
subservient, 93
supplicate, 160
supposition, 100
surfeit, 160
surmise, 30
surreptitious, 67
susceptible, 93
sybaritic, 150
synonym, 8

taurine, 116
tenuous, 38
theme, 111
thesis, 111
thwart, 167
tone, 7
torpid, 100
tortuous, 160
transcend, 23
transgress, 67
transient, 60
transmute, 67
turgid, 160

umbrage, 23
unctuous, 23
unequivocal, 144
unwieldy, 60
ursine, 116

vapid, 60
varnish, 150
vicarious, 67
vitriolic, 38
vulnerable, 86
vulpine, 116

wheedle, 38
winsome, 133